WILD EXUBERANCE

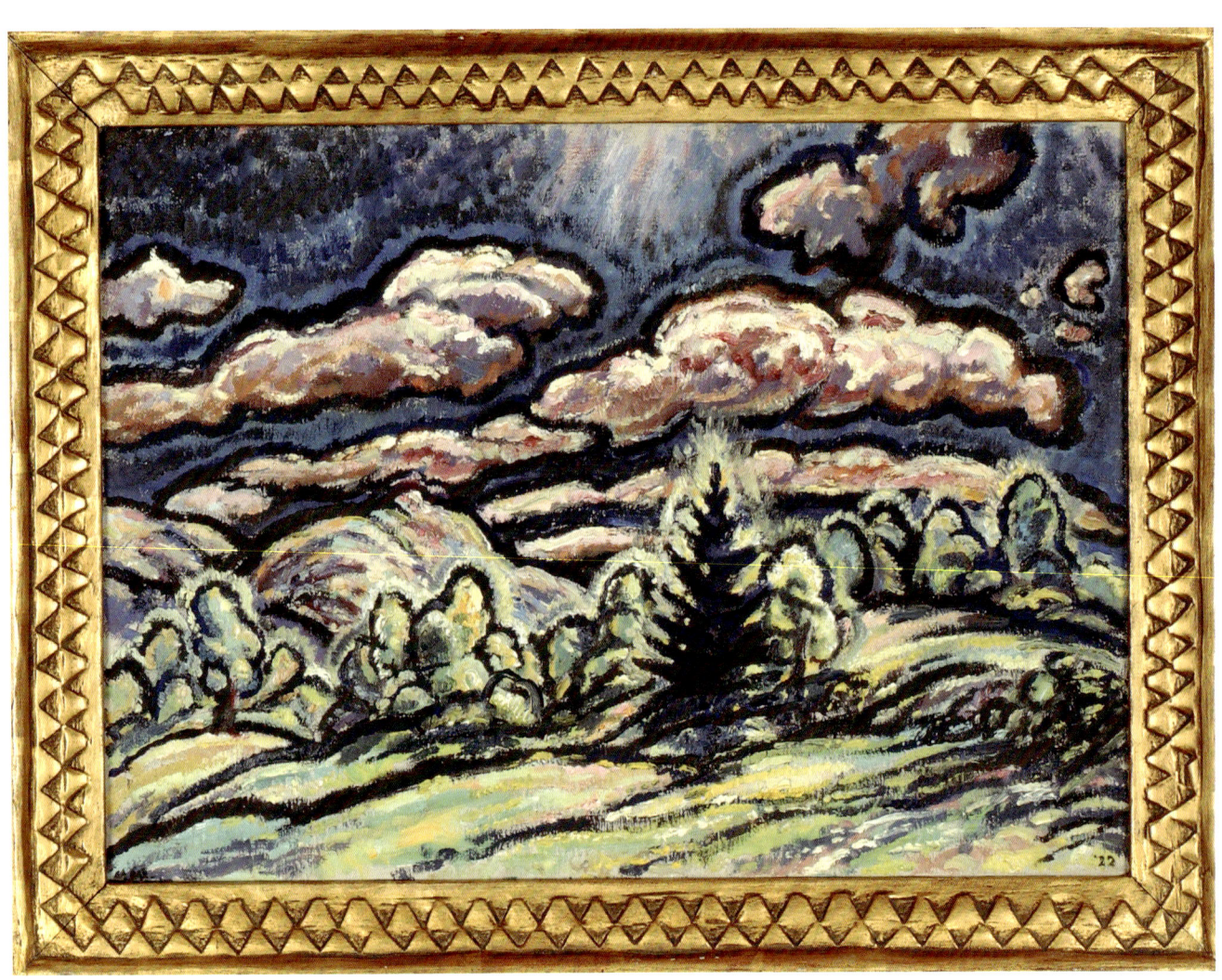

WILD EXUBERANCE
Harold Weston's Adirondack Art

Rebecca Foster

&

Caroline M. Welsh

With Contributions by
Theodore E. Stebbins Jr., Stephen Bennett Phillips,
Kathleen V. Jameson, *and* Nina Weston Foster

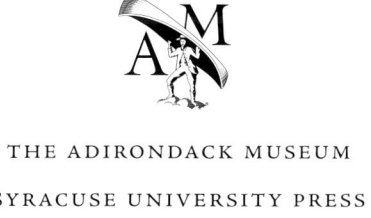

THE ADIRONDACK MUSEUM
SYRACUSE UNIVERSITY PRESS

ALL RIGHTS RESERVED
First Edition 2005
05 06 07 08 09 10   6 5 4 3 2 1

Exhibition: The Adirondack Museum
May 27, 2005–October 22, 2006

Project director and curator: Caroline M. Welsh
Guest curator and associate editor: Rebecca Foster
Copy editor: Fronia W. Simpson
Design: Christopher Kuntze
Photographers: Richard and Elizabeth Walker, George W. Adams,
Ben Blackwell, Kevin Burget, Katya Kallsen, Robert Lifson

FRONTISPIECE: **1.** Harold Weston, *Noonday Sun*, 1922. The Adirondack Museum.

The paper used in this publication meets the minimum requirements of American National
Standard for Information Sciences—Permanence of Paper for Printed Library Materials,
ANSI Z39.48-1984.∞™

LIBRARY OF CONGRESS CATALOGING-IN-PUBLICATION DATA
Foster, Rebecca Feldman.
    Wild exuberance : Harold Weston's Adirondack art / Rebecca Foster, Caroline M. Welsh ;
with contributions by Theodore E. Stebbins Jr. . . . [et al.]. —1st ed.
        p. cm.
    Catalog of an exhibition at the Adirondack Museum, May 27, 2005–Oct. 22, 2006
    Includes bibliographical references and index.
    ISBN 0-8156-0809-8 (cloth : alk. paper)—ISBN 0-8156-0834-9 (pbk. : alk. paper)
    1. Weston, Harold, 1894–1972—Exhibitions. 2. Adirondack Mountains (N.Y.)—In art—
Exhibitions. I. Weston, Harold, 1894–1972. II. Welsh, Caroline Mastin. III. Stebbins,
Theodore E. IV. Adirondack Museum. V. Title.
    ND237.W55A4 2005
    759.13—dc22   2005008617

Printed in Canada by Friesens

Contents

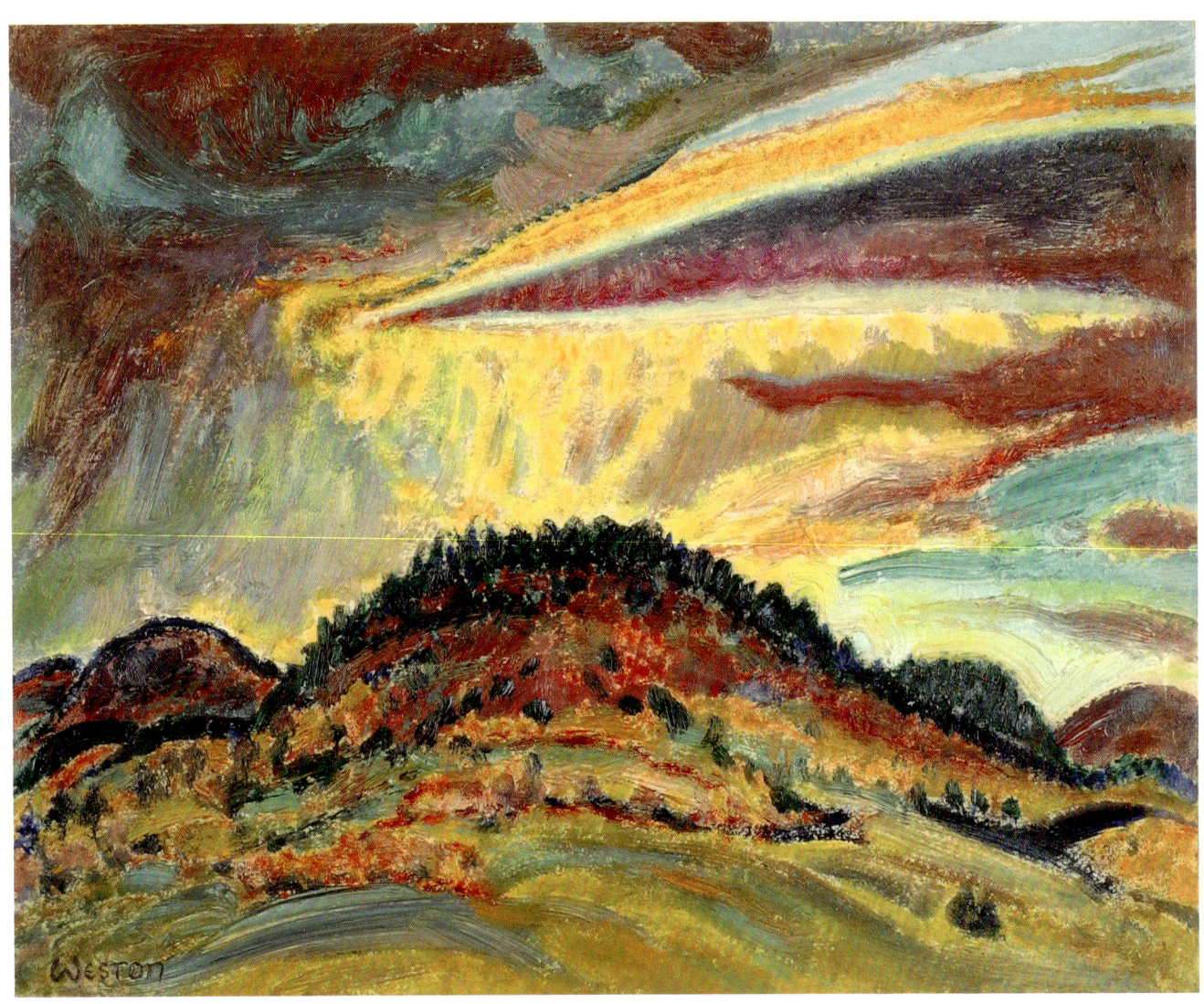

2. Harold Weston, *Sunset over Baxter Mountain*, 1920. St. Huberts Trust.

On 1 October 1923 Harold and Faith Weston climbed Haystack Mountain, one of Harold's favorite vantage points in the Adirondack high peaks. As evening clouds gathered, they descended to the col between Haystack and Basin Mountains to a newly constructed lean-to whose hastily made floor of tree trunks still had sharp, protruding branch stubs. Harold gathered springy fir boughs and tried, unsuccessfully, to cushion the bed while Faith started a smoky fire of wood chips in the first drops of a rainstorm. Their miserably wet, cold, smoked-out night was rewarded, finally, by a dawn transformed by hoarfrost that lined every crystalline twig, fern, and spiderweb at their high elevation. They climbed to the top of Basin in time to see the clouds clearing over the high peaks in riotous disorder. At once under the clouds came a peek of the autumn crimsons, greens, and golds of the valleys. Then it was gone, and the shoulder of Haystack appeared. Clouds and shadows swept up the side of nearby Gothics and, suddenly, were dissolved by brilliant sunshine. In a frenzy Harold painted four oil sketches to capture, as he wrote later in Freedom in the Wilds, *"the wild exuberance of the day and its successive orgasms of wilderness beauty."*

— Rebecca Foster, Guest Curator

Figures

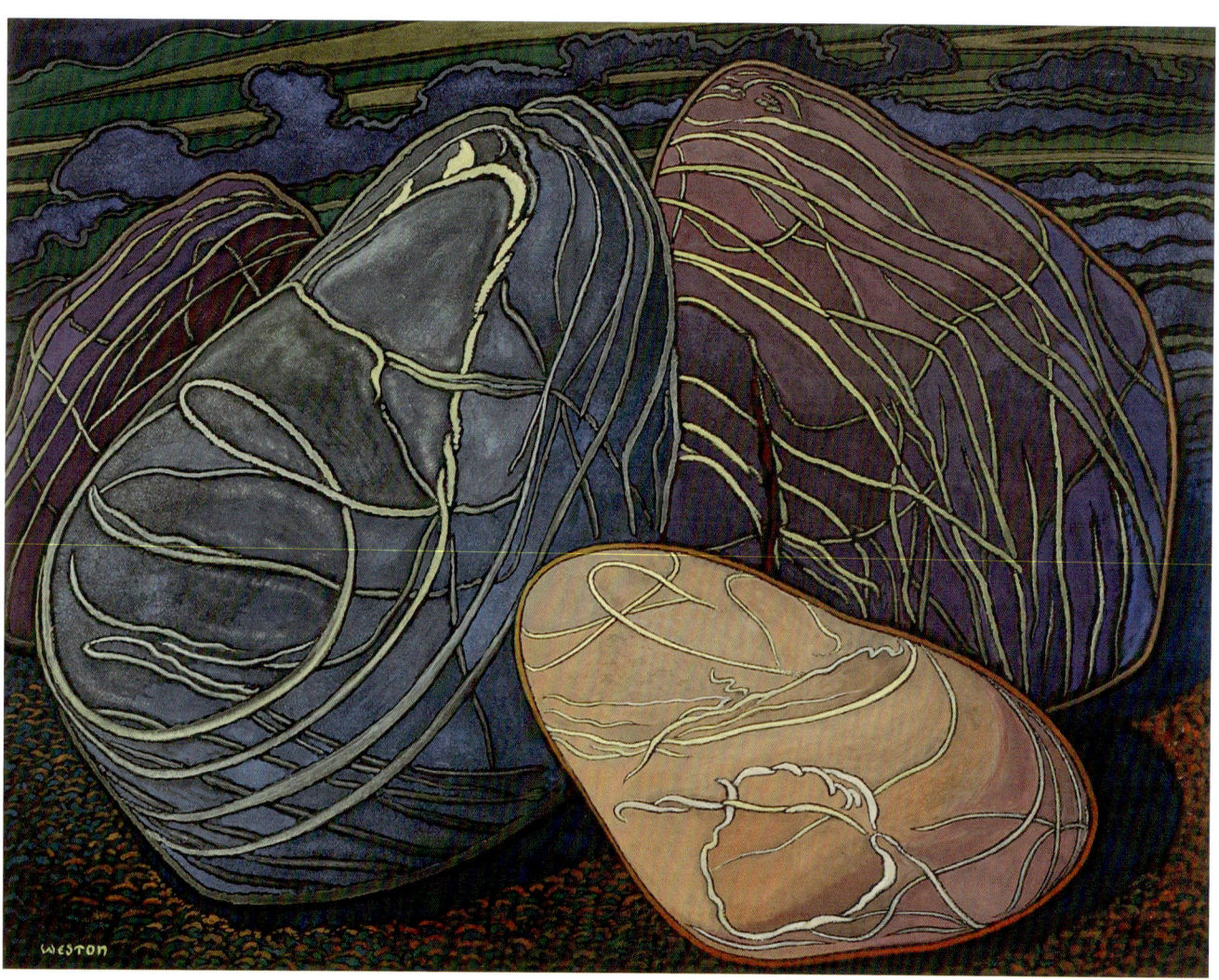

3. Harold Weston, *Conference*
(Stone Series No. 3), 1968.
Harold Weston Foundation,
courtesy of Atea Ring Gallery,
Westport, N.Y.

Lenders to the Exhibition

The Adirondack Museum, Blue Mountain Lake, New York
Atea Ring Gallery
Jackie Day and David Hansen
D. Wigmore Fine Art, New York
Baird and Nancy Edmonds
C. Corscaden Galbraith
Sarah Hamill
William H. B. Hamill
Harold Weston Foundation
Michael and Susan Mahoney
Katherine Merle-Smith
Edward Bear Miller
Museum of Fine Arts, Boston
Donna and Michael O'Rourke
The Phillips Collection, Washington, D.C.
Stephen Bennett Phillips
Platt Fine Art
Suzanne and Seymour Preston
Kathryn and Robert Preyer
Private Collectors
Jonathan and Jennifer Ring
San Francisco Museum of Modern Art
Springfield Art Museum, Missouri
St. Huberts Trust
Bill Sudduth
Syracuse University Art Collection
Burns H. and Marta C. Weston
Charles and Marietta Weston
Laura Weston
Wichita Art Museum, Wichita, Kansas

Donors

The Adirondack Museum gratefully acknowledges the support of the following persons and organizations for the exhibition Wild Exuberance: Harold Weston's Adirondack Art and related programs.

Anonymous
Alice K. and William H. Boardman Jr.
Aurelia Garland Bolton
Reed and Lois Foster
John and Linda Fritzinger
Mark T. Gallogly and Elizabeth B. Strickler
GE Foundation
Mr. and Mrs. Thomas P. Saddlemire
Harold Weston Foundation
Ed and Caroline Hoffman
Steve and Judy Hopkins
Courtney and Idy Iglehart
Mr. and Mrs. John S. King
Anne Adams Laumont
Laumont Editions
Mr. and Mrs. Douglas S. Luke
The McLanahan Family Trust
Ellen and Bruce McLanahan
Annette Merle-Smith
Katherine S. Merle-Smith
James T. Morley
Robert and Mary Orben
William L. Paternotte Family
Seymour Preston Jr.
Mr. and Mrs. Eric Ridder Jr.
Atea Ring
Mr. and Mrs. Thomas P. Saddlemire
Arthur V. Savage
Nulsen Smith
Society for the Preservation of American Modernists
William and Elizabeth Stewart
Dan and Ellen Strickler
Phebe Thorne and Paul Wilcox
Mr. and Mrs. Wynant D. Vanderpoel
Anne H. Van Ingen
Julia B. Walker
Barrie A. and Deedee Wigmore Foundation

Foreword

The Adirondack Museum is located at the center of the Adirondack Park, a vast mosaic of state and private land that constitutes the largest public park in the contiguous United States. Since 1894 nearly half the Adirondack Park's 6 million acres have been protected as "forever wild" by the New York State constitution. Since the Adirondack Museum opened to the public in 1957, its exhibitions and publications have documented the complex interaction between people and the land as well as cultural attitudes toward nature. The American experience of the wilderness has been in part defined in this region, where the reality of everyday life and work has been transformed through the myth-making imagination of its artists—among them, Harold Weston (1894–1972) and other twentieth-century artists.

This exhibition and publication present for the first time a focused look at Harold Weston's Adirondack art and the role that Adirondack imagery played in his creative output. The museum is indebted to the scholarship of art historian and Weston biographer Rebecca Foster; art historians and curators Stephen Bennett Phillips, Theodore E. Stebbins Jr., and Caroline M. Welsh; and the assistance of the president of the Harold Weston Foundation, Nina Weston Foster, and of research associate Kathleen V. Jameson. Museum staff and consultants, under the exceptional leadership of chief curator and curator of art Caroline Welsh, have worked with great energy and commitment to bring this important study and its related publications and programs to the public through Wild Exuberance: Harold Weston's Adirondack Art.

David L. Pamperin
EXECUTIVE DIRECTOR

Acknowledgments

The Adirondack Museum's mission to collect, preserve, and interpret the history of the Adirondack region affords a unique opportunity to examine regional manifestations in relation to their national context. Its art collection has been used to study artists renowned in American art who have made Adirondack subject matter a serious part of their artistic work—including Winslow Homer, Jonas Lie, Arthur Fitzwilliam Tait, Levi Wells Prentice, Rockwell Kent, William Trost Richards, and now Harold Weston.

The life of Harold Weston encompassed a broad range of creativity, from his art to his humanitarian service. This multifaceted man is reflected in an equally multifaceted effort by the Adirondack Museum in offering the first exclusive museum exhibition of his Adirondack work, an exhibition catalogue, a documentary film on his life and art, and educational and public programs designed to illuminate the many contributions of this extraordinarily gifted artist.

The project was long in the making. The idea germinated in 1994 during a conversation with Nina Weston Foster—Harold and Faith Weston's daughter, longtime keeper of the artist's legacy, and president of the Harold Weston Foundation. She became the indispensable guiding light for the project. Rebecca Foster, independent writer and curator, is Harold Weston's biographer. Her thorough knowledge of and fresh insights into Harold Weston provided the foundation for the exhibition and catalogue. Theodore E. Stebbins Jr.—noted authority on American art, curator of American art at the Fogg Museum, and summer resident of Keene Valley—shares an enthusiasm for the artist, which is enhanced by his knowledge of American art. Stephen Bennett Phillips has long been a Weston devotee, a dedication enlarged by his work at the Phillips Collection. Kathleen V. Jameson, curatorial assistant at the Museum of Fine Arts, Houston, researched and assembled the checklist and bibliography with the essential assistance of Nina Weston Foster. Filmmaker Kevin Burget and his team have added dimension to the story through the interweaving of interviews, archival materials, and paintings. It has been a wonderful privilege to work with the artist's family and friends and with scholars in the field to bring the Adirondack art of Harold Weston to attention.

Many people and institutions deserve thanks for their assistance with this exhibition. The lenders' generosity has been paramount; without their collaboration and support there would be no exhibition. Staff in every department supported this project at all its stages: Tracy Meehan, collections manager; Doreen Alessi, conservator; Angela Donnelly, assistant curator; and Scott Chartier and Robert Holford, exhibit preparators, deserve special mention. Susan Dineen and the museum educators worked creatively to plan and execute the programs. David Pamperin and Hillarie Logan Dechene led the fund-raising efforts with the essential assistance of the Weston Steering Committee. Words cannot adequately express our thanks for the Steering Committee's efforts and the project funders' generosity and enthusiasm. We are indebted to Christopher Kuntze for this volume's handsome design and production and to Fronia W. Simpson for gracefully and intelligently editing our work. As always, it is a pleasure to work with the staff of Syracuse University Press.

Caroline M. Welsh
CHIEF CURATOR AND CURATOR OF ART

WILD EXUBERANCE

INTRODUCTION TO HAROLD WESTON'S ART

Theodore E. Stebbins Jr.

HAROLD WESTON WAS WIDELY HONORED and much admired throughout his lifetime for his paintings and for a host of other contributions to the arts and to human welfare, but since his death in 1972 there have been few major exhibitions and very little critical discussion of his art.[1] Though Weston's memory is revered in Keene Valley and elsewhere in northern New York State, he and his work seem in danger of being forgotten in the world at large.

The present exhibition and its catalogue are presented in the beliefs not only that Weston was one of the great twentieth-century artists of the Adirondacks, but that he deserves recognition for having made some of the most compelling and original paintings of his day. Those who have ignored his work in their written histories of American modernism and of such areas as the spiritual aspect of twentieth-century painting have missed, in our view, an artist of importance.[2]

From the beginning, Weston's family supported his interest in the arts, and in 1909, when he was fifteen, he was taken to Europe for a year. The family chose an uncommon itinerary for Americans on the grand tour, living in Lausanne, Switzerland, and Hannover, Germany, with side trips to Holland, Belgium, and Italy. Weston later recalled that he had filled his diary with watercolor sketches and that he had found the museums "almost as thrilling as the Alps."[3]

By 1912—the year after polio had left one of his legs permanently damaged—he was producing creditable oil sketches of Giant Mountain, which he could see from his family's summer cottage at Keene Valley. He was already as concerned with the fluency and expressiveness of brushwork as he was with recording the color and shape of his favorite peak.

At Harvard from 1912 to 1916 Weston majored in fine arts. As a freshman, he was admitted to the advanced painting and drawing course, and in his sophomore and junior years he studied painting with the illustrious Denman W. Ross, who was himself an important, highly eclectic collector while being also an assiduous, if not highly gifted realist painter. Weston at Harvard studied the arts of Spain, Italy, and the ancient world (in the latter course the teaching assistant was James Munn, who became a friend of the aspiring painter and an important early collector of his work).[4] His other teachers included the color theorist Arthur Pope and the Fogg Art Museum's director Edmund W. Forbes. He also took a course on the Greek poets and another—conducted entirely in German—on Goethe's *Faust*. Weston's superb academic record enabled him to be excused from several final exams, and he graduated magna cum laude.[5]

Like many of his generation, Weston was anxious to join the allied war effort even before the United States became officially involved. From July 1916 to November 1919, he served with the Young Men's Christian Association (YMCA), first "at a garrison fort 7000 feet up in the foothills of the Himalayas," then in Baghdad, where he "organized construction of three theatres, large palm gardens for the [British] troops, revised a Turkish harem for a hostel, ran an art club and several concert parties, and was first to take 'movies' from an airplane."[6] He left Baghdad in May 1919 and traveled widely through Asia on his way home. During these years, he found time to make a number of small oil sketches of the scenery, largely in the Persian desert, in a competent realistic style not unlike that practiced by his teacher Denman Ross.

During his college years Weston became familiar with modernism. He did not see the Armory Show of 1913, nor did the conservative Harvard faculty introduce him to the new art, but during the summer of 1914 he attended on his own the pioneering Ogunquit Art School run by Hamilton Easter Field. Field was a devoted modernist who had been influenced by the work of Pablo Picasso and Henri Matisse in Paris, and who had purchased a work by Jacques Villon at the Armory Show. He opened his school in 1913 and in the first year taught Marsden Hartley and William Zorach, among others. Weston had his eyes opened. He reported that Field provided his "first contact with modern art." He went on, "I became so convinced about the new approach that … half of my oral exam for honors [in 1916] was taken up with an attempt to persuade the professors of the Department of Fine Arts as to the validity of modern painting."[7] Seeking other ways to supplement his Harvard training, Weston also worked for a month during the summer of 1915 with Homer Boss, Robert Henri's successor as head of the Henri School and himself an adventurous realist. Later, after returning from Asia, Weston spent four months in 1920 in New York with William Schumacher, another veteran of the Armory Show, who worked in a fauve manner influenced by Matisse.

In 1920 Weston built his studio in the Adirondacks, several hundred yards away from the Ausable Club. During the short summer season he found himself in the midst of a busy resort community, but during the long, brutally cold months of winter he was the only resident of a mountain plateau in St. Huberts, which lies some three miles south of the small town of Keene Valley, New York. For three years, he devoted himself wholly to painting. He began by making dozens of quickly executed, small oil sketches—rough, expressive works whose emphasis on light and color renders the topography barely recognizable. They are somewhat reminiscent of the sketches of Maine made by Marsden Hartley a decade earlier; Hartley's small oils are more carefully composed and more disciplined, but Weston's have a special spontaneity and energy of their own.

In his studio during the winter of 1920–21 Weston began to make larger oils of the same Adirondack subjects. His finished compositions, both the vertical ones seen as *Pine*

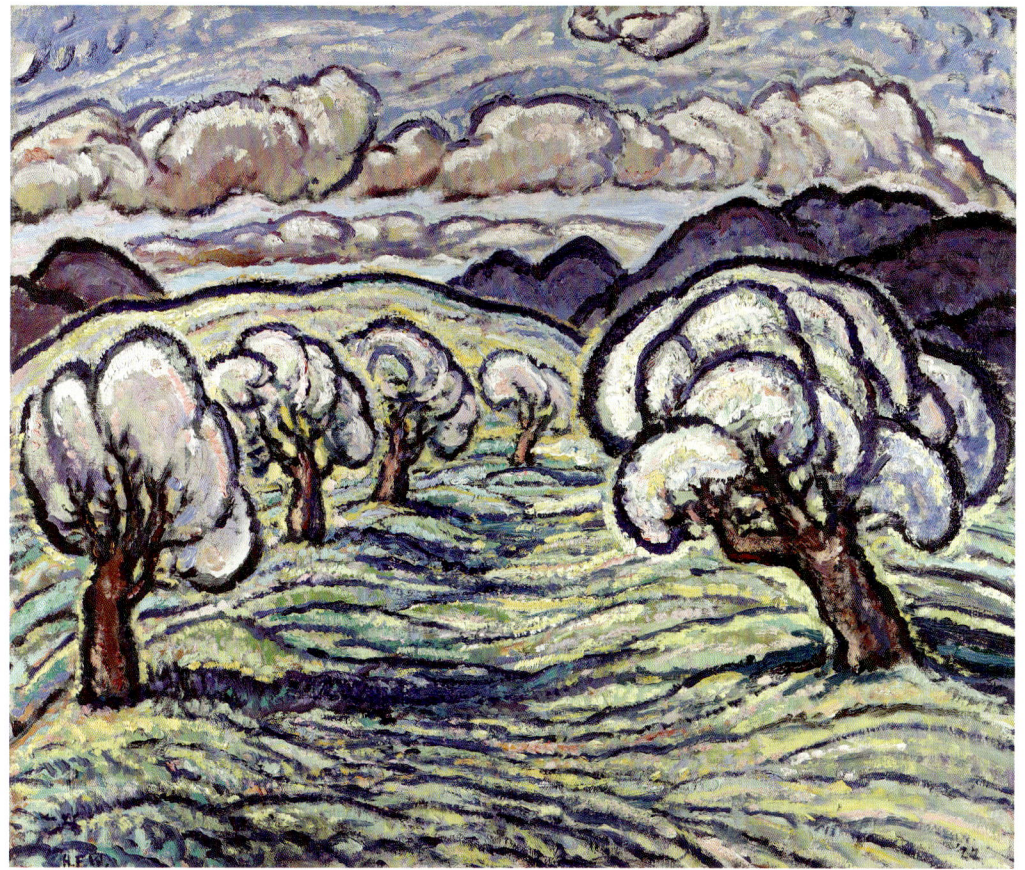

4. Harold Weston, *Apple Trees—Spring*, 1922. Courtesy of the Fogg Art Museum, Harvard University Art Museums, Anonymous Gift.

Tree, 1920 (Phillips chap., fig. 64), and the more typical horizontal ones such as *Winds—Upper Ausable Lake* (Phillips chap., fig. 68) or *Wilderness—Marcy, Dvôrák New World Symphony, Largo* (Welsh chap., fig. 99), both of 1922, suggest the curve of the earth, the vast power of nature, the very rhythm of creation. Mountains, trees, and lakes are outlined and abstracted; sky reflects the earth, and strong colors—blues, lavenders, yellows—unify each work. In his *Apple Trees—Spring*, 1922 (fig. 4), Weston employed rich impasto of mixed whites, greens, and pinks, and outlined trees, mountains, clouds, and fields with dark blue borders to create a work of electric intensity.

John Marin, Arthur G. Dove, Charles Burchfield, and other contemporary Americans and Europeans painted nature in the same way, as vibrant and alive. During his three isolated years in the mountains, living alone, painting with huge energy and passion, Weston produced a series of paintings that rivals theirs. He would have been familiar with Wassily Kandinsky's belief that "human emotion consists of vibrations of the soul, and that the soul is set into vibration by nature."[8] For Franz Kupka and the theosophists, "the essence of nature was manifested as a rhythmic geometric force." And Ralph Waldo Emerson, whom Weston had studied at Harvard, believed in the "Over-Soul" that "reveals the day of days . . . in which the inward eye opens to the Unity of Things." Weston's painting *Sunrise*,

1922 (fig. 5), is an archetypal illustration of both theosophical and Emersonian theory: man (here, the artist himself) stands naked before the immensity of the mountains, surrounded by a halo of light, immersing himself in nature and at one with it.[9] Weston's *Sunrise* is a descendant of Caspar David Friedrich's *Monk by the Sea*, 1809 (Schloss Charlottenburg, Berlin), where the lonely figure at the edge of the ocean "explores his own relationship to the great unknowables, conveyed through the dwarfing infinities of nature," as Robert Rosenblum put it.[10] There can be no doubt that in identifying with the mountains, Weston found both his art and his God.

The moment was short-lived. After two and a half years as a self-described "hermit" in the mountains, Weston exhibited his paintings at the Montross Galleries in New York in November 1922. The show was a triumph, and the work was highly praised by the critics. But Weston inexplicably reacted negatively to his success, seemingly embarrassed by what he accurately called the "semipantheism" of his work. He wrote of himself as a "youth running to the mountain top, beating his chest and declaiming, 'I have seen God.'" Always highly idealistic, he also noted that he had "no desire to produce work for an established market."[11]

Weston gave up his isolated life and married in the spring of 1923. Still living in Keene Valley, he modified his painting style and turned to a new subject, concentrating on painting the female nude for the next two years. Using his wife, Faith, as his model, he made a series of heavily worked, encrusted oils depicting the naked female body. The compositions are cropped in ways reminiscent of Alfred Stieglitz's remarkable nude photographs of his wife, Georgia O'Keeffe. The subject's face is often seen from behind, giving her anonymity. She is usually seen lying on bedsheets on her back or side, or face down. They are labored, difficult paintings—Montross refused to show them—yet they are moving and deeply felt. There is nothing pretty about them, but they are passionate, memorable works. They have a toughness and darkness that remind one of such German expressionists as Max Beckmann or Oskar Kokoschka, and there is little like them in American art.

In 1925 illness intervened in Weston's work, and in 1926 the Westons moved to France for four years. The result was a third stylistic shift within the decade. The painting and gouaches Weston made in France are landscapes and figurative studies in primary colors—yellows, blues, reds, and greens—sometimes used in strong intensities and other times in pastel tones. Both the Adirondack landscapes of 1920–23 and the nudes that followed seem Germanic in character; both series rely on a dark palette, and both express the artist's deepest feelings. They are expressionist works in a broad sense. In France, however, he took on a postimpressionist sensibility, turning as he did to more decorative interior scenes, landscapes, and figurative studies made in the traditionally cheerful colors of the School of Paris. Duncan Phillips wrote of Weston's apparent admiration for the French painters

Pierre Bonnard and Edouard Vuillard, but concluded that his concept of color was closer to "the symbolical, almost mystical realism of Van Gogh."[12]

Weston developed his mature style during the 1930s, combining elements from each of his earlier phases into a successful realist mode. Duncan Phillips in 1931 correctly called him "an artist of abstract tendency although a realist at heart."[13] Weston himself confirmed that he had turned away from his earlier, more spontaneous approach when he wrote: "I find that an oil takes me considerably longer than it used to, perhaps because the design is more thoroughly worked out before I begin."[14] Outstanding in these years were several still lifes (such as *Squash Enthroned*, 1932 [Phillips chap., fig. 75], or *My Snow Shoes*, 1934 [Phillips chap., fig. 76]) that are carefully drawn, interestingly composed, warmly lit works. He continued to paint handsome, but more conventional Adirondack views. He worked hard to sell pictures and to expand his reputation, each year sending one or two of his works to a dozen or more venues, including many of the then-leading institutions, such as the Corcoran Gallery, the Pennsylvania Academy of the Fine Arts, and the Whitney Museum of American Art in New York. Weston enjoyed good sales during the early 1930s, but by 1939 times were harder for him (as for all American painters); as he wrote a friend, "We could not possibly live on what I earn nowadays."[15] Phillips continued his crucial support, buying works regularly, providing friendship and financial backing, and giving Weston one-artist shows, the last in 1939.[16] Weston's final one-man show at Montross came in 1932, the year of the dealer's death. After this he was energetically represented by Philip Boyer, who showed Weston's work in the early 1930s at his Philadelphia gallery, then in New York beginning in 1936. During these years Weston won the respect and affection of his peers and of some important writers, but he never again enjoyed the warm critical reception of 1922.

In 1936 Weston won a commission under the Treasury Relief Art Project to paint twenty-two murals covering 840 square feet for the General Services Administration Building in Washington, D.C. His subject was the exterior and interior of a number of federal buildings around the nation, which he chose to paint in a literal, photographically based, realist style (Foster chap., fig. 45). A Washington critic reviewing Weston's 1939 show at the Phillips Memorial Gallery summed up the decline of Weston's critical reputation when she wrote, "There are times when [Weston's] work is more illustrative than aesthetic. But it is always thoughtful and soundly executed."[17]

Between 1949 and 1952 Weston executed an ambitious series of six large vertical paintings illustrating the construction of the United Nations headquarters in New York. They begin with a view of the structures being framed in steel and end with a grand, perhaps overly dramatic description of midtown Manhattan, including the completed United Nations. He did these paintings on his own, without a commission, hoping they would be purchased and hung at the site that inspired them, but this dream was never realized.

By 1940 Harold Weston's career on the cutting edge was largely over, but in many ways his greatest contributions lay ahead. He was a true polymath who possessed a multitude of talents. He was the rare artist who—as he had demonstrated in Persia—was a gifted and effective leader, administrator, and lobbyist. These talents, together with his personal warmth, drive, and high ethical standards, led him to serve humanity in a variety of important ways, as Rebecca Foster describes in her essay in this catalogue.

Weston began to paint prolifically again during the 1950s, continuing his long series of views of the Adirondack peaks, now in brighter tones with flatter brushwork. Through the last two decades of his life he experimented enthusiastically with modernism. Though the results were mixed, he deserves credit for his courage and his constant willingness to take risks. In some works he appears to have in mind the surrealists, both French and American. His palette becomes more intense, and his view of nature more stylized; some of the later paintings recall those of Georgia O'Keeffe, whereas others relate to the "pattern paintings" being made in New York by a younger generation of artists. He was drawn to abstraction, yet he never embraced cubism fully, and he could not leave his beloved landscape behind. In his final works, the Stone Series on paper, Weston accomplished much of what he had been aiming for in his late years. Laying meandering lines over the images of veined, abstracted stones while simplifying form and color, he successfully resolved his dedication to the real with a new acceptance of the flattened picture plane of modernism. Here he achieved a synthesis that expressed his deepest feelings about nature, his love of color, and his own adventurous spirit.

Notes

For their assistance in the preparation of this essay, I am grateful to Rebecca Foster, Atea Ring, Judith Hoos Fox, and Maria Di Raimo.

1. See the excellent discussion of Weston in Jean C. Harris, *A Retrospective Exhibition of Paintings by Harold Weston (1894–1972)*, exhibition catalogue, (South Hadley, Mass.: John and Norah Warbeke Gallery, Mount Holyoke College, 1975).

2. For example, the important study by Maurice Tuchman et al., *The Spiritual in Art: Abstract Painting, 1890–1985* (New York: Abbeville, 1986), makes no mention of Weston.

3. Harold Weston, "A Painter Speaks," *Magazine of Art* 32 (Jan. 1939), 18.

4. Munn became a professor of English at Harvard. In 1941 he presented the Fogg Art Museum with his collection of twelve works by Weston, including a watercolor, a self-portrait etching, two early oil sketches, three important oils from 1922, and a group of other paintings dating from 1925 to 1931.

5. Harvard University Archives.

6. Harold F. Weston, "Report," in *Records of the Class of 1916*, 5th Anniversary (Cambridge, Mass.: n.p., 1921).

7. Weston, "A Painter Speaks," 18.

8. Kandinsky quoted in Tuchman et al., *The Spiritual in Art*, 35.

9. See the print *Man as Seen by Clairvoyant (4-Dimensional Vision), and by Ordinary Human Sight*, in Claude Bragdon, *A Primer of Higher Space* (1913), illustrated in ibid., 26.

10. Robert Rosenblum, *Modern Painting and the Northern Romantic Tradition: Friedrich to Rothko* (New York: Harper and Row, 1975), 14.

11. Weston, "A Painter Speaks," 19.

12. Duncan Phillips, "Harold Weston," in *The Artist Sees Differently: Essays Based upon the Philosophy of a Collection in the Making*, 2 vols. (New York: E. Weyhe; Washington, D.C.: Phillips Memorial Gallery, 1931), 136.

13. Ibid., 137.

14. Harold Weston to Peppino Mangravite, 18 Nov. 1939, Harold Weston Papers, 1916–72, Archives of American Art, Smithsonian Institution, Washington, D.C.

15. Ibid.

16. Duncan Phillips died in 1966; after his death, the Phillips Gallery began to show Weston's work again. In 1976, for example, in part 3 of a series of exhibitions devoted to American artists in the collection, fifteen Westons were exhibited together, and in 1982 twenty-seven works from the Stone Series were shown.

17. Jane Watson, "Weston in One-Man Show at Phillips," *Washington Post*, 23 Apr. 1939, sec. 6, 6.

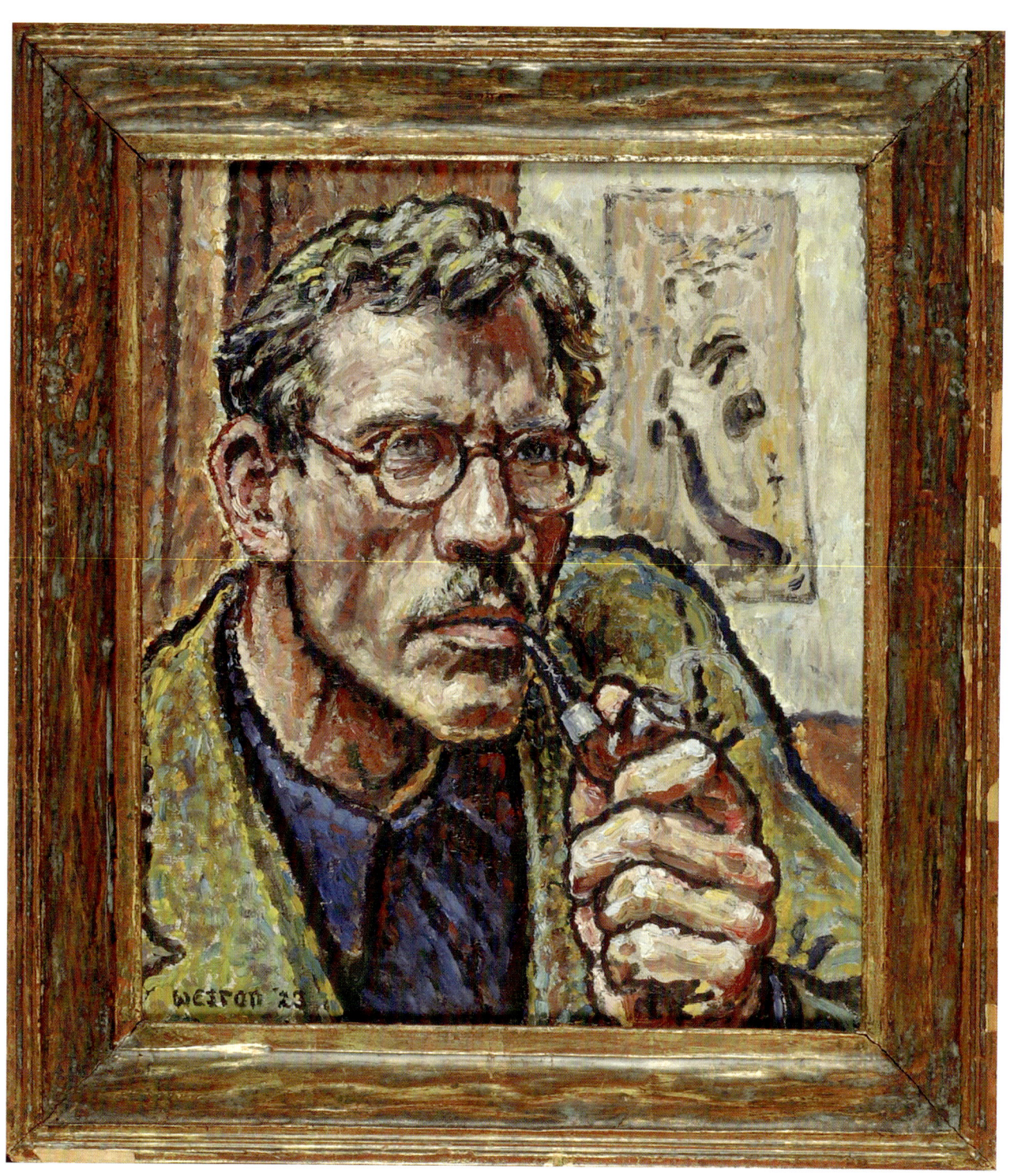

SPIRIT OF INTENSITY
The Life of Harold Weston

Rebecca Foster

This morning was the sort of day so perfect that the beauty of it seems to surge up and overwhelm your senses, exhilarates every pore as cool water after a plunge, and you simply have to sing, paint, or swim to keep afloat. And so I sketched quite madly for a while.

—Harold Weston to Faith Borton, 5 June 1922,
Weston Papers, Harold Weston Foundation

FACING PAGE

6. Harold Weston, *Self-Portrait,*
1923. Charles and Marietta
Weston.

To create anything worthwhile, an artist must raise his feelings and energies to an intense pitch, observed the critic Clive Bell.[1] Nature, sexuality, politics, and even, it seemed, the ordinary things of day-to-day life raised Harold Weston to that intense pitch. He lived to plunge into cool waters, and, as Duncan Phillips wrote, he painted what he lived.[2] He was intensely up or intensely down, and his painting followed the serpentine course.

Many of the decisive transitions in Weston's work were driven by life changes, but some were a result of his inability to stay still. His was a condition of continual experimentation—by disposition and professional resolve. "If you stop to watch yourself performing," Weston wrote, "you won't get beyond your mirrored self."[3] He feared that repetition and self-consciousness would dim the authentic, original passion of his creativity. The poet Archibald MacLeish agreed that self-imitation ruins an artist and praised Weston's experimentation.[4]

Although Weston's career was defined by a spirit of change, it had a fundamental integrity. In 1932 an *Art News* review noted that Weston's style had evolved over ten years, but that he had "remained curiously and courageously himself." The explanation, the review concluded, was his early contact with nature.[5] The poet who is bred in the woods will always be able to conjure nature's lesson, wrote Ralph Waldo Emerson. "At the call of a noble sentiment, again the woods wave, the pines murmur, the river rolls and shines … as he saw and heard them in his infancy. And with these forms, the spells of persuasion, the keys of power are put into his hands."[6] Weston saw and heard such forms of nature in his own infancy and would reconjure them time and again.

The Spells of Persuasion

Harold Francis Weston was born on 14 February 1894 in Merion, Pennsylvania, in a mansion built by his maternal grandfather, Charles Hartshorne, who was vice president of the Lehigh Valley Railroad. Hartshorne had spent summers in the Adirondack Mountains since the 1880s, and in 1887 he helped purchase twenty-eight thousand acres of the Adirondack High Peaks to prevent their ruin from logging. As a child, Weston spent summers in St. Huberts, New York, with that enormous tract of wilderness, called the Adirondack Mountain Reserve, right outside his door.

Weston's parents, Mary Hartshorne and S. Burns Weston, met in St. Huberts. Mary, a pianist whose family was religiously conservative and lived on Philadelphia's wealthy Main Line, passed on an aesthetic sensibility to Harold. Burns was the impecunious son of a Maine farmer whom the Unitarian Church refused to ordain because of his religious freethinking. Although inept in the aesthetics department, sometimes making "amusingly stupid remarks" about his son's art,[7] Burns gave Harold an "integrity of purpose."[8] While leading the Society for Ethical Culture in Philadelphia through the Progressive Era and into the 1930s, the senior Weston founded settlement houses, schools, labor and peace organizations, and literary and art centers. The social activists he brought home, such as Jane Addams and Booker T. Washington, left an impressionable young Harold aware of a world of invigorating ideas and the importance of social justice. Harold also grew up surrounded by the sons of American transcendentalism—the philosophers and religious leaders who were drawn to the Adirondacks, such as William James, John Dewey, and Felix Adler. For them, nature, aesthetics, and spirituality were fundamentally linked.

7. The Weston family in 1909 in Merion, Pennsylvania. *Clockwise from top left:* Carl, Harold, Mary Hartshorne, Esther, and S. Burns Weston. Harold Weston Foundation.

Weston always liked to say that winning a pair of ice skates at age eleven in an art contest for his painting of a wildflower was pivotal in his decision to become a "nature composer."[9] As a teenager, he studied the ancients and old masters when the family lived in Europe in 1909 and 1910. He was most riveted by Europe's "modern" paintings, which he felt spoke to emotions and an inner self, not merely an objective technique. "Each picture was a world crying out for admittance in my mind," he wrote.[10] In the summers he walked with his father and brother, Carl, through the French, Swiss, and Italian Alps, sketching in his diary and painting in postcard-perfect style as he went.

When the family returned to America, Harold attended Phillips Exeter Academy and spent the following summer in the Adirondacks. The seventeen-year-old was at the peak of his physical powers when he set out with Carl on 4 August 1911 for a sixteen-day hiking and canoeing trip across the heart of the Adirondack High Peaks, the Saranac Lakes, and the Blue Mountain Lake region. He trotted over trails with a seventy-pound canoe, swam around his island camp before heading off for the day's journey, and on the final day on the way back to St. Huberts he walked and rowed thirty miles—running the last three and one-quarter miles in fifteen minutes.[11] The following day he played seven sets of tennis and that night danced and played the mandolin at a campfire gathering.

On 24 August he wrote in his diary, "pains begin." He spent the next day in bed, and the next. It was several weeks before he stood up again, but he could not walk, and the doctors said he would need a wheelchair for life. Instead of finishing his senior year at boarding school, he went home to Pennsylvania to regain the physical strength and emotional equilibrium seized by the polio that had struck his left leg. Below the knee, the nerve was so shattered that it

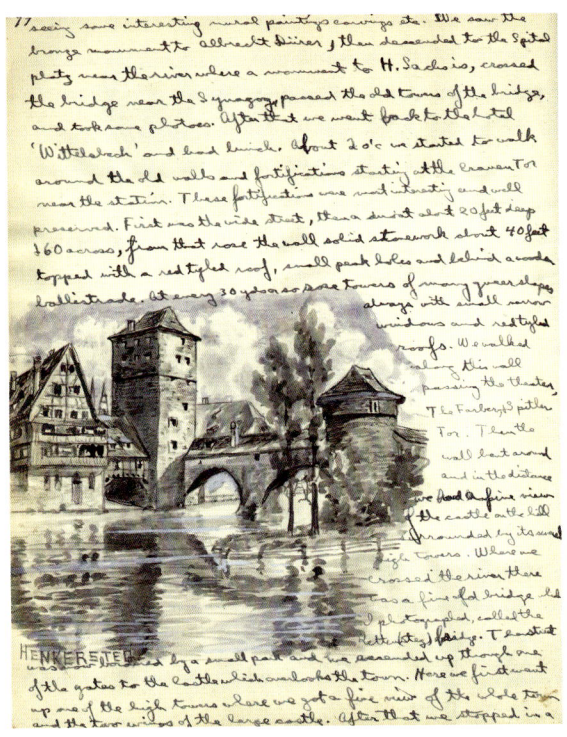

8. A page of Harold Weston's diary from 1910. Harold Weston Foundation.

9. Harold Weston, *Mountains and Farm Buildings*, 1909. Harold Weston Foundation.

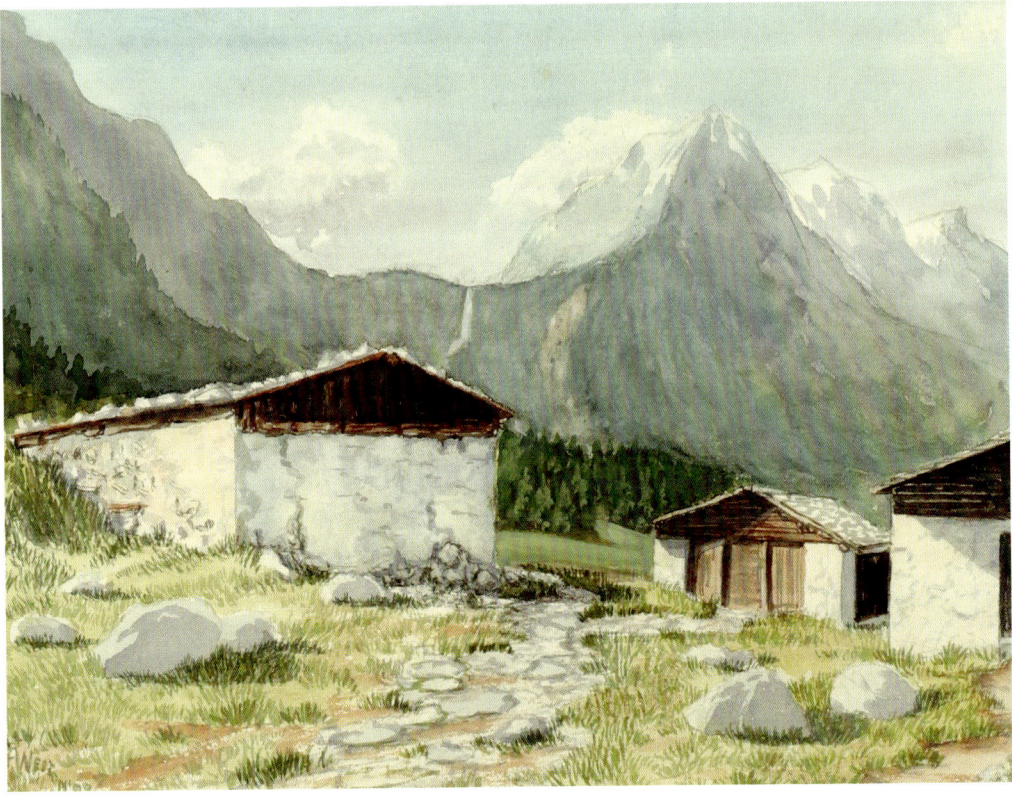

was useless. Determined to climb mountains again, within a year he built up strength to use crutches, and before long he figured out how to balance with one cane. Instead of portaging canoes and covering vast distances at great speed as he once did, he would learn to pick his way over the mountain trails more carefully, committing details to memory and pausing to record his observations in paint.

Polio was the crucible by which Weston became an artist. Before polio, he had the talent, the passion, and the intention to be an artist, but, still, as a precociously intelligent, good-looking, privileged boy whose talents were extensive, he could have done anything. Harold had spoken about his future with his father just three weeks before the peculiar chance of contracting polio in the Adirondack wilderness and had written in his journal: "Occupation art worthy, but??"[12] This ambivalence subsided after losing the full use of his exceptionally vigorous body. Life as an artist seemed fated. The social stigma and cruel timing of the polio during emerging manhood forced an emotional maturity on the boy that made him look years older than he was, gave him added ambition, and suited his developing artistic temperament.

10. Harold Weston, *Wiamo*, 1913. Harold Weston Foundation. On the back of the painting Harold Weston wrote: "Singled out by Dr. Denman Ross for favorable comment when I showed to professors of Dept. of Fine Arts at Harvard some 30 of my sketches to illustrate modern principles during my honors exam—granted magna cum laude."

Training the Heart to Paint

Harold's parents offered to send him to art school, but he chose to follow his brother to Harvard University. "I felt too many painters had a facile ability or proficient technique," he wrote, "and nothing significant to express."[13] He studied philosophy, literature, languages, and art history. The cartoons he drew for the *Harvard Lampoon* are more revealing of his characteristic strong line than the academic paintings he was made to do in his studio classes. Not content with either, however, he was searching for a third approach and thinking about modernism, or what he called "the spiritual side of things."[14] During the summers

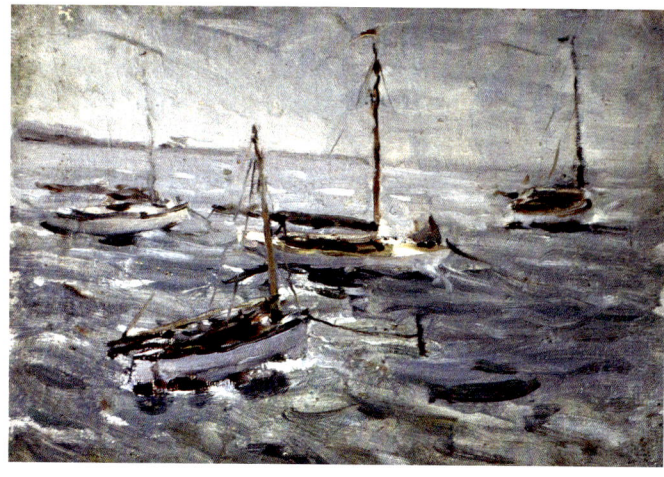

he painted in the Adirondacks, and in 1914 he studied under the important proponent of modern art Hamilton Easter Field at his Summer School of Graphic Arts in Ogonquit, Maine. If he were going to be the "modern" who cried out for admittance in people's minds—not merely in their aesthetic sensibilities—he would have to look inside himself for self-expression. "Give me faith, give me hope, give me courage, give me strength," he pleaded in his journal.[15]

After graduation in 1916 he discovered faith and courage when he volunteered for the war effort. The United States had not yet declared war, but Europe was fresh in Weston's mind. He and just about everyone else seemed to believe that the world crisis would be followed by a spiritual regeneration. He wanted to be in the middle of the action, "to literally see the heart of humanity laid bare." Witnessing this moment would train his heart, he thought, and help him to become a better artist.[16] Many Harvard graduates, such as classmate and friend John Dos Passos, volunteered for ambulance service, but Weston's lame leg disqualified him. The Young Men's Christian Association (YMCA) accepted him to run one of its many "huts" for recreation and religious services that were located in army bases, concentration camps, and prisons.

The YMCA sent Weston to Mesopotamia (now Iraq) with the British troops. What he thought would be one year turned into three and one-half years. In Baghdad, where he was based at the YMCA headquarters, he managed three theaters and arranged for a full roster of lectures, readings, cinema, songs, checkers tournaments, indoor stunts, and concerts. His greatest innovation came when he sent for one thousand dollars' worth of art supplies to launch the Baghdad Art Club. The soldiers took so much interest in the club's evening studio hours and the "sketching excursions" to the desert that Weston arranged two exhibitions of the men's work.

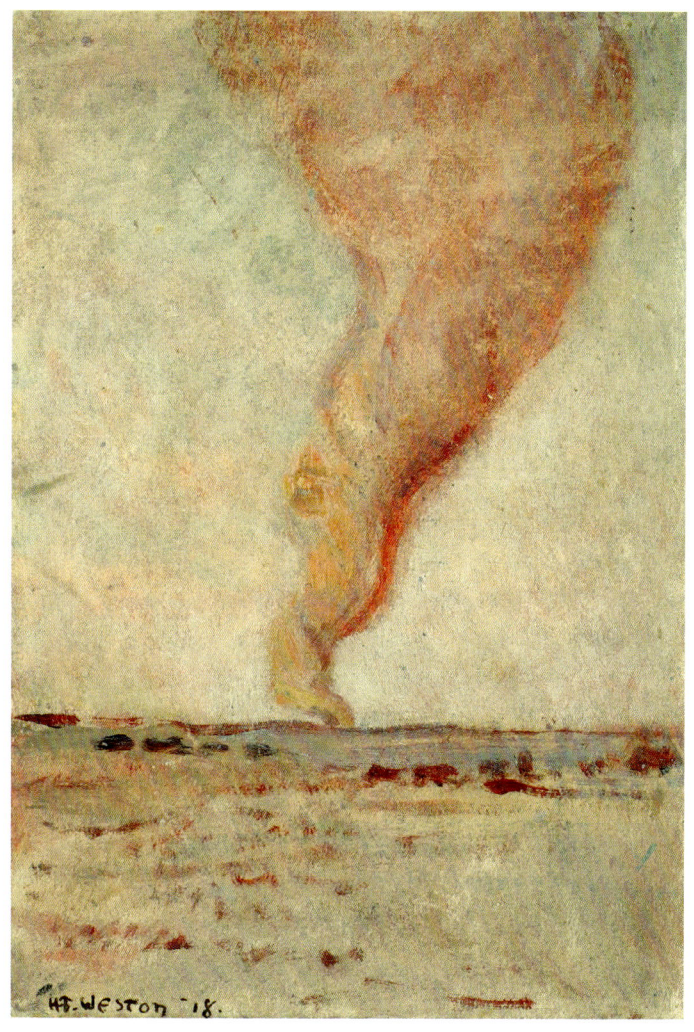

11. Harold Weston, *Dust Storm and Nomad Huts*, 1918. Private Collection.

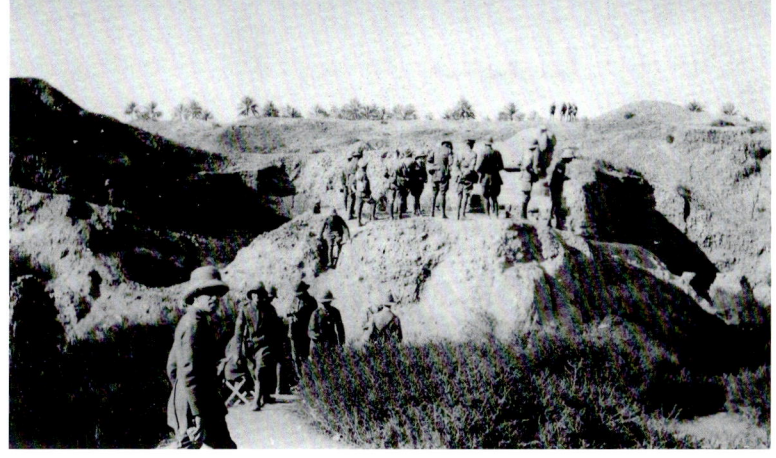

12. The Baghdad Art Club on a sketching trip to Babylon. Photograph by Harold Weston. Harold Weston Foundation.

On the face of it, it was congenial work—and important because there were four hundred thousand troops and untold numbers of refugees from Armenia, Egypt, Great Britain, India, and Turkey. But the work had to be done in some of the worst conditions of the war. Warfare was not Weston's biggest problem: his closest brush with fighting came one moonlit night when Turkish airplanes dropped bombs two hundred yards from the open-air theater in which he was showing films. In the summer of 1917, however, the temperature in the shade measured 128 degrees Fahrenheit, a heat that killed four hundred people a day. And there was famine. Weston saw children chase a dog away from a dead donkey so they could get at the meat. It was difficult to conscionably take the time to paint or sketch, so he did not for about two years. Nevertheless, he could not stop himself from seeing. "Color oh what color!" he wrote. "Sunset red and gray brown of utmost delicacy . . . a marvelous display of yellow green quite clearly vibrated with orange, and below great violet shadows . . . fields of a green such as I have never seen, pure emerald only more vigorous and substantial . . . while above great violet blue shadows under a huge white, absolutely neutral cloud, above strays of gold, behind over the horizon traces of pink. And the moon, green! like green!!"[17]

By 1918, after hostilities were over in that part of the world, Weston made time to paint. His sketches of the open, arid, and, to him, exotic terrain have strong colors, patterns, and bold outlines. Away from art teachers, away from Western civilization even, he was developing his first independent expression. His conviction held fast that art was nature was spirituality. "My best prayer always was and will be before the God of the open—of nature," he wrote while in Mesopotamia. "My best words spelt in paints."[18] In 1919 he

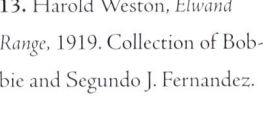

13. Harold Weston, *Elwand Range*, 1919. Collection of Bobbie and Segundo J. Fernandez.

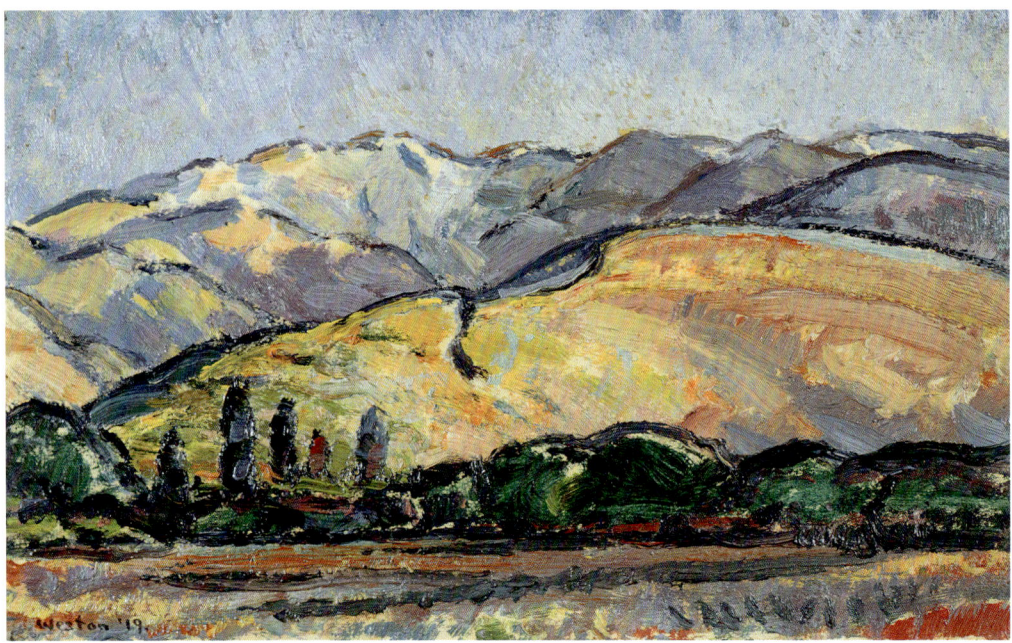

convinced a friend to travel home with him through Persia (now Iran) and Asia. They had adventures of the highest order, waving off murderous bands of robbers with the new technology of a flashlight, being lavishly entertained by the shah's uncle, riding on donkeys for nights on end to avoid the heat in the daytime, and nearly dying of malaria. "If I get back before I am toothless and gray," Harold wrote to his parents, "I want to live in a wild desert place—I want to live in the slums—I want to live."[19]

He moved to New York City in January 1920 and indeed lived in the slums, working in one of the city's many settlement houses that kept thousands of immigrants in adequate shelter. Weston took drawing classes with Boardman Robinson at the Art Students League, painted in the evenings with a group of moderns, and in the mornings painted under the affable tutelage of William Schumacher, a symbolist who used whimsy and color in his paintings of simplified forms.[20] Weston attended modernist exhibitions, explored dusty corners of the Metropolitan Museum of Art, and critiqued the opera, symphony, and theater in his journal. The intense cultural immersion made up for the years away in the desert, but it also galvanized disquiet. "Damn! Where getting to?" He was not pleased with his painting. One day he pulled out some old sketches of the Adirondack Mountains and remembered how much he loved them. Wishfully, he quoted Luke in his journal: "And he withdrew himself into the wilderness, and prayed."[21]

Into the Wilderness

"I have wasted time," Weston scrawled scathingly in his journal while on the deck of the Albany night boat in May 1920. "Egoist, painter without real vision. Sentimentalist and think you are analytical. What power have you?"[22] The day-and-a-half journey from New York City into the wilderness of the Adirondack High Peaks ended at the Weston camp at St. Huberts. Like an

14. Weston's one-room studio, 1920. Harold Weston Foundation.

15. The interior of Weston's studio, 1921. Harold Weston Foundation.

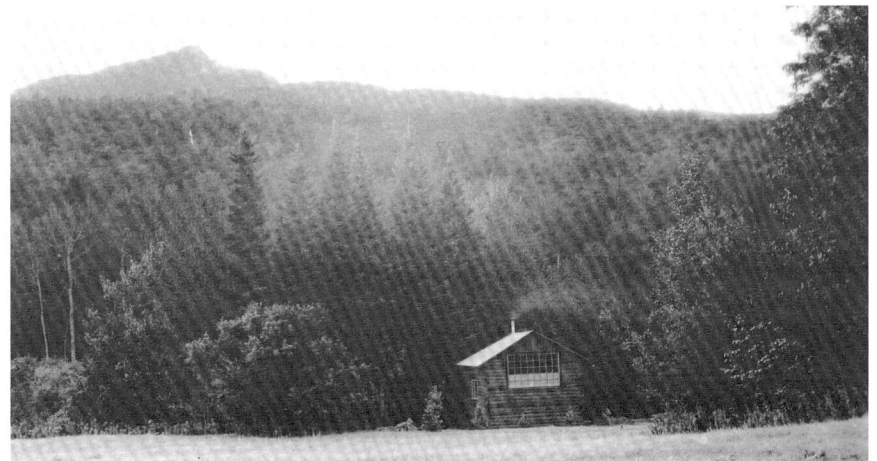

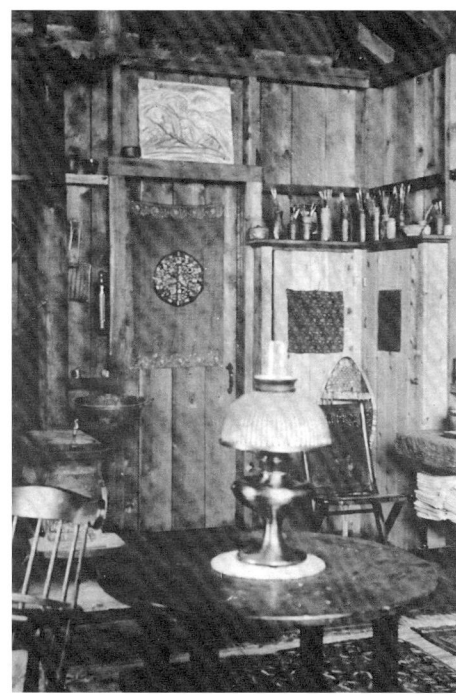

impatient character from a romantic Russian novel, Weston lamented after only one day, "What proving?" A few days later he was extolling the "stolid, unflinching, eternal" rock cliffs by Chapel Pond and the "woods, glorious woods."[23] To him this was God's land, a subject that moved his brush. He resolved his mission: to stay and paint the glory of God in nature.

Weston helped local craftsmen construct a one-room studio. It was primitive. In the winter he kept the temperature between forty-five and fifty-five degrees Fahrenheit to minimize contrast with the cold outdoors. He tacked a Persian rug over the door and laid six more over the rag rugs on the floor to fight the drafts. When there was enough snow, he banked it against the outside walls for insulation. Mice sometimes stole his apples and ate them by his feet while he painted. Thrushes and chimney swifts found their way in. It was a rustic and orientalist haven with Persian saddlebags tossed on the bed and Japanese prints and Buddha statuettes propped on the open cross studs. When he was perfectly content, he would sit by the fire watching the moon rise over Giant Mountain while smoking one of the cigars that Dr. Felix Adler, the founder of the Society for Ethical Culture, had given him.

Weston's family was concerned about his paralyzed leg and his well-being in the wilderness. Accounts in his journal of walks and hikes and one-hundred-pound camp baskets filled with woolen blankets for overnights seem ordinary until he recorded: "only fell once." He lunged, hopped, and swung himself from powerful arms across ranges of wilderness. He climbed elevations to get views, to see and study every change in the light, colors, and forms. The fearlessness with which he did his research, staying on the tops of mountains to paint while the light was just so, only to stumble down in the dark, came from a reckless pursuit of the perfect subject.

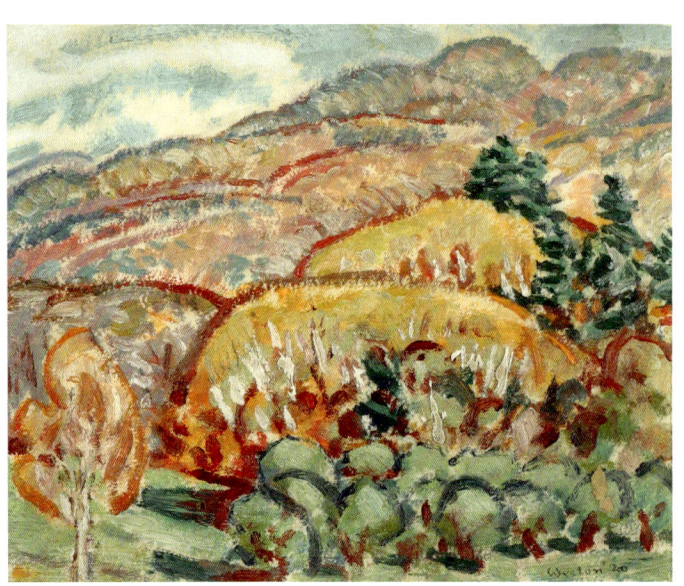

16. Harold Weston, *Spring Light*, 1920. St. Huberts Trust.

"Not yet sure of my point of view, just what paint can and cannot express," he wrote to his former teacher Hamilton Easter Field. "If I have anything vital to say I must work it out with this great and ever changing source of inspiration about me."[24] In the brilliant autumn weather he packed a knapsack with a tin sketch box that had paints, pencils, and small pieces of cardboard, usually about nine by six inches. Bobbing in a canoe or emerging from the woods to an outcropping of rock, he would be struck by a composition. He was in a state of constant readiness to attack the cardboard, urged on by the Adirondacks' fast-moving light and clouds no less than by his desire to get an unmediated first impression. Vigorously, expressionistically, ecstatically, he daubed and smeared reds, blues, yellows, and greens, sometimes in unlikely combination and frequently with swirls and swoops of pencil running through the wet paint for texture and definition. Spots of raw cardboard render the sketches in process and ever changing.

The sketches, which took anywhere from ten minutes to an hour to complete, are more mature than the Middle East sketches. They have more meteorological drama, and it is as if the mountains grew larger as he grew more familiar with them. The same way color opposites highlight each other, he was impressed by the Adirondacks' greens and blues after the reds and purples of Persia. He painted more than fifty oil sketches in two weeks in October 1920. When the local guide and workman Frank Hale came to drop off a pail of milk at the studio one day, he could recognize the subject of only two sketches. Weston was not an academic painter who strove for realistic depictions. He sympathized with the moderns, calling their work "spiritual," and yet he also understood Walter Pach's warning that there can be "a modernist academism as deadly as the academism of the academy." So Weston tracked his own way, progressing logically from what he knew. After four months he warned his parents that things were getting "rather wilder."[25]

Solitude in the wilds suited his passions. "It is the amount of life which a man feels," wrote William James, "that makes you value his mind."[26] James proposed that emotional excitement creates memory by leaving a "scar" on the mind.[27] In perpetual excitement Weston nimbly remembered arcane details of trails he walked, words people spoke, and

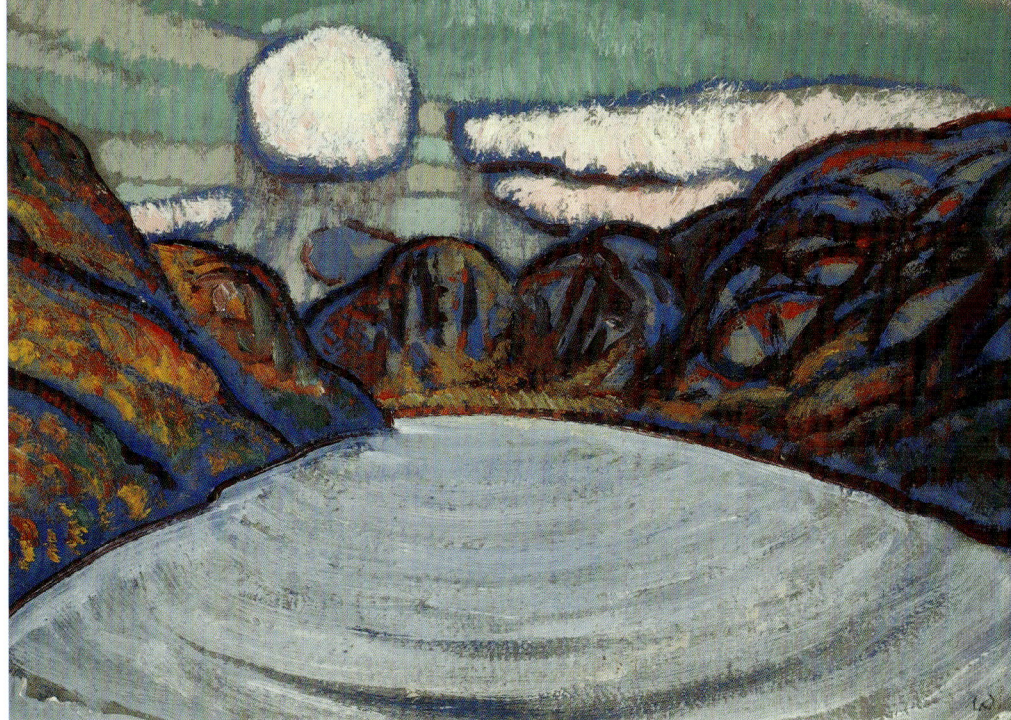

17. Harold Weston, *Lower Ausable Lake*, 1921. Baird and Nancy Edmonds.

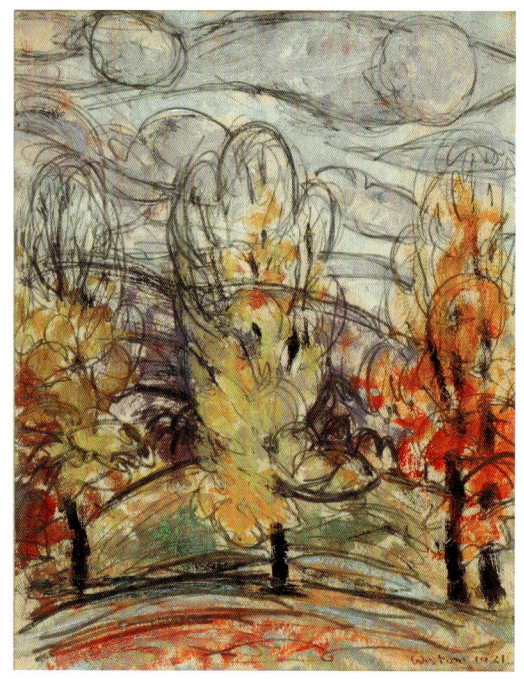

colors they wore. He wrote, in an expression much like the ancient Greek idea that memory is drawn onto a wax tablet, "The hand of nature traces a pattern upon our nerves as the etcher on the waxed plate and contact direct with it pours acid into those lines which bite deep into memory. There was too something acrid about the sunset, in the sense of burning, almost painful, brilliance. Stenciled lines of gold jazzed up from behind ocherish purple ranges of looming hills. Then suddenly the current of gold played out, the molten metal ran down, a few eddies lingering, down behind the western range."[28] Created in moments of elation, Weston's sketches of red clouds, green snow, and purple trees, made of lush, racing impasto and pencil, gave him a visual and emotional cue back to the creativity he hoped for in the studio paintings.

He finally shut himself in the studio in January 1921 and started tacking linen on stretchers, propping along the walls bedaubed canvases with their charcoal underdrawing. Working on several at once, he looked to the world—if there were a world to see him—the profile of the mad

18. Harold Weston, *Autumn Trees*, 1921. St. Huberts Trust.

19. Harold Weston, *Nubble—Coming Night*, 1921. Private Collection.

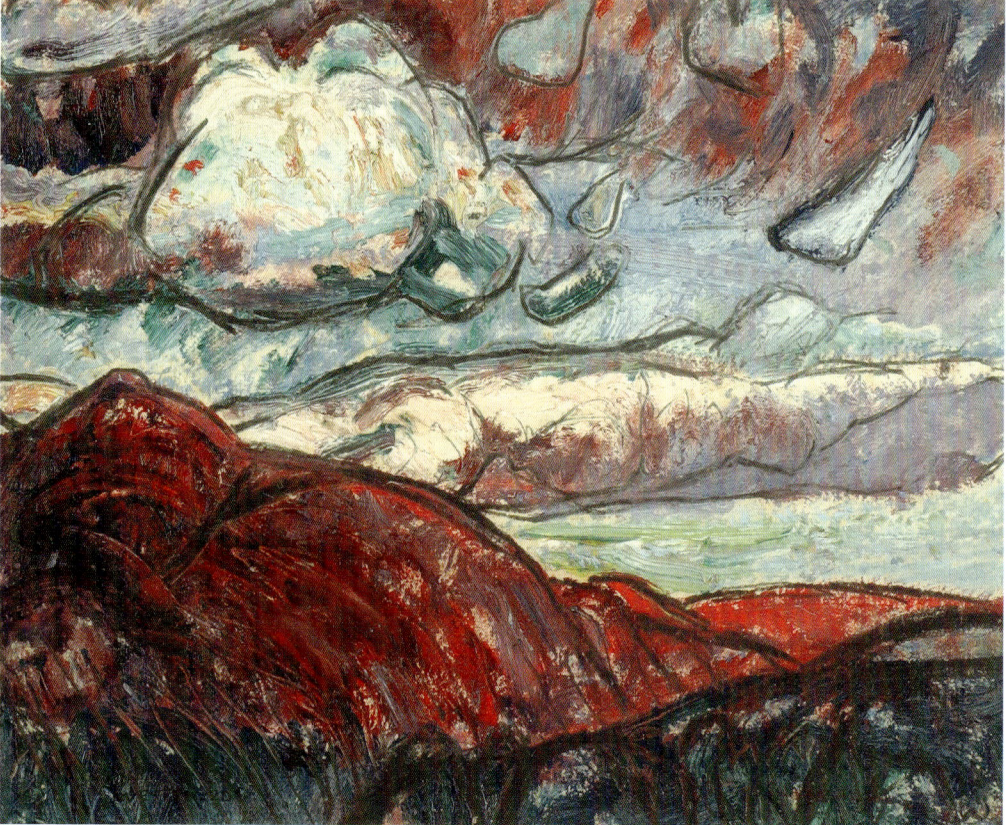

artist, hair hanging around his ears and "wornout, bald, hairless paint brushes" in his hand.[29] Each new phase—from sketches to canvas, from charcoal to paint—brought on unbidden insecurity. "Paint is being progressively spread on canvas even though it seems to progress towards art, the expression of the inner soul, about as fast as maple syrup drips out of a tapped tree in mid winter," he wrote.[30] But the beginning of being is doubt, wrote Descartes. And somehow Weston's strokes on canvas came out trembling with being, bold with confidence.

"There is so much rhythm in some of these forest scenes," a critic exalted, "that one well believes the trees can 'clap their hands together,' and indeed, make any gesture of joy and abandon."[31] At first, large stands of trees served as models for cathedrals, but, over time, trees came to be seen to resemble cathedrals. Weston's house of worship was formed of cloisters of trees and vaults of branches. The uninhabited landscapes ignore the human relationship to earth and reach back to something primal, to a time "before anything had a soul / While life was a heave of matter, half inanimate," as D. H. Lawrence wrote in a poem

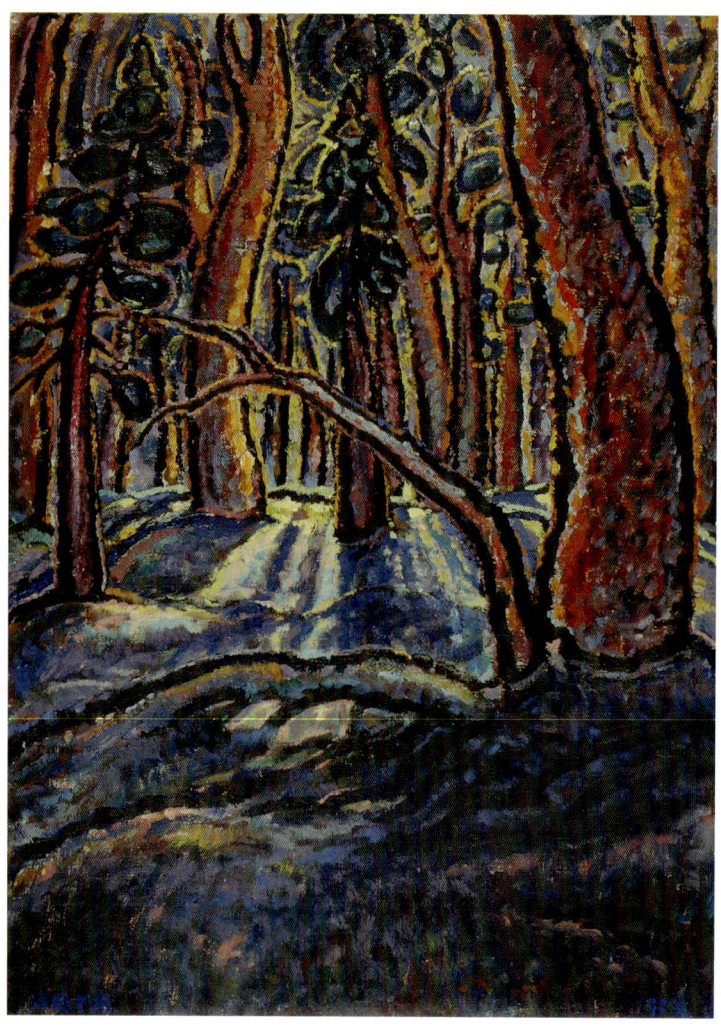

21. Harold Weston, *Forest Winter No. 2*, 1922. Michael and Susan Mahoney.

that Weston clipped from a magazine.[32] Weston was discovering the birth of the world, especially in the aerial optimism and snow-frozen forms of his winter canvases. Painters of the northern romantic tradition, such as Caspar David Friedrich, often used blue— the color Wassily Kandinsky called spiritual, infinite, heavenly—to paint religious landscapes in lieu of religious iconography. Weston, whose winter landscapes are awash with blue, is a descendant of this tradition, but his work also exhibits a "joy and abandon" not often found in a Friedrich, Ferdinand Hodler, or Edvard Munch. Weston's sure stroke, strong forms, and dark outlining of tree trunks, clouds, and mountains give some of the paintings a cloisonné effect. His paintings are expressionist in technique, slightly symbolist in feel, high in color key, and harsh "to one who was used to looking at paintings from the older point of view," according to Weston.[33] He had found his style. His nature forms were heightened, bowed, distended, and furled, but not unrecognizable. The paintings were challenging but not alienating, and it was unlikely he would be charged with insanity, as many modernists had been.

In the fledgling stages his work was largely private. But in April 1922 Weston was ready to roll up thirty-one canvases and subject them to critique in New York City. He boldly took them to the Montross Galleries, a leading venue for modern art. Montross had held Edward Hopper's first commercial gallery show as well as the first Vincent van Gogh exhibition in the United States. Within an hour the dapper, white-haired Newman Emerson Montross offered Weston the gallery for an exhibition in November. Thrilled at the opportunity, Weston, in an extravagant act of creative unity, carved frames for all the oil paintings in the show. Wharton Esherick, the "poet in wood" who lived in Paoli, Pennsylvania, inspired Weston's own frame carving, though he worked in a completely different style.[34] The profiles of Weston's frames were more muscular, rough hewn, and composed of abstract designs of grooves, circular shapes, or troughs that curled up like waves. (See figs. 6, 23, 32, 40; Phillips chap., figs. 65–67, 75; and Welsh chap., figs. 106, 121.) Carved of three-inch-square lengths of pine, each frame was different and related to the painting it compassed.

Weston had them gilded in New York City. At Montross he hung sixty-three oil canvases with hand-carved frames, twenty Persian sketches, and seventy Adirondack sketches.

Weston stayed at the gallery every day during the show's run from 8 to 25 November to discuss his work with visitors and critics. Henry Tyrrell from the *New York World*, whom Weston called one of the few progressive critics, lingered for two and one-half hours, telling Weston that his work was the "biggest thing of its kind to hit the New York art world in the last two years." His printed review was hardly more restrained, calling the picture-

22. Harold Weston, *Giant Mountain from Windy Brow*, 1922. Kathryn and Robert Preyer.

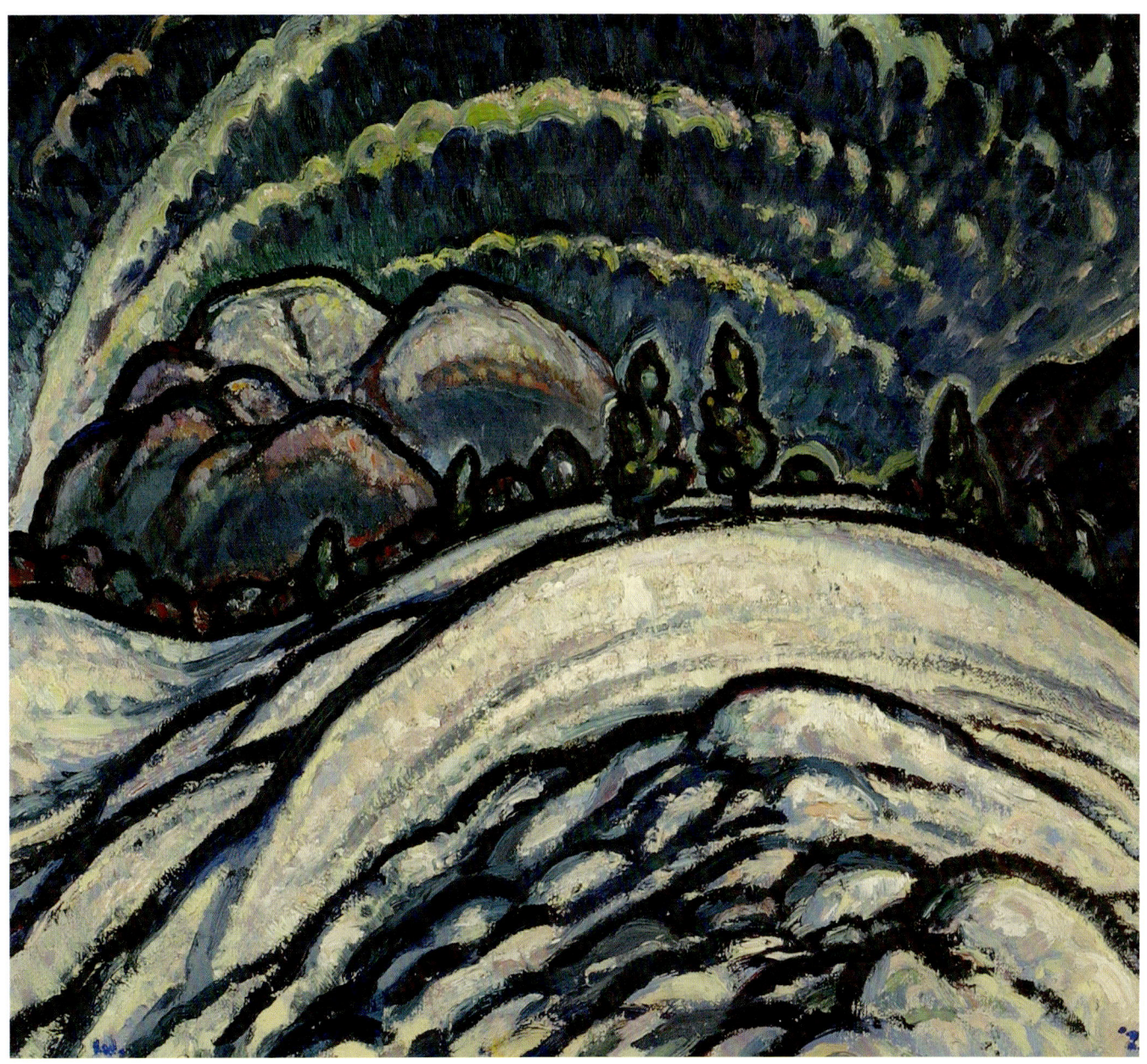

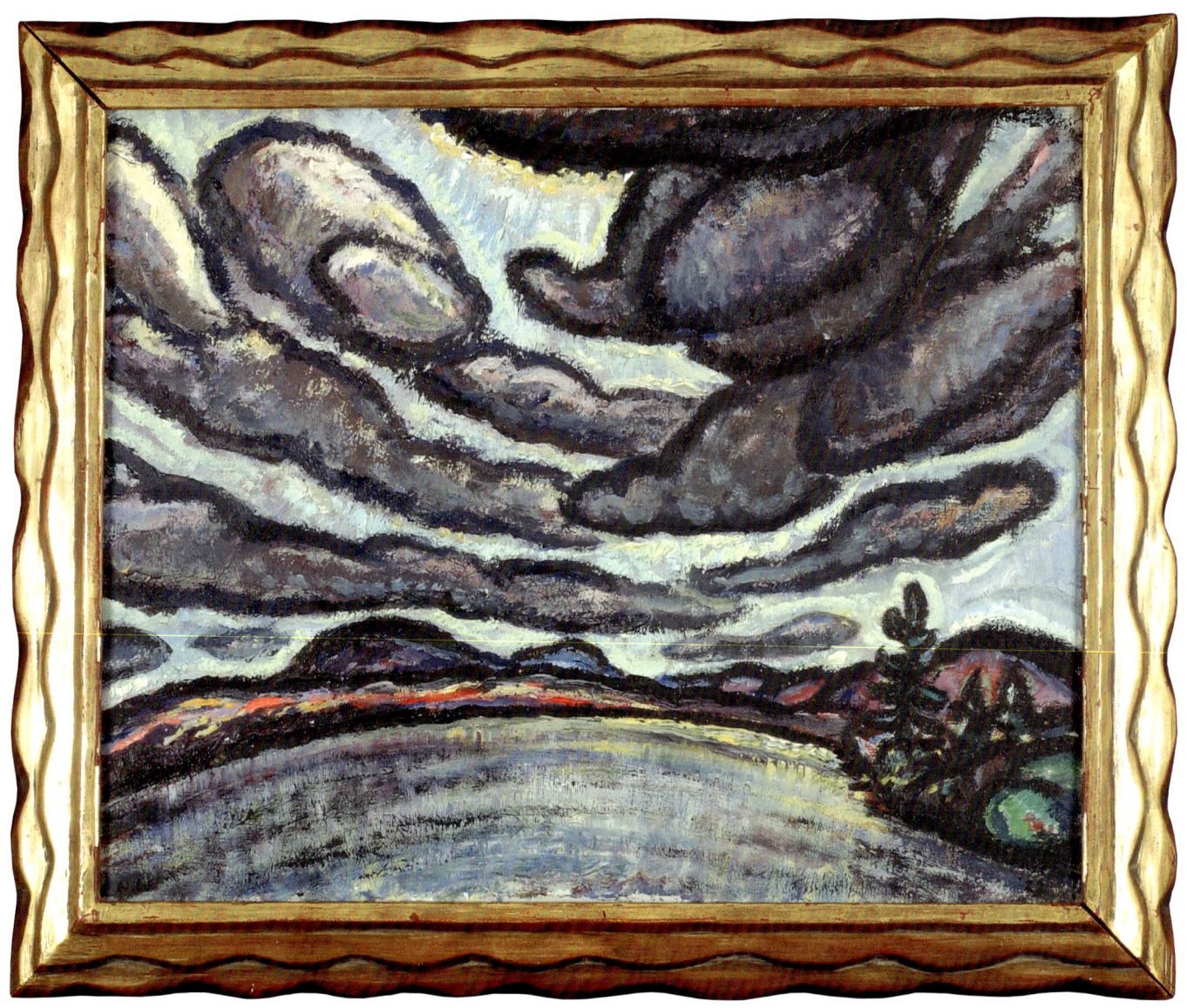

23. Harold Weston, *Clouds—*
Upper Ausable Lake, 1922. Private
Collection.

hymns to nature "symphonic."[35] A poet friend of Weston's saw in each of the paintings, which he called "musical," a different composer—a welcome comment to the painter, who once thought he might compose music and whose Dvôrák-, Debussy-, and Chopin-playing Victrola made lonely winters endurable. Tyrrell explored, as other critics did, the work's connection to the oriental and mystical, quoting the artist's own assertion that the East had given him "a direct and summary style of expression which made me a modernist without my knowing it."[36]

Art critics for the *New York Evening Post*, *American Art News*, *Art Review*, and *Vanity Fair* agreed that Weston's paintings were highly personal, not of any one school, and certainly not academic.[37] Most important was the critical approval of Henry McBride, the longtime champion of modernist work, in the *New York Herald*. Accustomed to making and breaking careers, he anointed Weston "likely to have a career." He called Weston heroic for pursuing his wilderness solitude and claimed that most of the great American artists, such as Thomas Eakins and Winslow Homer, had been recluses, too. McBride admired Weston's sincerity and enthusiasm, but chided him for his breathless haste to discover the world, to do too much, to attempt too many themes.[38] Most critics had no reservations at all. "The boy has a strangely beautiful and haunting vision of the woods," wrote the critic Christian Brinton, who thought Weston was a "near genius in his deeply personal and mystic vision."[39]

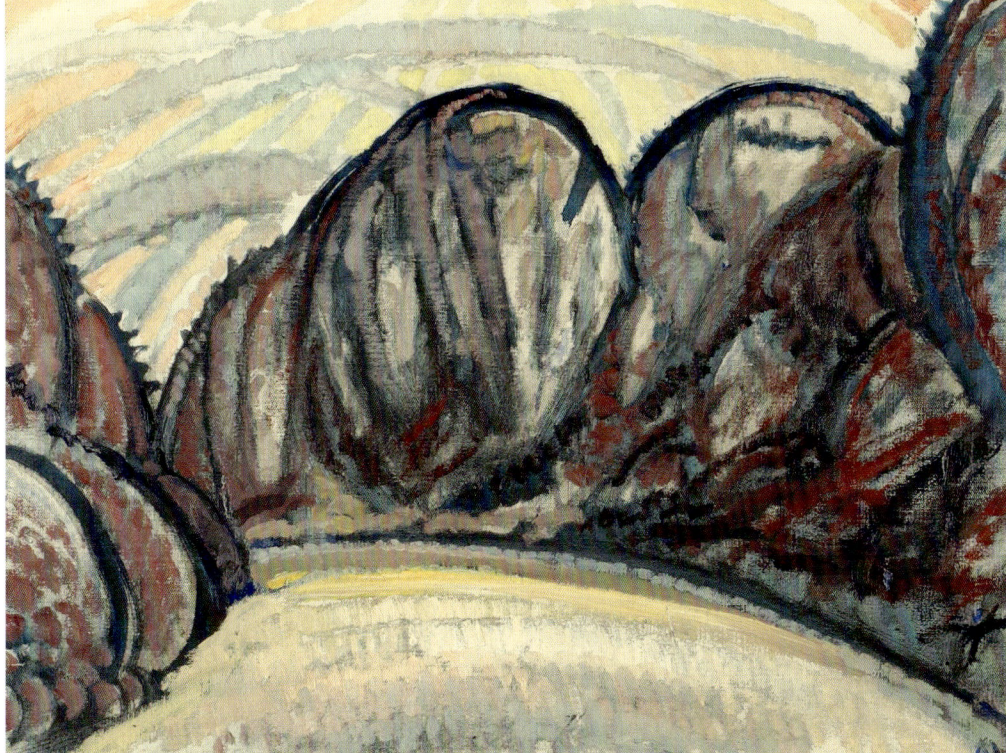

24. Harold Weston, *Winter Lower Lake*, 1921. Harold Weston Foundation.

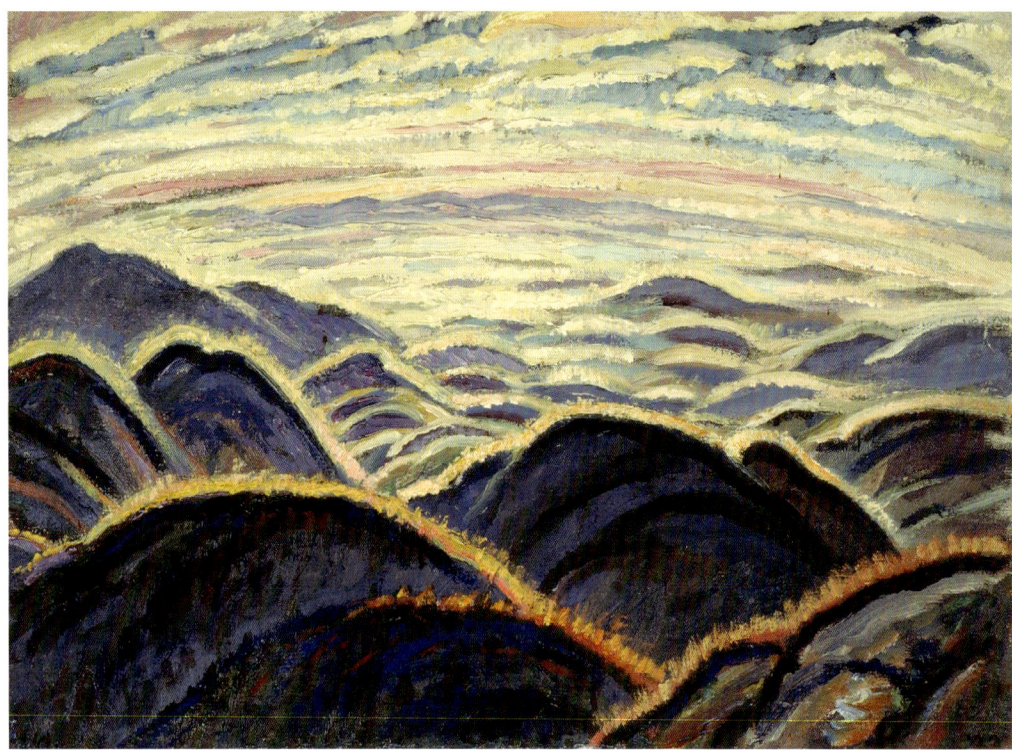

The *Christian Science Monitor* declared the show the highlight of the season: "In his pictures [there is] something different, something stirring and magnificently bold, a proclamation of a bigger belief in beauty than is usually heard in the galleries."[40]

Weston was wary of his good fortune and positive reception, however. After seeing a gallery show of the Russian artist Leon Bakst, he was more convinced than ever that artists suffer from success. "Repetition kills the spark of inspiration from which all Great Art takes its life. There is a terrible danger," he wrote, "in doing too well one isolated type of thing."[41] Without the self-conscious "mirrored self" that success brought, Weston might have continued with the landscapes. If so, it would not have been for long. He had a new, more powerful source of inspiration.

Faith

Faith Borton had a liveliness and poise that Harold noticed immediately. She was brought up in Moorestown, New Jersey, on Quaker principles of generosity, contemplation, and social awareness, as well as an assiduous reverence for the everyday. Upright and God-loving, the Bortons let loose by playing word games around a large holiday dinner table. "Thee would have nearly died," Faith wrote to her brother, "to hear mother trying to work in the sentence 'Do Fords have magnetic breaks' while talking to Aunt Caroline."[42] Faith—a classmate of Harold's sister, Esther, at Vassar College—caught his eye when he stopped by for a visit. She came to the studio for a winter party he hosted in February 1922, and the placid pattern of her life was forever shattered.[43] They watched ice cutting on the lake, balanced on a load of logs drawn by horses charging downhill, drove bundled in furs across frozen lakes in ten-degree-below-zero weather, and got lost while snowshoeing through a blizzard in remote Marcy Swamp. She was impressed by Harold's passion "to enhance the life of mankind," as he put it, and "to express the finer things in this existence."[44] They married in May 1923.

The union of Harold and Faith was a fusion of dynamic spiritual and physical attention to the great and small. The newlyweds spent long hours of comradeship together at the studio, which now had three more rooms. They cooked and cleaned, planted nasturtium seeds in the garden, and went on the daily evening walk for milk and mail. After dinner they sat by the hearth, reading out loud and darning socks. Faith was well prepared to parry Harold on nineteenth-century poetry and the moral and religious views of John Ruskin, Emerson, and Leo Tolstoy. After a week of marriage Harold wrote to a friend that he and Faith felt as though they had never really lived before.[45]

In good weather they walked to places where he could sketch and she could write. Once they were a pencil short, so he snatched the one she was writing with to press accents onto

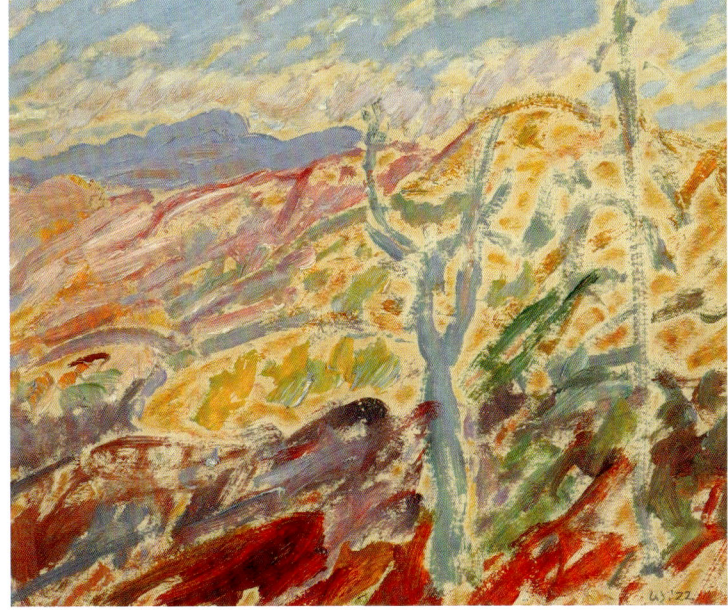

27. Harold Weston, *On McIntyre*, 1922. St. Huberts Trust.

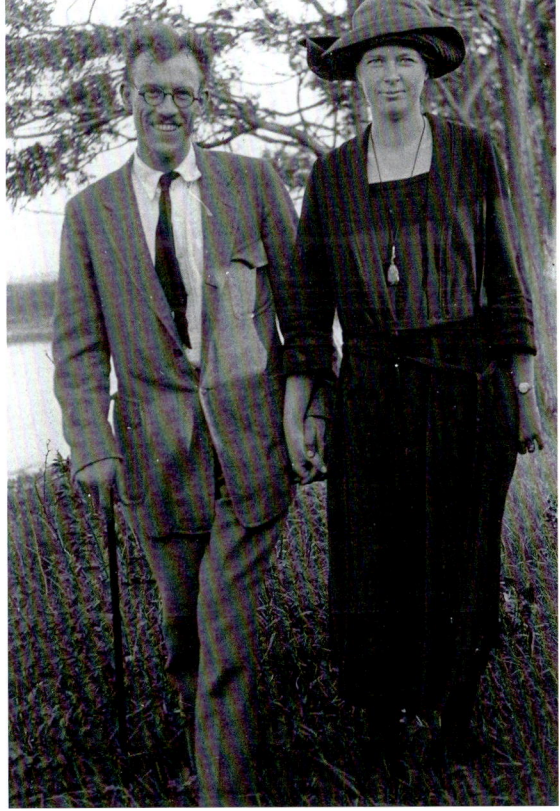

26. Harold and Faith Borton Weston in 1923. Harold Weston Foundation.

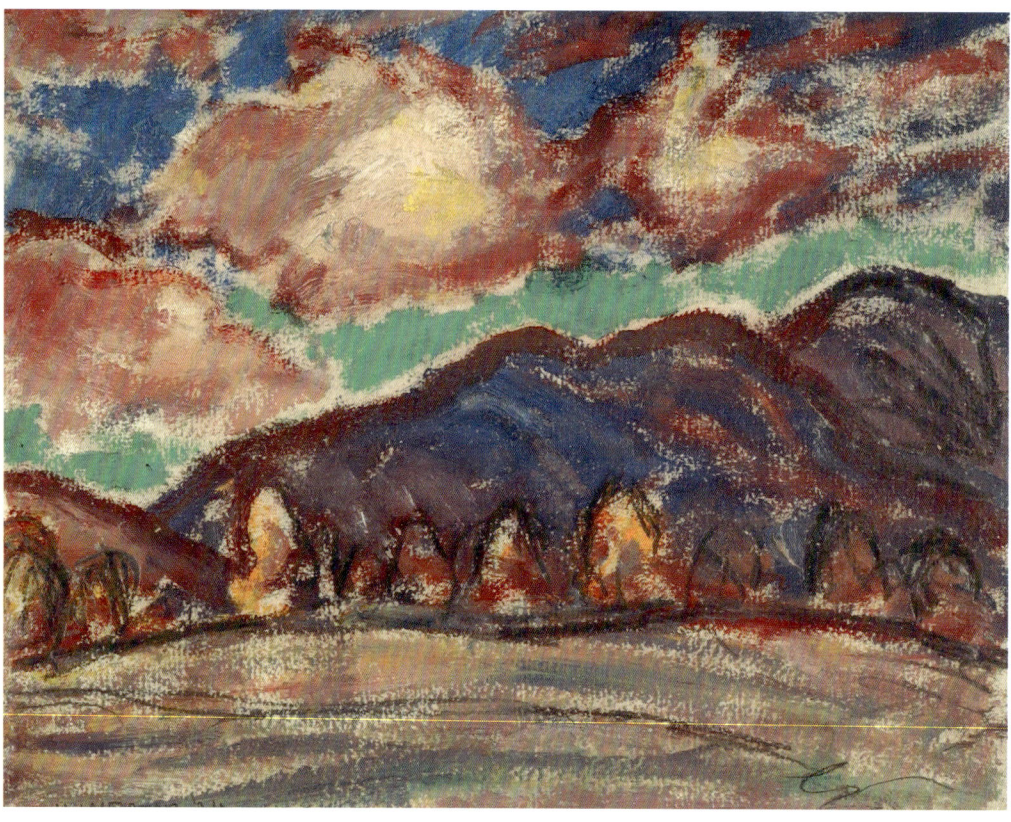

the yellow-green leaves in the sunset light on the side of Noonmark Mountain. They sat in the orchard while he sketched, stayed on top of mountains until the sun set, floated in a canoe on the Upper Ausable Lake. One afternoon they took off for a long hike up Giant Mountain carrying camp baskets with blankets and food. Wrapped in red wool blankets in the lean-to near the top, they saw the moon rise red, large, and mysterious over Lake Champlain and light all the High Peaks. Then, with the morning's sun, Harold painted. All that day they watched the shadows play across the mountains before descending in the late afternoon. "Somehow it doesn't seem fair for two people to have all that we have in our lives of beauty and love," wrote Faith.[46]

At a time when most people's domestic lives were being made daily more comfortable by clever inventions, Harold and Faith eschewed them. They built their life and beliefs around pure idealism and were too earnest to accept the "lightness, inconsequence, [and] bitter cruelty" of the swirl and throb of the city, which was, after all, quickly becoming the cultural, political, and social center of America in the 1920s.[47] Had it been an age of faith, their effort to live in the realm of the spirit would have been unremarkable. But it was an age of skepticism and machines. "To be a user of machines is to be of the spirit of this century," contended the Hungarian artist László Moholy-Nagy. "It has replaced the transcendental spiritualism of past eras."[48]

The spirit of machines had no place in the Westons' cabin in the wilderness. Harold and Faith had the mountains to themselves with oncoming winter. They ate their last bit of fresh lettuce in early November, scrubbed and oiled the floors, and cleaned the rugs, laying down extras. Their focus on each other intensified. He wanted to try nudes. It was cold, and the studio had never been airtight, so they stoked the stove until the room was warm enough for Faith to pose. At first they tried calculated poses but quickly realized that the positions Faith happened into were more natural and rhythmic. Bending over with the discomfort of menstruation suggested a composition. Sitting casually on the side of the bed another. Once, when she was on the couch with her knees drawn to her body, she saw her reflection in a glass and said to Harold, "That's nice in there." He came to sit by her and, seeing himself in the glass, too, threw the first canvas to the side and grabbed a larger one. Tearing off his clothes he drew them both, the man's hand on the woman's arm, his lips on her back. Faith called the result "monumental" and "thrillingly modern."[49] "It looks as if the mills of humanity had ground exceedingly fine," she wrote her mother.[50]

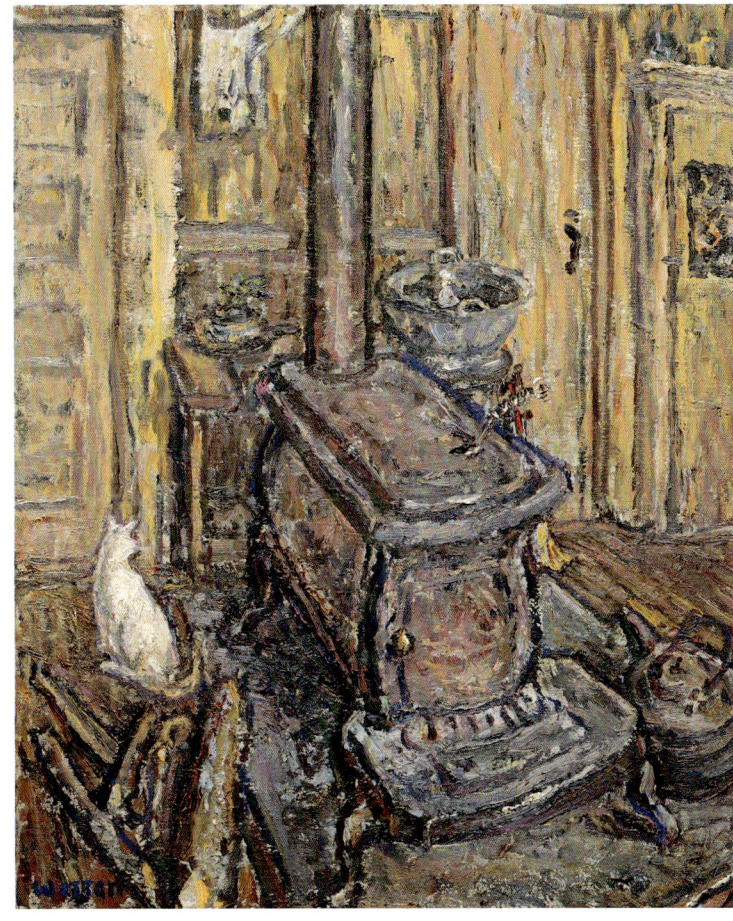

29. Harold Weston, *The Studio Stove*, 1924. D. Wigmore Fine Art, New York.

Almost all the nudes started out as charcoal drawings on paper. Then, in turpentine and a little paint, Harold drew outlines on the canvas. After getting each one started with Faith modeling, he worked on many simultaneously, much in the manner of the landscape paintings, propping them around himself and bringing them along to completion together. Working at a manic rate and in heavy impasto, Harold was in danger of running out of canvas and paint more quickly than he could order it. He cropped Faith's body, filling the canvas with increasingly bold and innovative heads and breasts, central torsos, backs, folded legs, feet, and hands. He called them "less composed and more vital" than his earlier landscapes.[51] His palette shifted from the blues of the Adirondacks' vast skies and waters to earth tones, paint that resembled the textured changes of earth on riverbanks and mountain faces yielding to a spring thaw. The paint is in constant motion, and yet the forms are monumental and solid—much like the relationship between the geologic permanence of a mountain and the busy, restive earth that covers it. The upper back in *Sleeping Nude*, 1925 (fig. 30), looks almost like a fallen branch growing a rich assortment of fungus, lichen, and

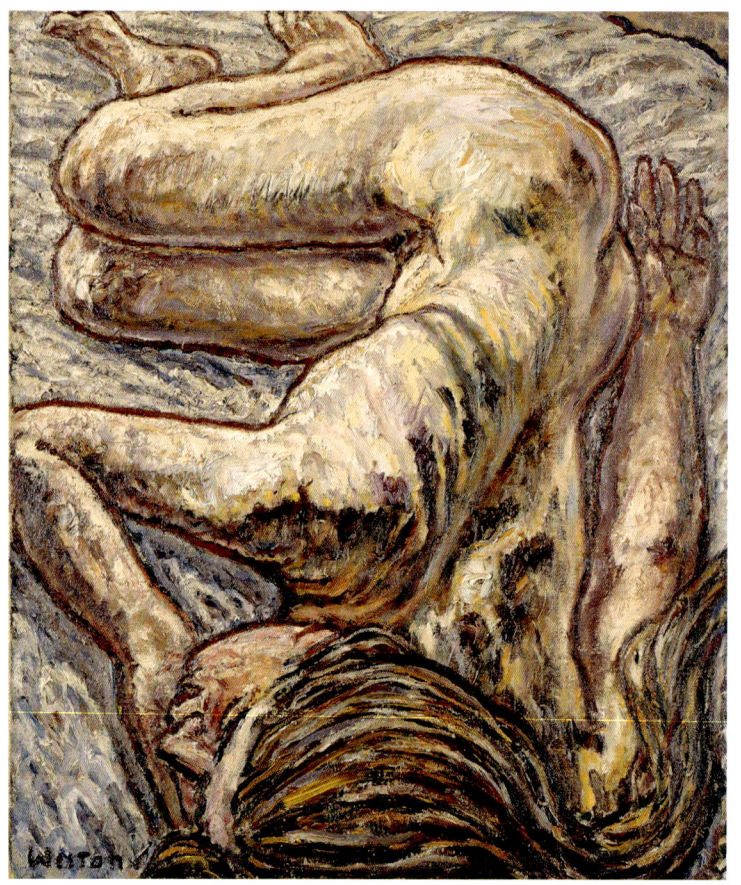

30. Harold Weston, *Sleeping Nude*, 1925. Wichita Art Museum Wichita, Kansas. Gift of Dr. Martin H. Bush.

mold. These works were painted with so much impasto of literal microcosmic hills and valleys that Georgia O'Keeffe remarked, "If you ran your hands over her, they would get splinters and bits of broken glass."[52]

In January 1925 the Memorial Art Gallery in Rochester, New York, held the first museum exhibition of Weston's work. The director wrote to Weston that the show of landscape, still-life, and a few nude paintings "is having an interesting effect upon our public, most of whom were not so wise as you in discarding the accumulation of the academies."[53] One critic wrote that other artists had asked deprecatingly how Weston could see such things. "Like [William] Blake he will find a small number of kindred natures whose emotions toward nature spring from similar sources," the critic continued. "He is merely a stray poet whom a few will listen to thankfully."[54] This stray poet was nevertheless dubbed "one of America's most significant living artists."[55] The Memorial Art Gallery acquired a landscape for its permanent collection—Weston's first museum placement. It was an ebullient affirmation of his past work, which was just radical enough to challenge, but not too radical to be collected by a museum.

The nudes, however, were proving to be too challenging. Montross was disturbed by the new work and refused to show it. Juliana Force, the director of the Whitney Studio Club, was shocked by the paintings but still invited Weston to join the club.[56] "I do hate to think of your giving up landscapes," wrote J. O. H. Cosgrave, the influential critic at the *New York World*, who had two of them. "The man who brushed them is a real painter."[57] The nudes deviated from a long tradition of beauty that aspired to perfection. These were no Botticelli or Titian Venuses, but cropped body parts painted as if with earth and flesh, whose primitive honesty complicated beauty with uncomfortably raw emotion and sex. These were not tame, pastoral scenes through which one could take a bourgeois stroll, but the wild. Unlike pretty nudes displayed for the male gaze, these were something more about the woman herself.

Faith and Harold tied up eighteen of the paintings and took them to show Alfred Stieglitz, the photographer and gallery owner. They unrolled them on the red plush carpet

31. Harold Weston, *Mountain Nude*, 1924. Collection of Springfield Art Museum, Missouri, S.A.M. 1977.19.

at the Anderson Galleries. Stieglitz quietly paced up and down in front of them. "You're painting yourself in all these," he said finally. "There's a great spirit of intensity at work here. I saw your things at Montross' three years ago and wasn't interested in them then but felt," he continued, "there was a fellow of promise." Then a sallow-faced man with long black hair, small keen eyes, and stooped shoulders walked into the room. He took in the nudes excitedly. "I feel the woods in these," he said. "Whose are they?" Stieglitz introduced the artist John Marin to Weston, and after Weston told Marin where the work was painted, Marin replied, "Ah, that explains it. I couldn't understand. Did you ever see mountains better painted than this?" He said he would like to see Weston's paintings shown in Paris. "It would give them a shock and show what purely American stuff is like. It has a direct, primitive quality."[58] The paintings have been called *landscape nudes* ever since.

Weston's "spirit of intensity" may have benefited the art, but it was hard on the artist. "He is goaded by an insatiable urge to work, *work, work,*" wrote Faith.[59] Harold told Faith, "I need thy laughter, thy smile, thy bit of song or cheerful word, thy lovableness. Intensity consumes me."[60] One day he fainted from the "nervous tension" of painting a canvas and did not paint again for four days. Another day, in July 1925, he painted four landscape canvases

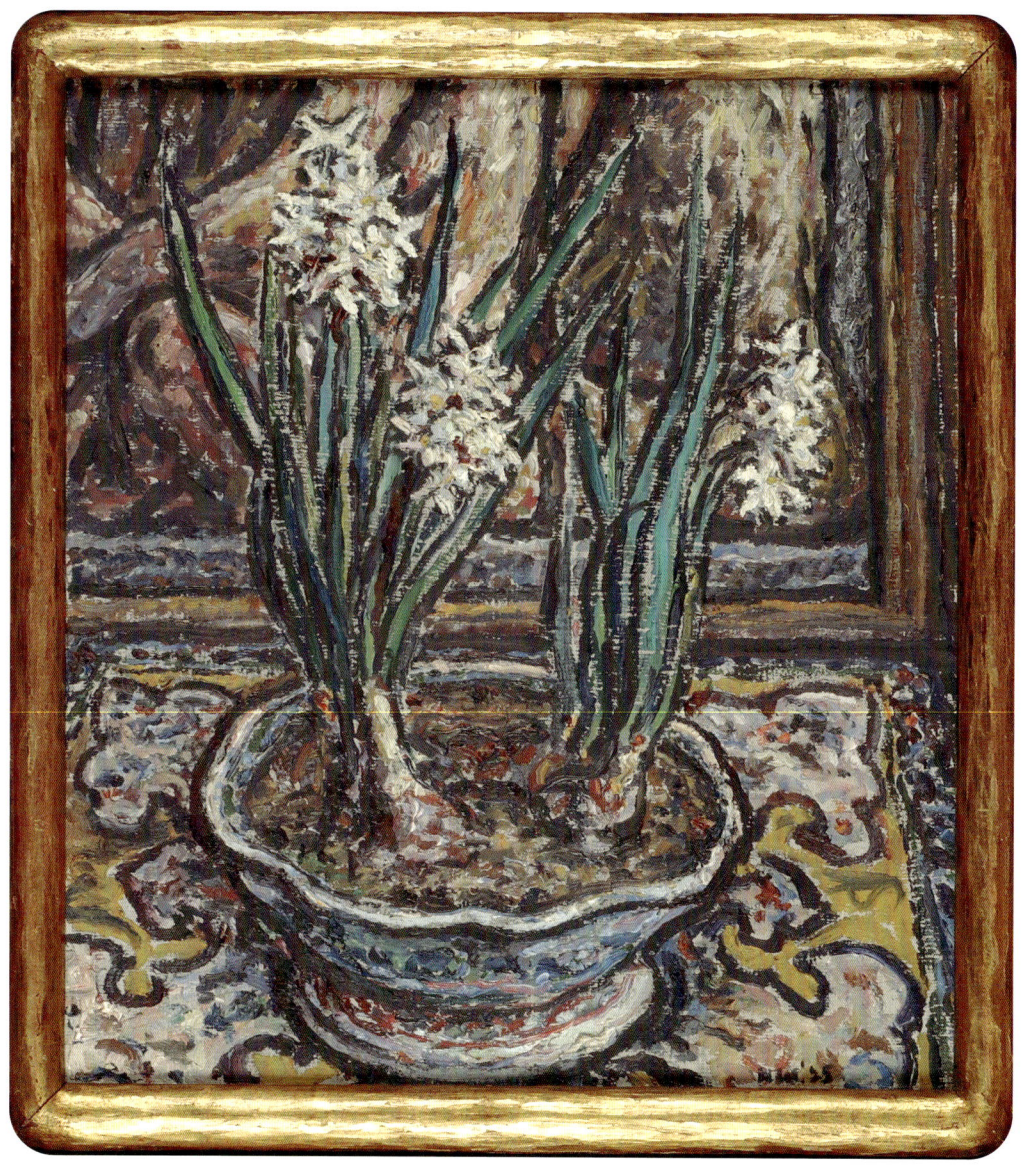

in a literal fever and then urinated blood. The next day, with unrelieved symptoms, he started two more landscapes and finished off with a self-portrait. The doctors in the hospital in Montreal determined that Harold had a diseased kidney, perhaps weakened by his malaria in Persia, and that it needed to come out. The surgery was successful, and before long the wound of the operation healed, but he still had a fever and was beset with a series of complications that went on for weeks. The doctors told Faith that they expected the worst. One excruciating month later the temperature in Harold's completely wracked body blazed up to 104 degrees and then, the doctors speculated, burned itself out. It was over, the end as inexplicable as the cause.

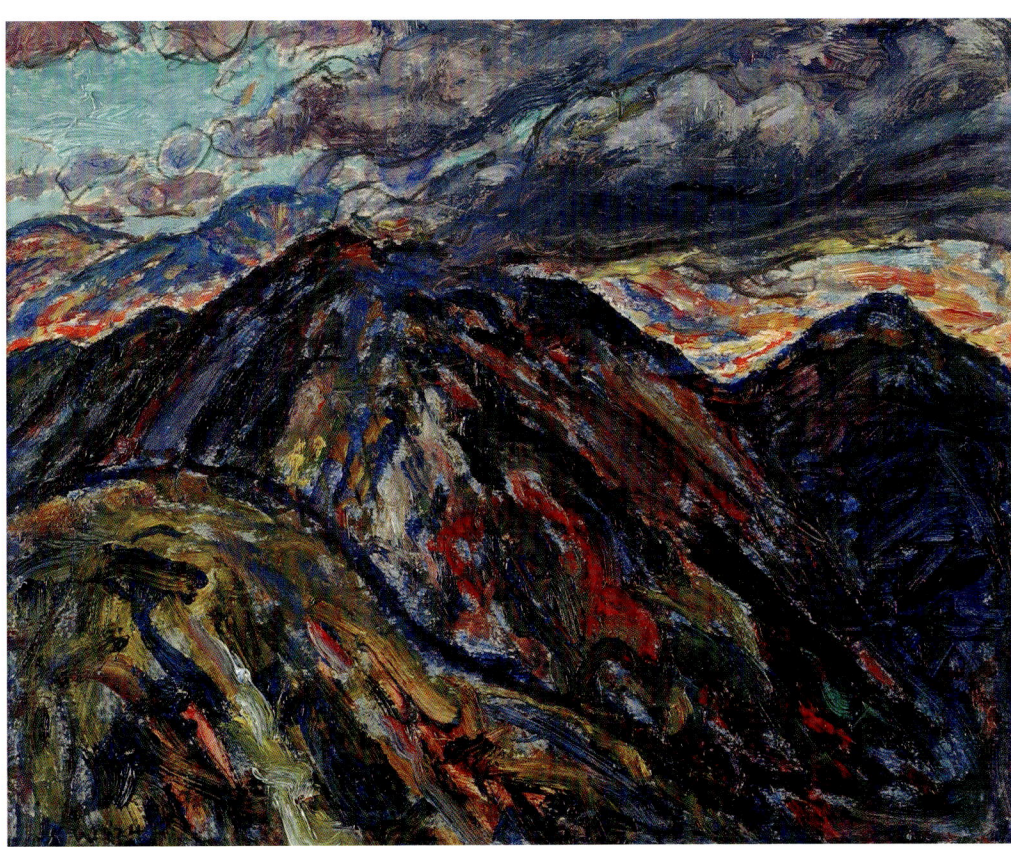

When the doctors learned of the emotional intensity with which Harold painted, they prescribed no work for six months. Harold and Faith decided to go to the South of France. Before they left, they visited Montross, who wanted to keep Weston in his "inner circle," and the Brooklyn Museum, where three Westons were hung—the nude upside down. Two of his paintings would be shown in the Whitney Studio Club later in the winter. And then, in January 1926, Harold and Faith settled into their second-class cabin on the SS *Colombo* for ten days of the ocean's even roll with portholes open to the springlike air.

We Have Made a Thing of Art out of Our Lives

"He has been wanting to paint," wrote Faith in her journal after two months of exploring the art of Italy and France.[61] Thinking of the doctors' prohibition, she wrote six days later: "He is again at the painting pitch. Have no idea what we can do. When he needs to paint, he needs to and does."[62] They wanted a place to settle and work. In Paris, Gertrude Stein told the Westons about her work in the Pyrenees during the war. It gave them an idea. Already feeling out of place in chic Paris, they thought that the Pyrenees seemed ideal. In the town of Prats de Mollo at the Spanish border, near the end of a bumpy, flea-ridden tram and train ride from Perpignan, they found a farmhouse with an eleventh-century chapel. From the terrace they could look up the valley beyond the Prats church tower or down over high-sweeping, cultivated, and grazed hills toward Perpignan. They lived in some ways as peasants among peasants, Faith cooking over an open hearth, walking to market every day for provisions, and getting water from the pump outdoors. Built on a hill, the house was designed to let sheep into the basement in the cold weather so that their warm body heat would rise through the slotted boards of the floor above. "Quiet, simple, intimate and hard," wrote Faith, "it is a region very sympathetic to the pioneer in H. Suited to the Quaker in me."[63]

In the fall of 1926 Harold started to paint canvases again. He took on any subject at hand, more varied than before—corn fields up close, interiors looking out, portraits of local people, babies. He seemed to find interest in everything. "H. has been working, *over* working," wrote Faith. "He has reached that terrific pitch of production which he attains only after painful, discouraged months of preparation."[64] The new paintings were less stylized than the Adirondack work and, unlike the work of the two previous periods, did not have one unifying idea. Nevertheless, the Westons felt that his experimentation revealed an admirable lack of dogma. Harold characterized the work, which now showed a greater command of material and color distinction, as "staid and stolid modernity with nothing flashy."[65]

The Spanish sculptor Manolo Hugué (known as Manolo), who lived down the valley, encouraged Harold to have a show in Paris, so the Westons took the train to Paris, where they stayed a few months. Living in an apartment that was frankly too small for stacks of

34. Harold Weston, *Ploughing*, 1926. Private Collection.

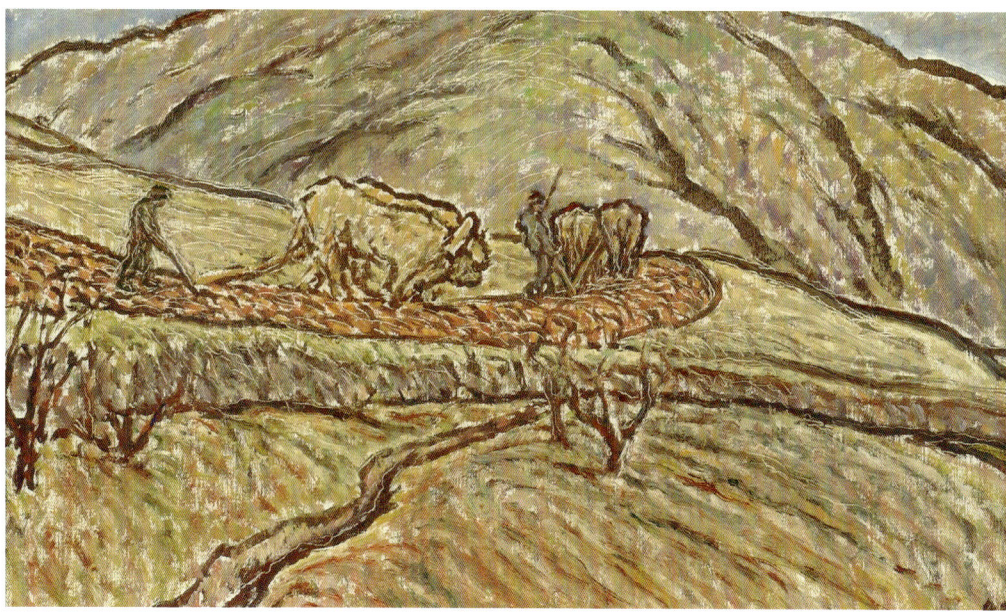

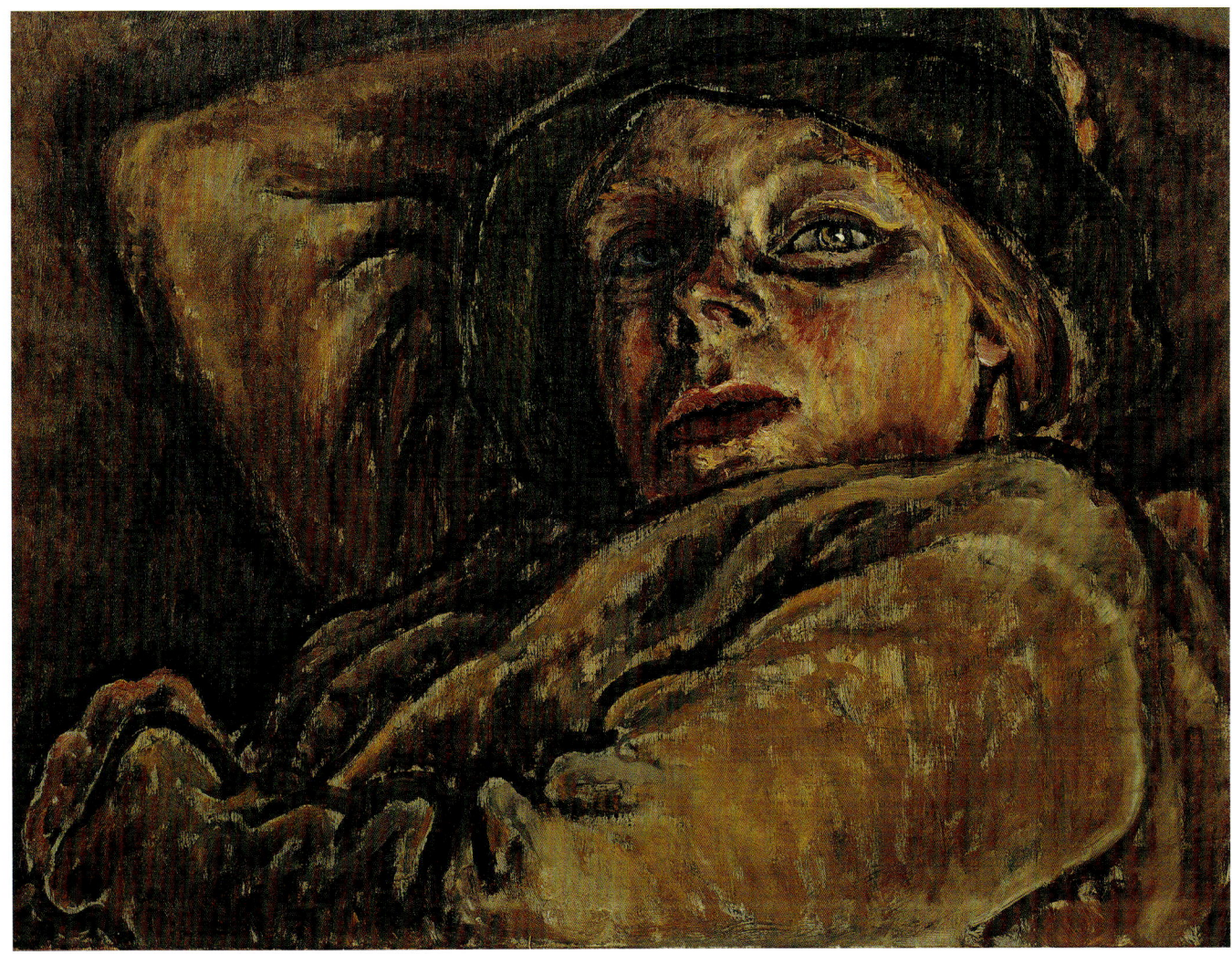

35. Harold Weston, *Green Hat*, 1927. San Francisco Museum of Modern Art. Gift of the Ladies' Auxiliary of the Palace of Fine Arts, 39.129.

drying oil canvases, he learned how to etch. "All day," Faith wrote, "paintings fever the smell of burnt sterno, the smell of stop-out varnish, the smell of nitric acid, a cigarette."[66] She watched Harold bend over a copperplate in complete absorption, combining the etching techniques of hard and soft ground, burin, dry point, and aquatint with brush and without. "I've never seen anything like them," Montross told the Westons when he saw them in Paris. "Most etchers take some subject and do the thing objectively, while these are part of your artistic expression, and say something unique in themselves."[67] (See figs. 36, 38.)

Weston's show at Galerie Joseph Billiet in July 1927 revealed a brilliant colorist who searched for strength over the pretty—as one French review put it, "What one expects least from an American."[68] The Billiet success was followed by an exhibition at Montross in New York in October. While in Paris, Montross had allowed Harold and Faith to choose the paintings for the show, and he approved the nudes Harold insisted be a part of it. To the

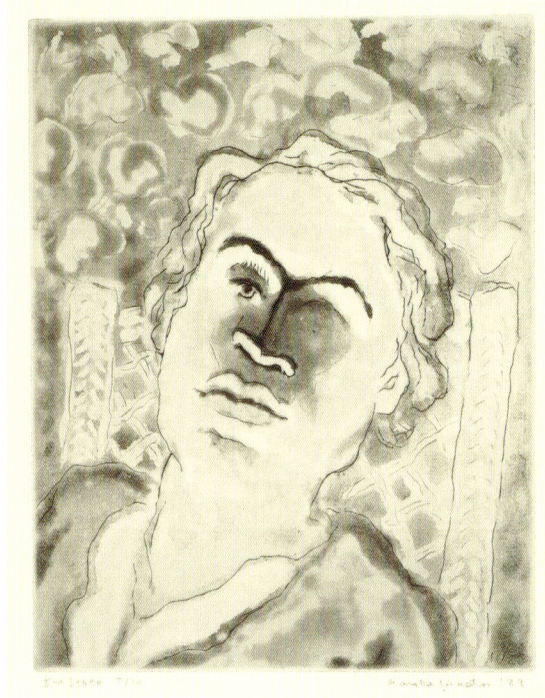

Westons, the nudes were his best and most important work. When they heard later that Montross had excluded the nudes from the walls, in spite of his verbal agreement to show them, Harold and Faith were devastated. "I have drunk perhaps the bitterest drought compromise will ever have to offer," agonized Faith. "I could not have believed things could have so fallen out against us," she wrote, after four years of trying to gain acceptance for the nudes.[69]

The nudes were their life work—their very lives even. It did not matter to them that the *New York World* critic wrote that Weston's landscape sketches at Montross "light up an entire room, shining from the wall like an Oriental temple mosaic."[70] For them, modernism was not just an aesthetic experience; it was about overcoming societal and sexual inhibitions to take lovers as they wished and to incorporate their explorations into art, in particular the nudes. That they were explorers in body and emotions and art in France in the 1920s would not be revolutionary except that in their case it was played out against the backdrop of the prohibitions of their conser-

36. Harold Weston, *Morning Light*, 1928. Harold Weston Foundation.

37. Harold Weston, *Church at Prats de Mollo*, n.d. Harold Weston Foundation.

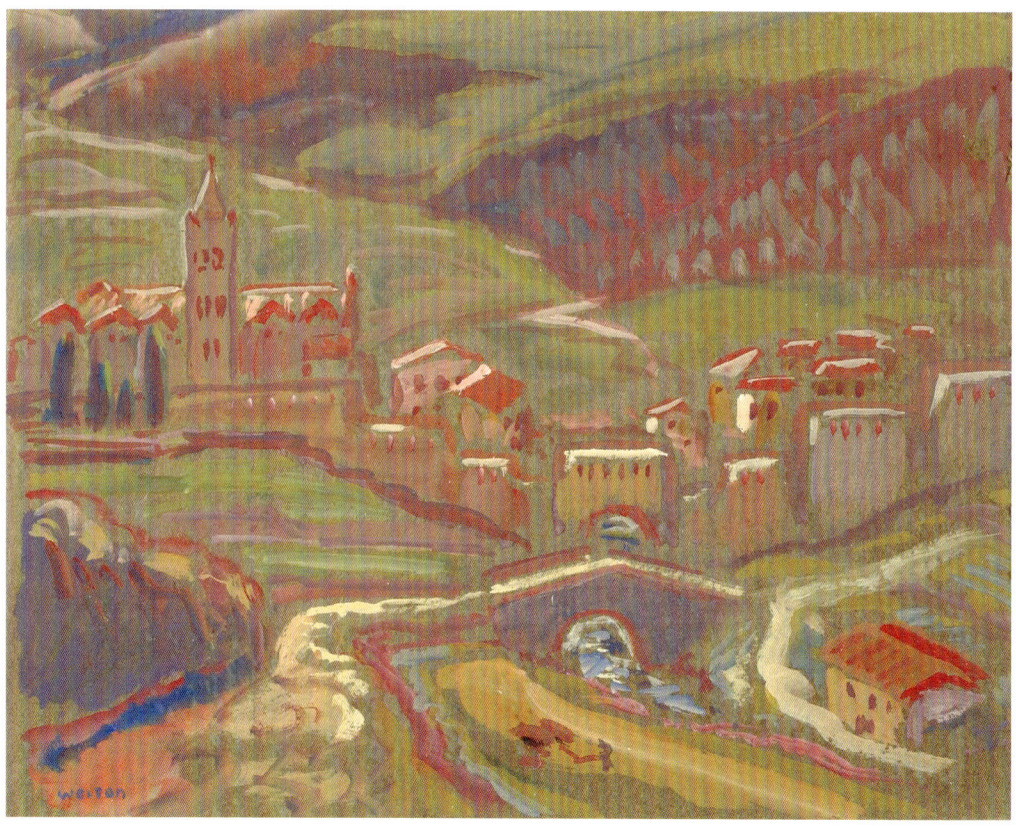

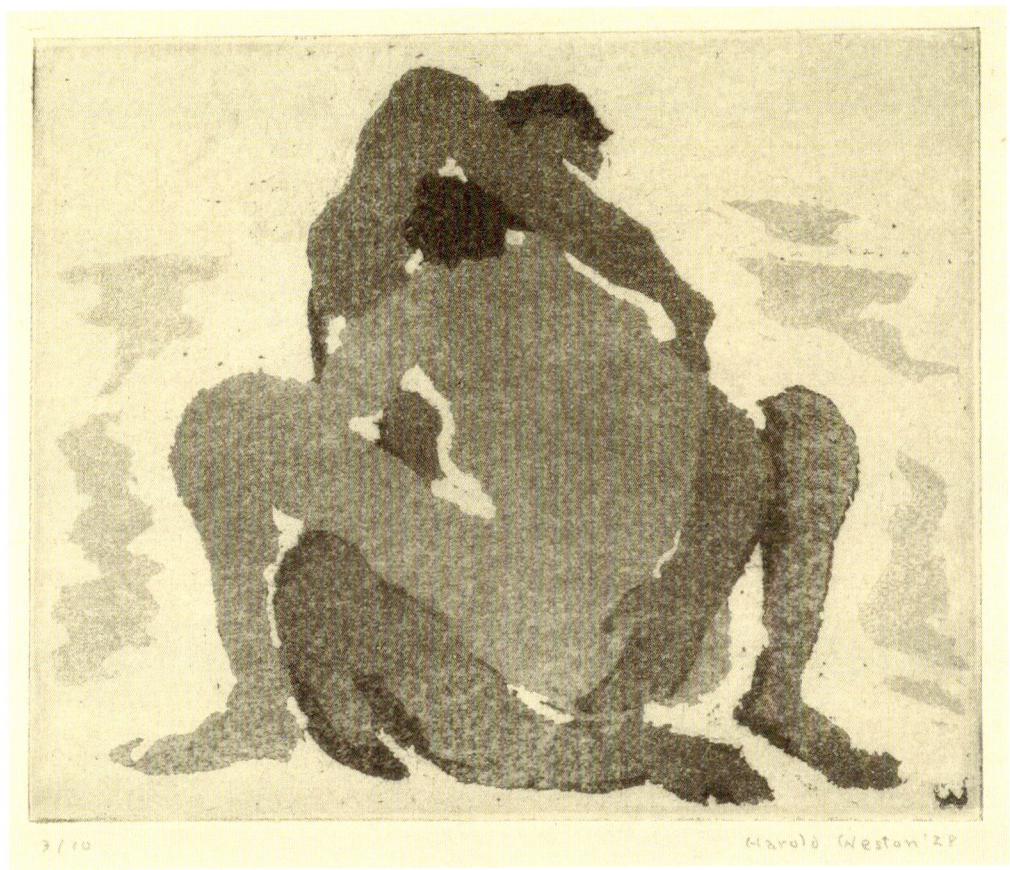

vative upbringings. Their sexual explorations, amazingly, were a mutual project that grew from their preternatural closeness and ultimately served Harold's art. Their loving and their lovers were their living was his art. "Oh gorgeous dangerous generous freedom," exclaimed Faith, who by then had resigned from the Society of Friends. Harold replied, "We have surely made a thing of beauty, a thing of art out of our lives."[71]

It was, of necessity, a split life as long as Harold's mother could say that some of the etchings "are too disgusting to show anyone."[72] The Westons were discreet about their intimacies, which would remain a secret between themselves, their lovers, and their closest friends. Most people preferred not to know or pretended not to understand or care about the life behind the nudes. Weston felt that the critic Paul Rosenfeld understood "the struggle towards liberation" that his nudes were meant to represent.[73] Rosenfeld wrote:

> Few of [Weston's] competitors parallel the fire and force of attack to which his moving torsos bear emphatic witness.... Those rude, bare shapes of his, resembling the knotted contours of roots, hard, wrinkled peasant flesh, primitive materials and things worn by the elements, convey

in a hundred degrees of intensity the quality of living stripped to the essentials; the acrid breath of the rough and solid earth beneath.... Certain of these juxtaposed forms convey a flush of the human intimacy so ludicrously rare in our civilization.... The spiritual implications of these paintings are important in a bourgeois America, dangerously removed from the simple realities and the struggle with nature by a thousand conventionalities and sentimentalities.[74]

The Westons stayed in France four years, splitting their time between the Pyrenees and Paris. They were productive years—"Weston is one of those prodigious workers who quite destroy the legend of the idle expatriate artist, for he returns each year bearing new sheaves of pictures with him,"[75] as one critic wrote. But with the stock-market crash and the dollar getting weaker, it was no longer an irresistible paradise for a poor artist. In the spring of 1930, with all of the paintings and the Weston babies—Barbara and Bruce (Dina would come later)—they returned to the Adirondack Mountains to eke out a living through the depression.

39. Harold Weston, *Torso Prone*, 1925. Private Collection.

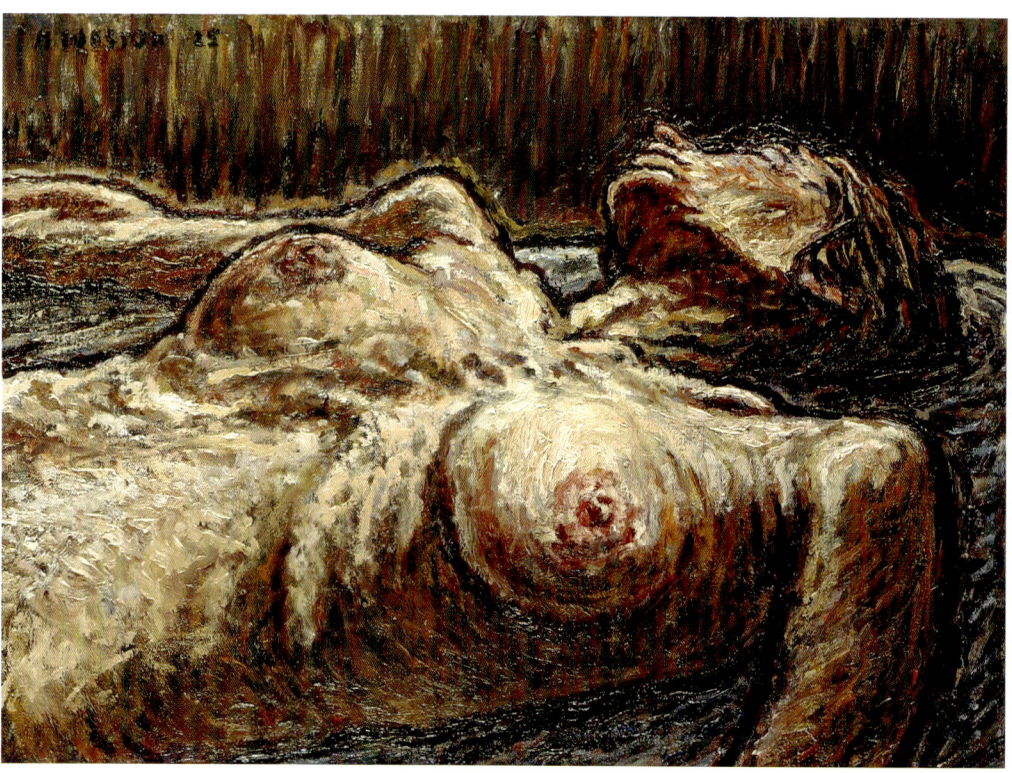

A More Powerful Outcry

Weston, exhibiting actively—even frenetically—in the 1930s, was now recognized as a major figure in American painting. In 1930, for instance, he had solo shows in New York, Washington, D.C., and Chicago. In 1934 he was represented in a dozen group shows (see Exhibitions, p. 123). He was exhibiting so much that when the Boyer Gallery asked to hang a group of Westons in the back room while other paintings were in the front, Weston, worried about overexposure, consented with some conditions: the critics should not be asked to review it; the Weston clientele should not receive notices about it; and only a few paintings that were not likely to be in his next show should be included.[76] At one of his many group shows, the Golden Gate International Exposition in San Francisco in 1939, his painting *Green Hat*, 1927 (fig. 35), won third prize in American painting and was purchased by the San Francisco Museum of Art.

Duncan Phillips, founder of the first modern art museum in America, started collecting Weston's work while the artist was in France. He became fond of the man as well as of the art and often asked Weston to come to the Phillips Memorial Gallery in Washington, D.C. In January 1931 he urged Weston: "[W]e need you in this course of Gallery discussions for there is no man now painting better able to discuss color as an instrument of emotional expression and of plastic design." He concluded that Weston's pictures "positively thrill me and I am convinced of their importance."[77] When Margaret Bourke-White started experimenting with color photography, she, too, was anxious to talk with Weston about color: "Will you teach me as much as you can?" she asked.[78] He had many admirers, but some viewers of his work were annoyed that he did not aim to please. The *New York Times* critic Edward Alden Jewell never gave Weston a favorable review, calling his work "disagreeable, harsh, or actually hideous."[79] Phillips laid some of the responsibility on the viewers: "[Weston's] austerity consists in being more outspoken and more scornful of airs and graces than is

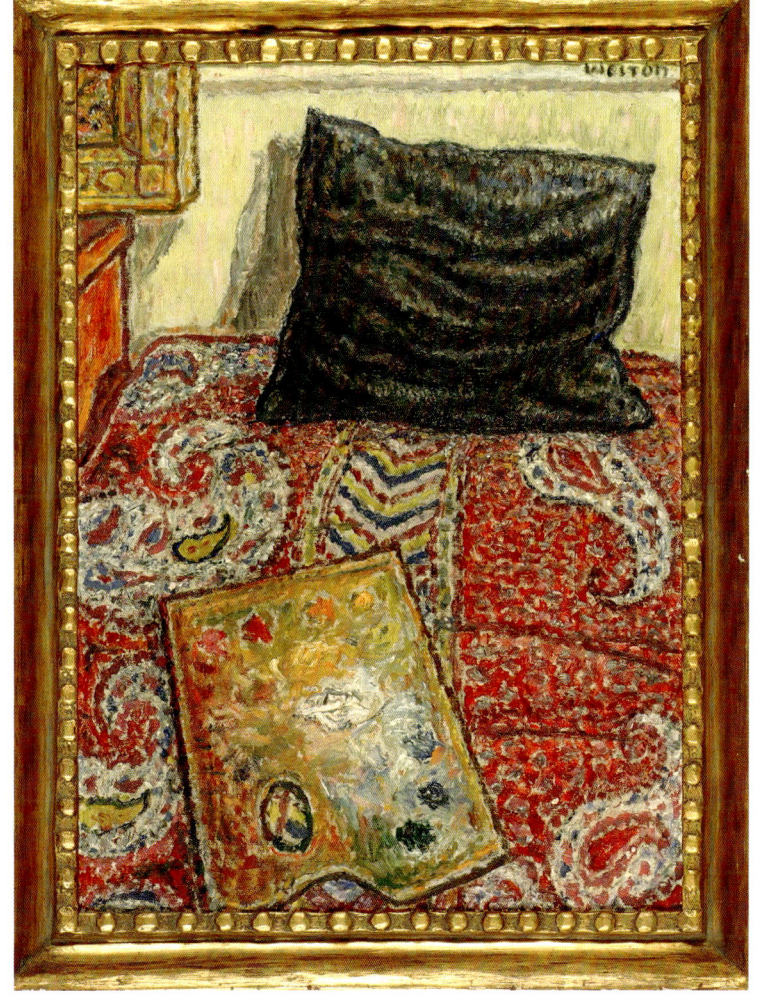

40. Harold Weston, *Palette on Couch*, 1931. Bill Sudduth.

either expedient or easy for us to enjoy." However, even he felt that Weston was sometimes more defiantly distorting than he needed to be.[80]

Weston painted in dull browns if he wanted to and in distorted forms if it pleased him, tackling whatever subject moved him, regardless of popular opinion. One could not say that his art was influenced by criticism, but he was emotionally affected by it. The comments that piqued him most were not delivered as criticism, but as statement of fact or even as praise: Weston's work was reminiscent of Van Gogh's. Critics noted similarities in linear qualities, heavy impasto, and energetic application. These comments first started when Weston's French work was shown in Paris in 1927 and were somewhat justified. But Weston was depressed and discouraged by them. He would look at a painting just after finishing it and say, "It's very van Goghy I suppose, but I like something in it."[81] The label dogged him throughout the 1930s even as his style changed drastically, ultimately raising more questions about the critics' derivativeness than about the artist's. Under a newspaper reproduction of the 1934 painting *Horizons* (fig. 41), which in technique and subject is about as remote from Van Gogh as one can get, the critic nevertheless talked about the Dutchman.[82] Much later, in the 1960s, Weston was still defending his early work against the Van Gogh charge.

41. Harold Weston, *Horizons*, 1934. Private Collection.

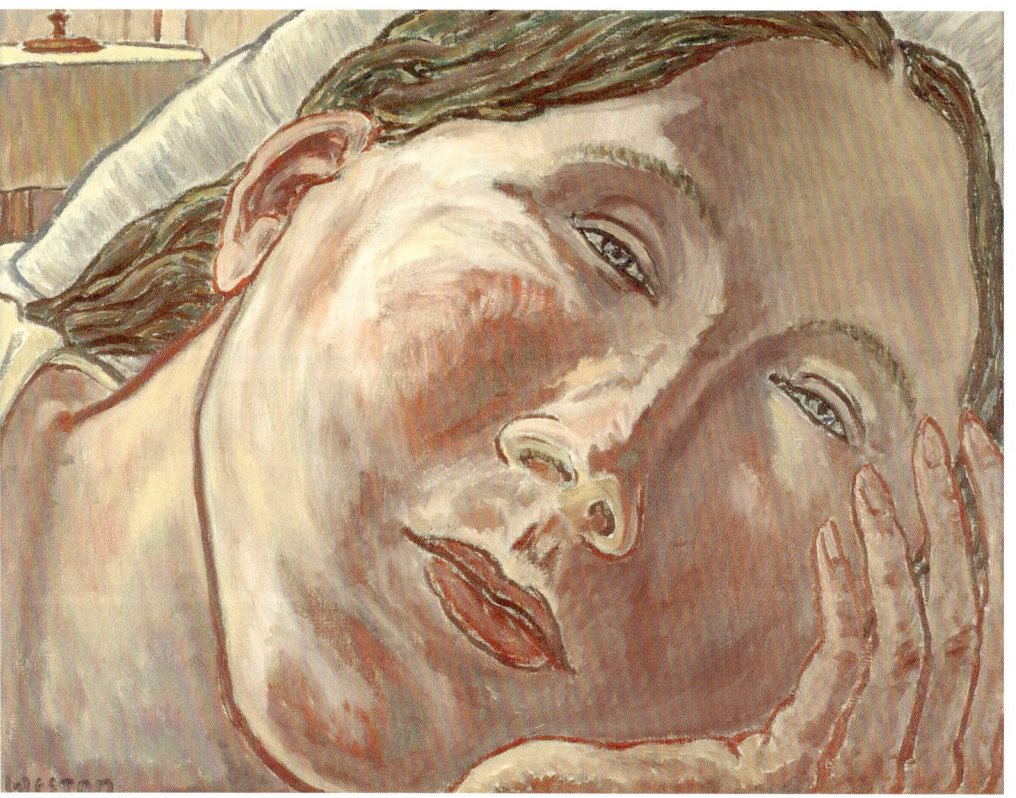

42. Harold Weston, *Gothics from Sawtooth*, 1935. Private Collection.

Most often, however, Weston was called an individualist, a sincere painter of personal convictions who was not affiliated with any school. The work of the early 1930s had no more than a peripheral affinity with American scene painting in that it conveyed values of a traditional America—hardy, independent, pioneering, and somewhat anachronistic. Weston himself was scornful of painters who "get on the bandwagon of whatever vogue is popular,"[83] and so he deliberately remained apart. Phillips felt that such an artist was rare: "The fact that our standardized world can still boast of such an individual is news of the most cheering and vital consequence."[84]

Weston was admired for his intensity, which could be sensual or rugged—or both. He could turn anything into an object of sensuality, even the side of a mountain, as in *Gothics from Sawtooth*, 1935 (fig. 42), with its surprising mass of writhing flesh. "Shall we call Weston's combination of austerity and sensuality a saint's love of the flesh or a lover's desire for holiness?" asked Lewis Mumford. "At all events, there is a touch of almost religious conviction in it, as in some of the best of D. H. Lawrence's prose and verse."[85] It became a cliché: Weston's work was "rough and rugged as hickory stumps" and depicted "rugged things" and a "rugged universality."[86] The "rugged" comments almost seemed to be a literal response to the lavish impasto that one reviewer quipped "must be a comfort to the color man lucky enough to furnish his supplies."[87] They may also have been an unconscious response to Weston's flaw theory, which held that a painting needed to show some mark of experimentation to have inherent life. If he did not feel an uncertainty of step or a bit of fumbling, then he was not convinced the work was experimental and genuine.[88] Art should have a flaw, not be too perfect, to be an accurate reflection of life's powerful and difficult emotions.

Weston's work was modern in that it was insistent and immediate—like an outcry, commented one critic, just as Tintoretto, Rubens, Eugène Delacroix, Van Gogh, and others made artistic outcries.[89] In the early 1930s Weston's outcry became more commanding as he magnified forms. A rhubarb bud dominates one canvas; in another we are presented with a head—no torso, no arm, just a monumental head. Mumford called the face in *Horizons* (fig. 41) "gigantic" even though the canvas was no larger than the nudes. Weston also had become more psychological in paint. The emotional range of a canvas such as *Profile*, 1931, 1933 (fig. 44), is limitless, a psychological counterpoint to the metaphysical limitlessness of the early Adirondack landscapes.

For several years Weston had been excited about the aesthetic challenge of wall murals. In 1935 he competed for a Treasury Relief Art Project mural commission and accepted one to depict the government's efforts to speed the end of the depression. The paintings showed the construction of government buildings as well as the movement of badly needed

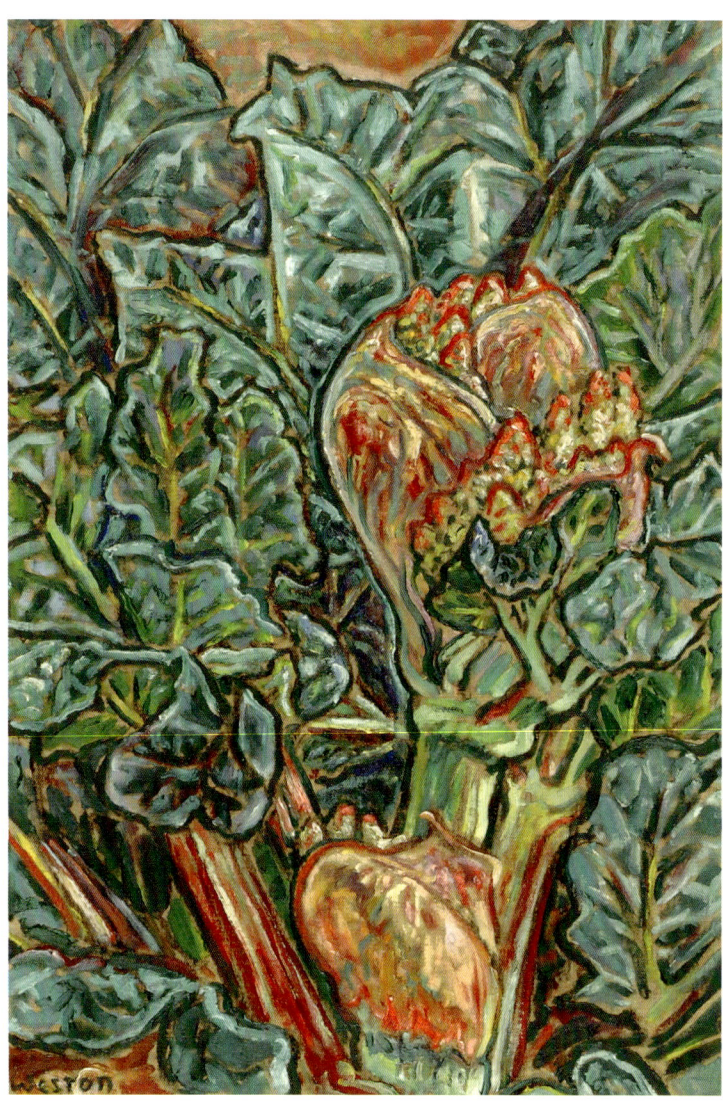

43. Harold Weston, *Rhubarb in Bud*, 1931. Private Collection.

supplies around the country. Weston collapsed intricate details into an integrated design "that makes one think of the weaving and interweaving, lacing and interlacing of Coptic tapestry," as his fellow artist and Adirondack neighbor Peppino Mangravite put it.[90] When the carpenter who built the extensions on the Westons' house at St. Huberts saw the highly technical panels of construction, he said: "If Harold hadn't worked with us, he never could have painted those pictures."[91] The 840 square feet of twenty-two mural panels done on canvas in his studio in the Adirondacks held Weston's rapt attention for almost three years. The panels were so large—some are 20 feet by 10 feet—that he had to build a special extension onto the studio. He did not see the panels in their entirety until they were mounted on the lobby walls of the General Services Administration Building in Washington, D.C., in 1938.

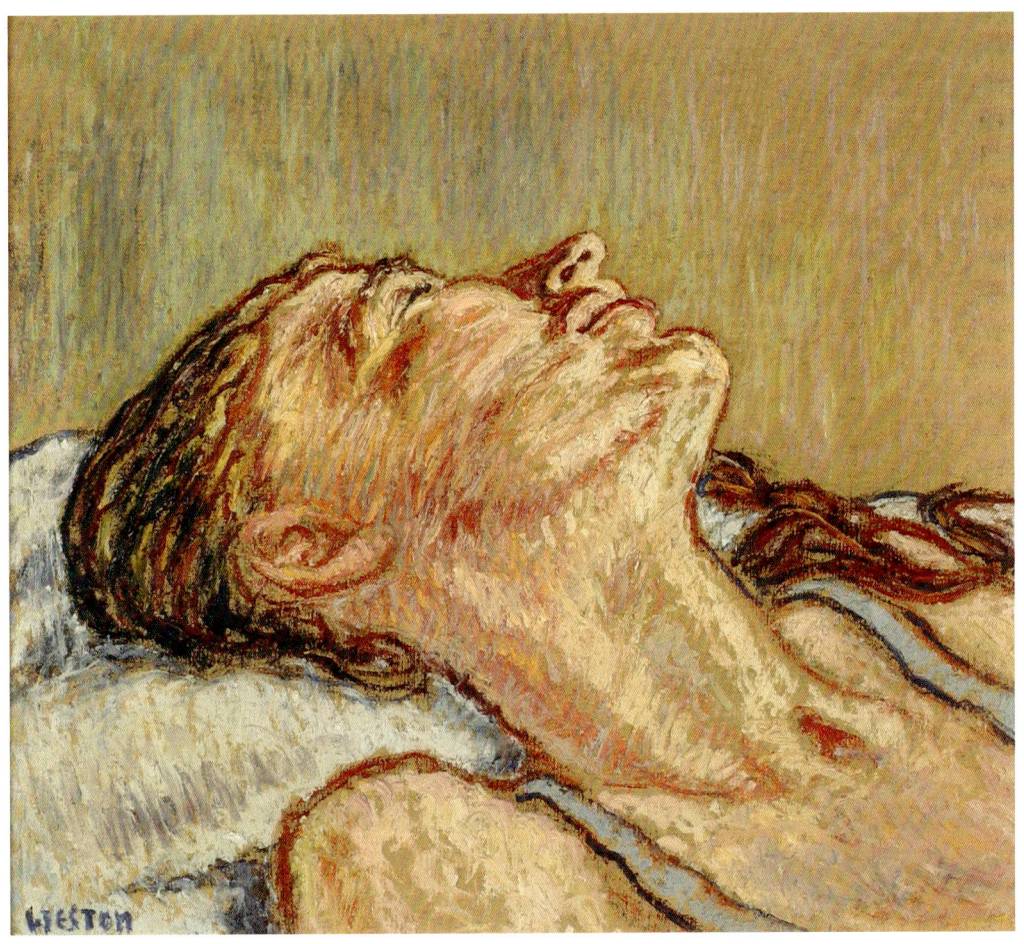

Murals were going up rapidly on walls of public buildings all over the country with varying degrees of success, leading some critics, such as Mumford, to surly condemnations of all federal art and architecture.[92] So it was not an insignificant accomplishment when Phillips wrote to Weston to say that his murals were "magnificent—the best by far of all the government murals."[93] Weston had wanted to make a mark on a long tradition of wall decoration, and he had wanted to try something new. He succeeded in both, but when he returned to easel painting, he discovered that his style had changed. The workmanship was more sophisticated, and a painting took him longer to execute. The flaw theory was no longer in evidence; even the outcry was silenced. But the work was saved from stagnation by a magnificent technique. The exquisite detail and control of his medium, which was now mostly watercolor or gouache, in the roadside snow bank of *Upstate Farm*, 1939 (fig. 47), or in the languishing feathers of *Pheasant* (Phillips chap., fig. 77), are reminiscent of the old masters. At the time he saw the change as a sign of maturity and a natural evolution of his work. "Maybe it was a mistake" doing the murals, he said years later. "It changed my style."

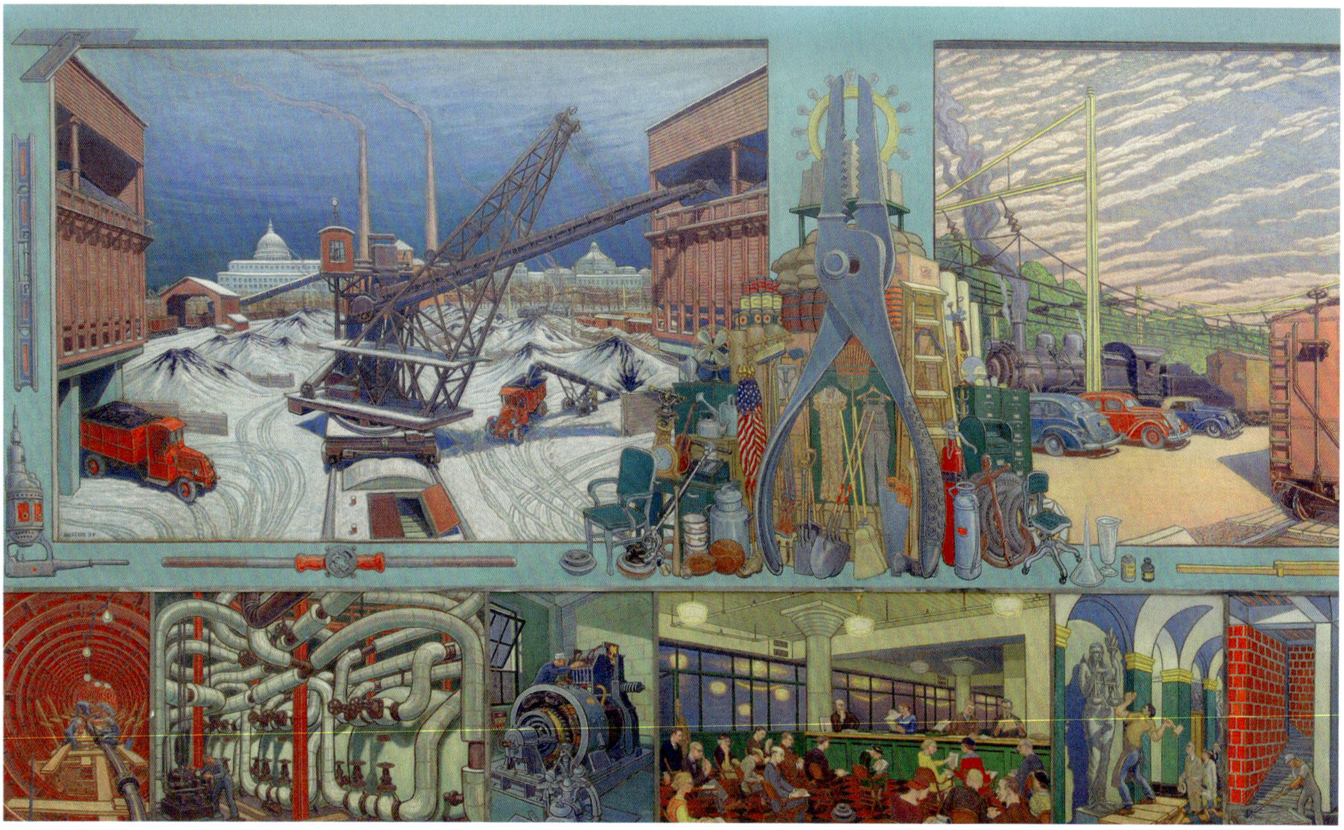

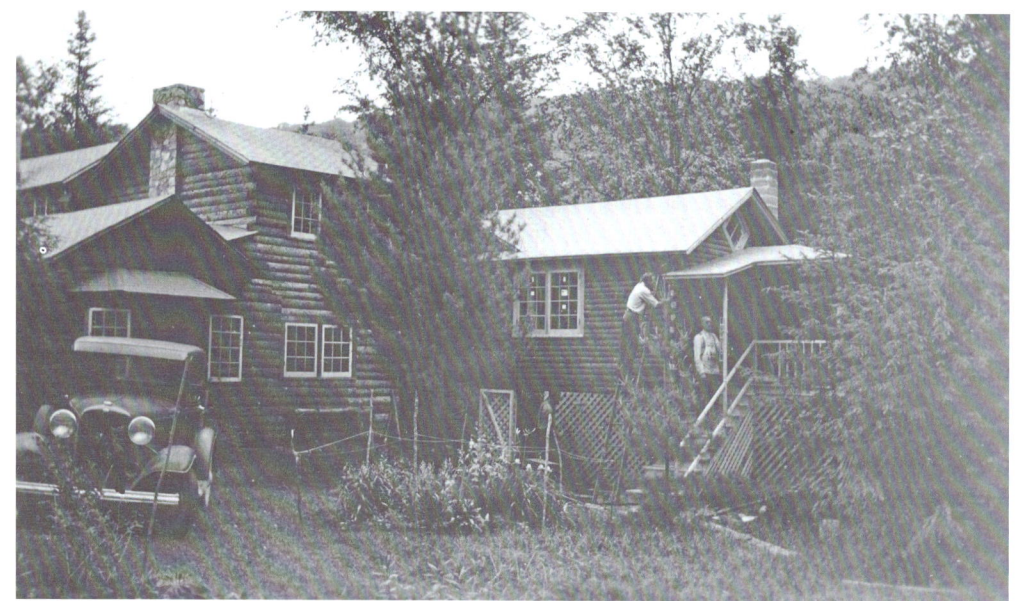

45. *Supply Branch of Procurement*, the north wall of Harold Weston's mural, 1936–38 (detail). General Services Administration Building, Washington, D.C.

46. Building the extension to the studio, 1936. Harold Weston Foundation.

47. Harold Weston, *Upstate Farm*, 1939. Harold Weston Foundation.

He added: "I think in the end it didn't do me too much good."[94] In retrospect, he might not have liked where it led, but the fact that it led somewhere different should not have been a surprise. "Weston is of the mental type of the American pioneer," Phillips wrote early on. "Probably he will keep moving."[95]

Something More Important Than Painting

In May 1940 Weston learned that Nazi military intelligence was so thorough that the Germans knew about the tiny grass-field airport near St. Huberts in Keene Valley, New York. With his father's legacy of social and political justice stirring, he anxiously listened to the daily news of events in Europe on the Philco upright radio that stood in the corner of the living room. When France fell to the Nazis in June, he started volunteering for the Committee to Defend America by Aiding the Allies. Within a year the group had organized eight hundred local chapters around the country. In the Adirondacks Weston organized a branch with eleven chapters. He was completely swept up in world events. "For the first time in my life," he said, "something seemed more important to me than painting."[96]

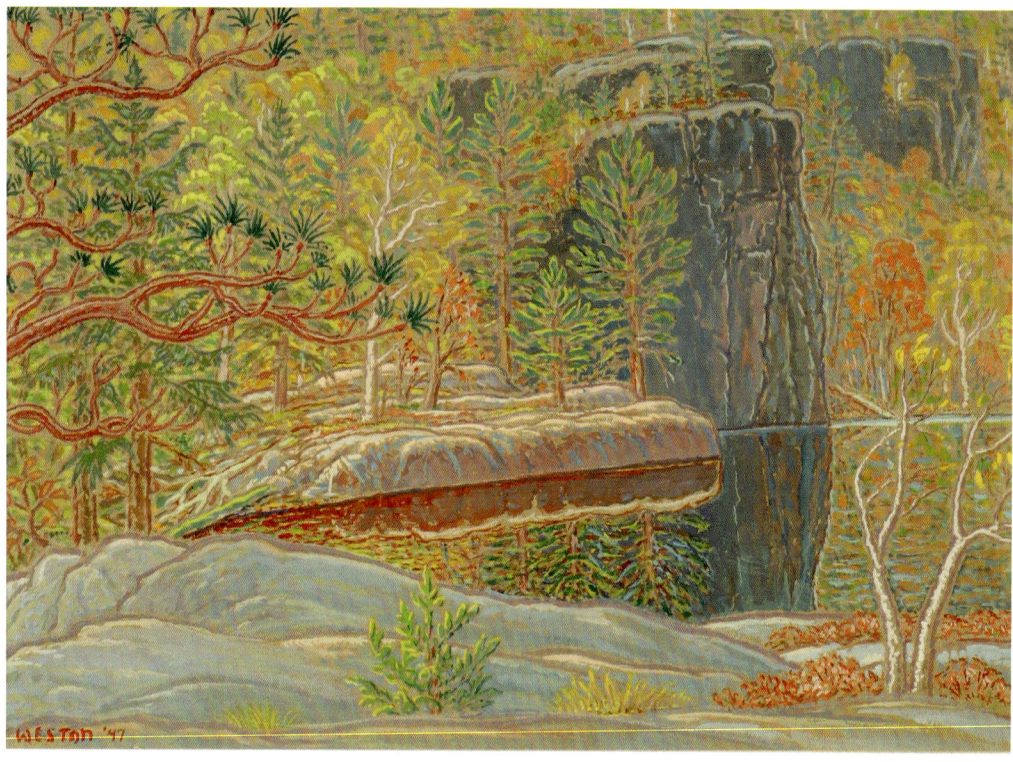

Weston projected beyond the war, in which the United States was not yet directly involved, to a victory that could be undermined by the chaos of famine. He remembered seeing a woman and her daughter stoned to death in Persia for killing a child and eating the body. He formulated some ideas about a special group of people who would be trained to go into liberated countries and quickly secure the basic necessities of life for the populace. He wrote up his ideas in a document. The journey of that document was a dizzying one. It started with a high-level committee of citizens that called Weston's plan the Reconstruction Service Committee; it then gained Eleanor Roosevelt's support; and ultimately it served as the outline for the United Nations Relief and Rehabilitation Administration (UNRRA), which was set up in 1943.[97]

Weston and his colleagues then established Food for Freedom, an organization to coordinate citizen participation in food relief for war-torn countries. "Food is a weapon. Hunger is a time bomb," they wrote.[98] Weston had not known anything about the food business or Washington politics, but he learned quickly, and for the next four years he worked to convince politicians, the powerful food lobby, and American citizens that peace and stability were not possible in a half-starved world. Having won the support of more than ninety national labor, church, and civic organizations whose members numbered 60 million, Food for Freedom was able to influence international food-relief policies.

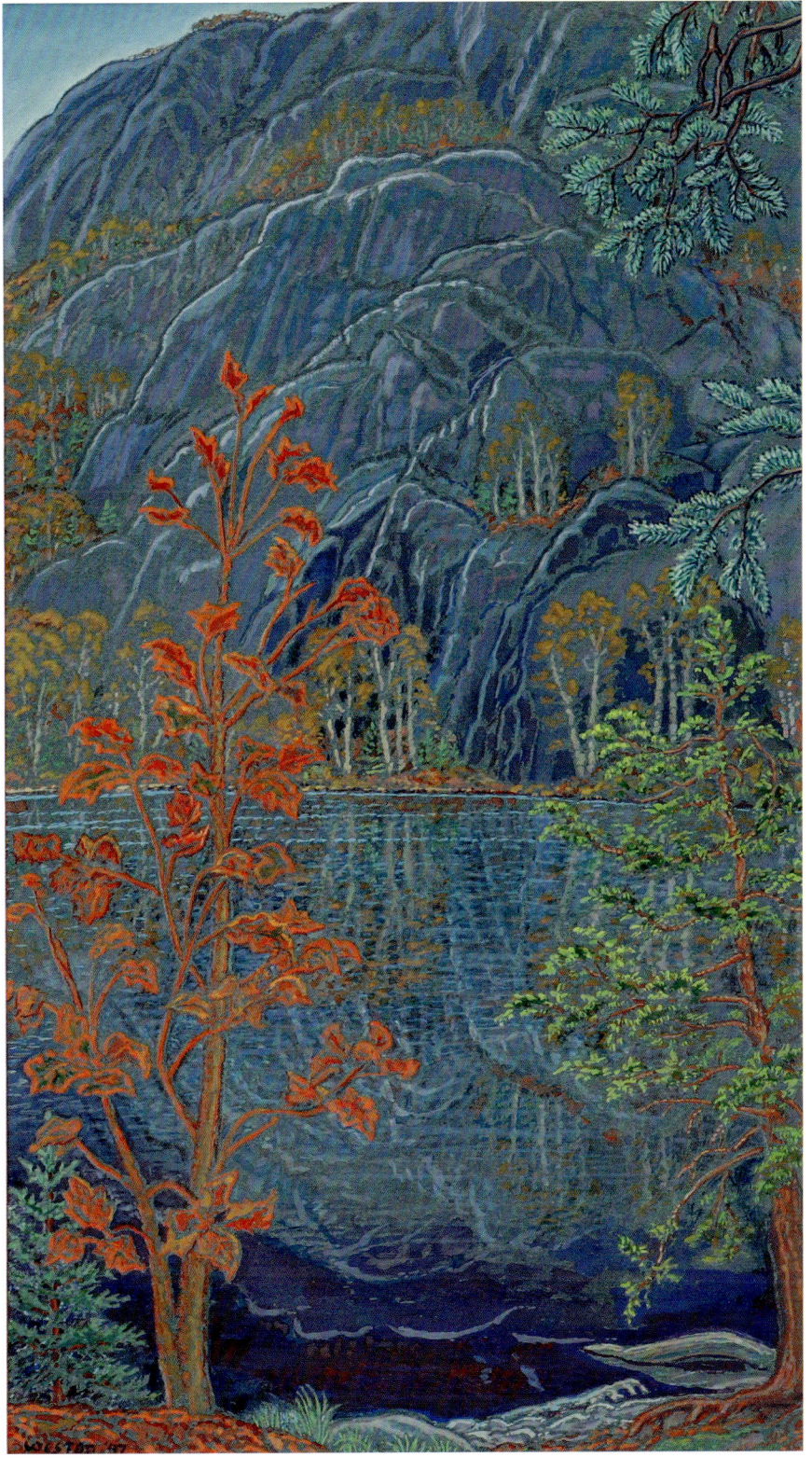

Harold Weston, *Chapel Pond*, 1947. Private Collection.

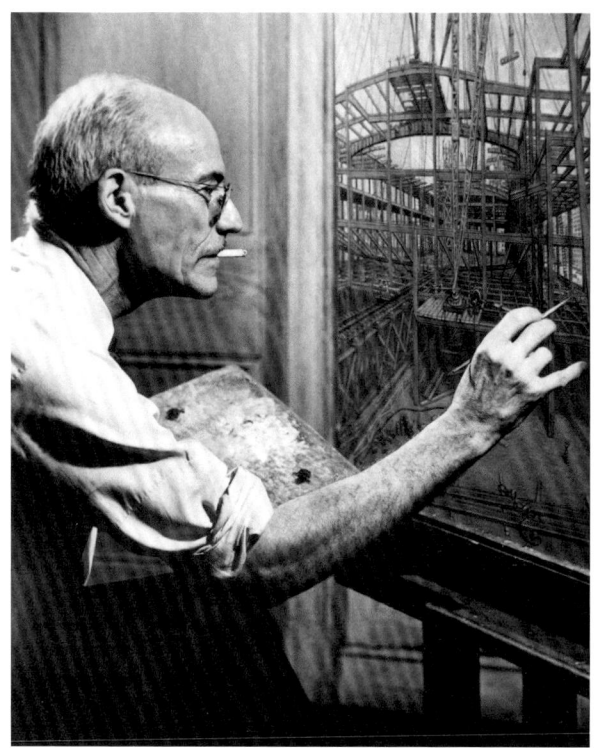

50. Harold Weston painting *Building the United Nations,* 1952. Harold Weston Foundation.

When it was all over, in 1948, Weston wrote a manuscript about his experiences titled "Battle of Bread." He was physically and emotionally exhausted from the strain of the high-powered work. He could not stay awake for more than half an hour. The doctor said that had Weston delayed seeing him by even two weeks, he would have suffered permanent dementia. He had pernicious anemia, for which he had to take weekly vitamin injections the rest of his life. The war effort had taken away his health and more than six years of painting. He was unsure where to start with painting again because he had sacrificed a sense of wonder and mystery that had been fundamental to his art from the early Adirondack days. By diving headlong into the war and the efforts to alleviate its horrors, he had displaced his belief in the sacredness of life with the grubby, Sisyphian work of trying to fix the world.

Weston hoped for much from the United Nations, whose headquarters were being built in New York City. In 1949 he began to make sketches of the construction. Over the next three years, on his own initiative, he made six large easel pictures of heroic skeletal structures with riveted tie beams, hefting cranes, and earth-moving backhoes. He devised a complex and expensive plan for the paintings to travel to industrial centers in the United States and to member countries of the United Nations, demonstrating along the way the symbolic construction of international cooperation. The plan called for the making of a short film dramatizing the urgency of world peace, and ultimately the paintings would rest at the United Nations headquarters.

The paintings were praised by Duncan Phillips; Lewis Mumford; René d'Harnoncourt, the director of the Museum of Modern Art; and even Eleanor Roosevelt, who offered to help place them at the United Nations. They were, however, a "re-creation of reality far more convincingly real than any photograph," as the artist Theodore Fried put it.[99] The precision finish and lack of gestural brush strokes—to say nothing of the optimistic outlook—were anathema to the new art of abstract expressionism that had gained ascendancy in the three years it took Weston to paint the series. Many in the older generation were confused and dismayed by the turn of events in art. Some artists, such as Hopper, retrenched, fought back, and published a manifesto called *Reality*.[100] Others adapted their style to the times.

Weston had called on high-profile friends to help raise money and support for his plan. But money was difficult to find, and the United Nations rejected the paintings. In the end,

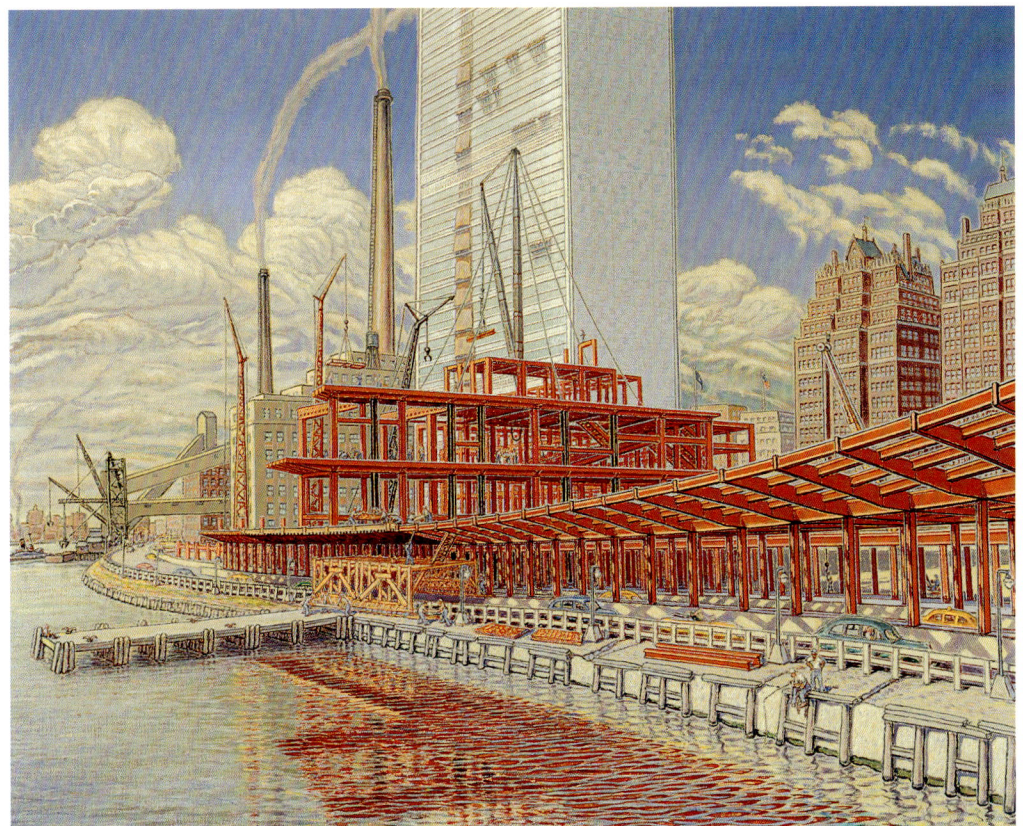

51. Harold Weston, *Building the United Nations—No. 2—Ramp over F.D.R. Drive*, 1949–52 (detail). Smithsonian American Art Museum, Washington, D.C. Gift of the Committee of the Weston United Nations Paintings.

the series went from a hoped-for one-hundred-thousand-dollar touring show to a simple gift to the Smithsonian Institution. Weston had failed, and he was poor. The ignominy was profound and complete. Faith lived in the Adirondacks during much of this period to help cut costs, while Harold, somewhat frayed without her advice and companionship, patched together an existence at the Hotel Wellington in New York, where he had a small, dingy room with a hot plate for a kitchen. "This strangely quiet period," she wrote to him, "seems to hold within itself the dissolution of long-held relationships." She continued:

> With the silent dropping of the golden leaves, the ticking of the faithful cuckoo clock, the gentle lapping of the rose-colored flames on the hearth, where the wonderful, immortal photograph of thee and the U.N. painting dominates the room, a whole cycle of existence here slides gently to a close. I went to the fireplace, laid my head on my hands under thy picture and sobbed so loudly that Frisky barked and came in from the kitchen to see what was up. Weeping in great deep drafts, not from sadness or disappointment or discouragement, but from a huge excess of accumulated emotion quite beyond one human heart to bear.[101]

52. Harold Weston, *Fungus*, ca. 1959. Sarah Hamill.

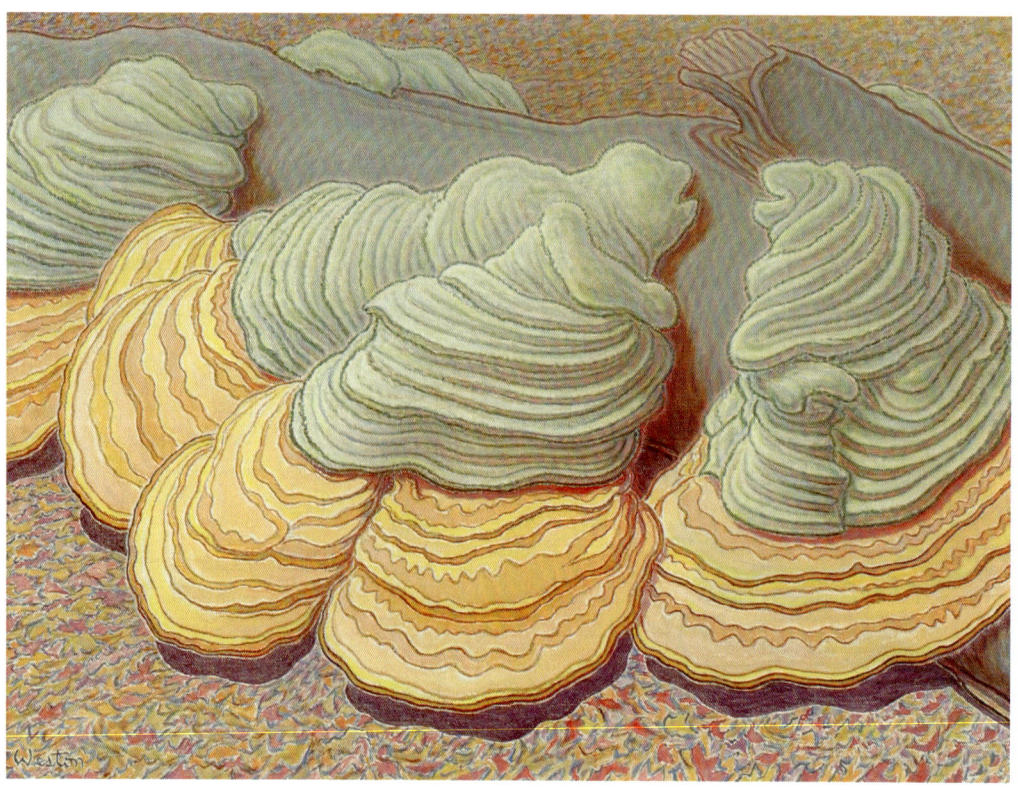

The Doer of What Had to Be Done

Weston was not sure where he should live or what he was going to do next. He did believe, however, in the goals of the Federation of Modern Painters and Sculptors, the oldest modern art organization in the country, to promote its members' work and to maintain solidarity among a generation of freethinking artists. As materially poor as he and Faith were themselves, he was concerned about the artists in New York City who were having "a hell of a time getting enough to pay for rent and food."[102] Although he had been a charter member since 1940, Weston did not attend a federation meeting until January 1953. He was soon elected president. His chief innovation was the promotion of contemporary art and artists through a trilateral arrangement in which donors bought works from artists for donation to museums. This had never been done in any systematic way. Within a few years thirty-five gifts had been made to museums all over the country, including three Louise Nevelson sculptures that helped launch her career and an oil by Will Barnet for the Museum of Fine Arts, Boston—its "first really modern American painting," according to Weston.[103]

Committed now to activities in New York City, Harold and Faith moved their winter home from the Adirondack studio to a dingy railroad apartment located at 282 Bleecker

Street in Greenwich Village over a bakery that kept them warm in the winter and unbearably hot in the summer. Local drunks used the stairwell as a latrine until the Westons forced the landlord to fix the lock; sometimes there was no water; and Faith frequently threatened to call the board of health. But it had a separate room for Harold's studio and a patio in the back that got plentiful sun where they could read the paper and grow flowers and tomatoes.

As the federation's president, positioned in the center of the art world in New York City, Weston was invited to join other causes in the arts. He had the federation become a member of the U.S. Committee of the International Association of Arts (IAA), an organization to support artists that was established by the United Nations Educational, Scientific, and Cultural Organization (UNESCO). As an IAA delegate, vice president, or president, he attended all of the group's international meetings between 1954 in Venice and 1966 in Tokyo. "He managed to make it all seem, and be, so valuable and important," said Richard Carline, Weston's colleague from the United Kingdom. "Many years I might not have bothered, but Harold's sense of urgency kept me at it." Even in his late sixties Weston "had the vigor of a man in his 50s" and astonished colleagues with his pace. A meeting without him, concluded Carline, was "hopelessly inadequate."[104]

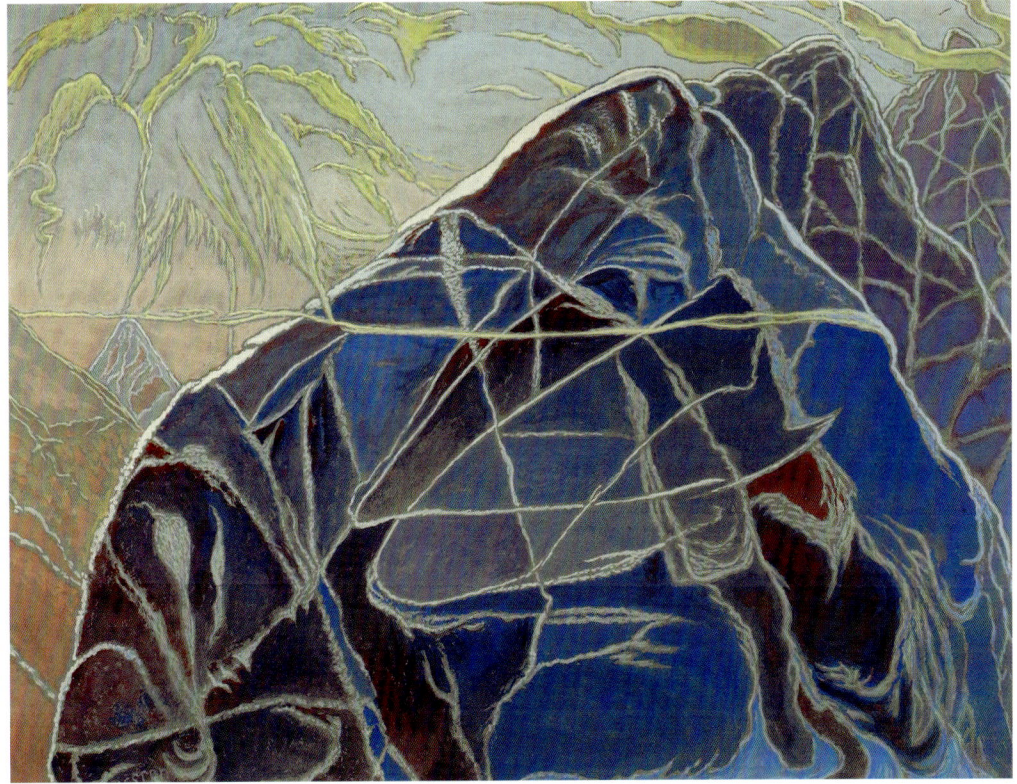

53. Harold Weston, *Silent Barriers*, 1961. Laura Weston.

In the winter of 1955 Lloyd Goodrich, assistant director of the Whitney Museum of American Art, invited Weston, as the federation's president, to join a discussion of what could be done to encourage government support of the arts. This group, which included the actress Lillian Gish, developed three principles: the arts deserve recognition by the federal government; the arts should be used for international cultural exchange; and the government should seek advice from professional artists rather than political appointees. Heartened by President Eisenhower's January 1955 announcement that a federal advisory commission on the arts should be established, Weston drafted an outline for such a body on his manual Olivetti typewriter.[105] The statement of purpose he wrote remained almost exactly intact in the legislation that established the National Endowment for the Arts ten years later.

As he had in Food for Freedom, the Federation of Modern Painters and Sculptors, and the IAA, he quickly became the driving force behind the cause, which this time was the artists' lobby for government support of the arts.[106] He testified before Congress, wrote letters, and launched campaigns on arts legislation. Simultaneously, he was organizing overseas exhibitions of American art, starting up the IAA, and working on the federation's museum gift plan. "Is it sensible to give up so much of one's time and energy to a cause that few artists seem to give a damn about?" he asked Goodrich, who himself had books to write, exhibitions to organize, and a museum to run.[107] It probably was not sensible because there was little to ensure success: they had no support from politicians, the public, or artists. But a few zealous, romantic believers—Weston, Goodrich, Gish, and their early colleagues, who called themselves the National Council on Arts and Government (NCAG)—were pioneers who did not need to be sensible to be right.

"Almost everyone was against us," Weston said of the early years when it was considered subversive to talk about government subsidies for the arts.[108] Fear of control, censorship, and mediocrity persisted as the NCAG was accused from the left of bureaucratizing the arts. From the right, the "Red" label stuck to national arts bills in an obtuseness unique to the times, despite the fact that the NCAG was loudly in favor of using art as a weapon in the Cold War. "The arts are the sharpest weapons in the competition for men's minds," pronounced Senator Robert Lehman of New York, an NCAG ally.[109]

Before federal legislation could pass, Weston and the NCAG paved the way with dozens of small arts bills, such as reduced postage for sheet music and improved tax provisions for self-employed artists. Although each bill was insignificant alone, such legislation cumulatively established a central place for the arts in society. "Many provisions of the statutes now on the statute books were largely proposed by [Weston]. And when I say by him, I mean by him and not by us," declared Goodrich, speaking on behalf of the NCAG. "He was our leader and we backed him completely, but it was he who did all the work."[110]

By 1959 the NCAG had secured support for the Federal Advisory Council on the Arts from fifty-one national organizations representing all of the arts. Others did their part, too. Congressional sponsors of arts bills and their aides worked the language of the bills to suit political imperatives and skillfully manipulated backroom politics to ensure the votes. And President Lyndon Johnson put the arts on the Great Society tide that was so huge and inevitable that nearly everything on it rose to completion. Over the ten years that the NCAG worked toward the goal of federal legislation, the American way of life was radically transformed. The initial language and concepts behind the National Endowment for the Arts legislation, however—first worked out under one bare ceiling bulb on Bleecker Street—were remarkably stable. Only the arguments around them, the majorities in Congress, and the preoccupations of the public changed.

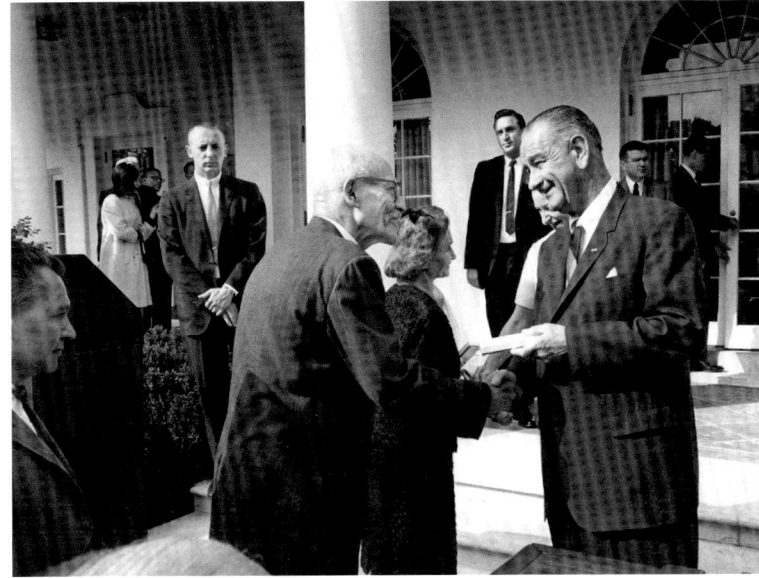

54. Harold Weston and President Lyndon B. Johnson in the Rose Garden at the signing of the National Foundation on the Arts and the Humanities Act, 1965. Harold Weston Foundation.

Even before the National Endowment for the Arts legislation passed in 1965, many of the NCAG's cooperating organizations scrambled to honor Weston. They described "tireless service" and "imaginative effort" and asserted that "there is nowhere a man who knows and understands the problems of artists as you do."[111] Goodrich wrote that Weston "more than any other private individual played a key role in the improvement of our government's relation to the arts in our time."[112] Edward Steichen considered Weston the one with the vision for the NCAG and "the doer of what had to be done."[113] Being the tireless one, the doer, and the leader came at a physical cost, however. Over the NCAG years Weston suffered flaring arthritis, lumbago back pain attacks, shingles, bursitis, thrombosis, and an ulcer—to say nothing of the regular maintenance of his bad leg, bad eyes, anemia, and the occasional broken tooth. But no one knew of these personal trials except Faith.

"There must be many times," sympathized Helen Treadwell, the president of the National Society of Mural Painters, "when you yearn to be at your easel instead of your typewriter."[114] The press accorded Weston an adulatory profile at the IAA congress in Vienna in 1960: "It was Harold Weston," the article states sweepingly of his war work, "who supplied half the world with food." The "likeable elderly gentleman" who looked a "trifle undernourished" leaning on his cane got the final word in the article, however: "If I should once again be interviewed about my paintings before I die, I'll know that I'll have been a little successful in my real vocation, too."[115]

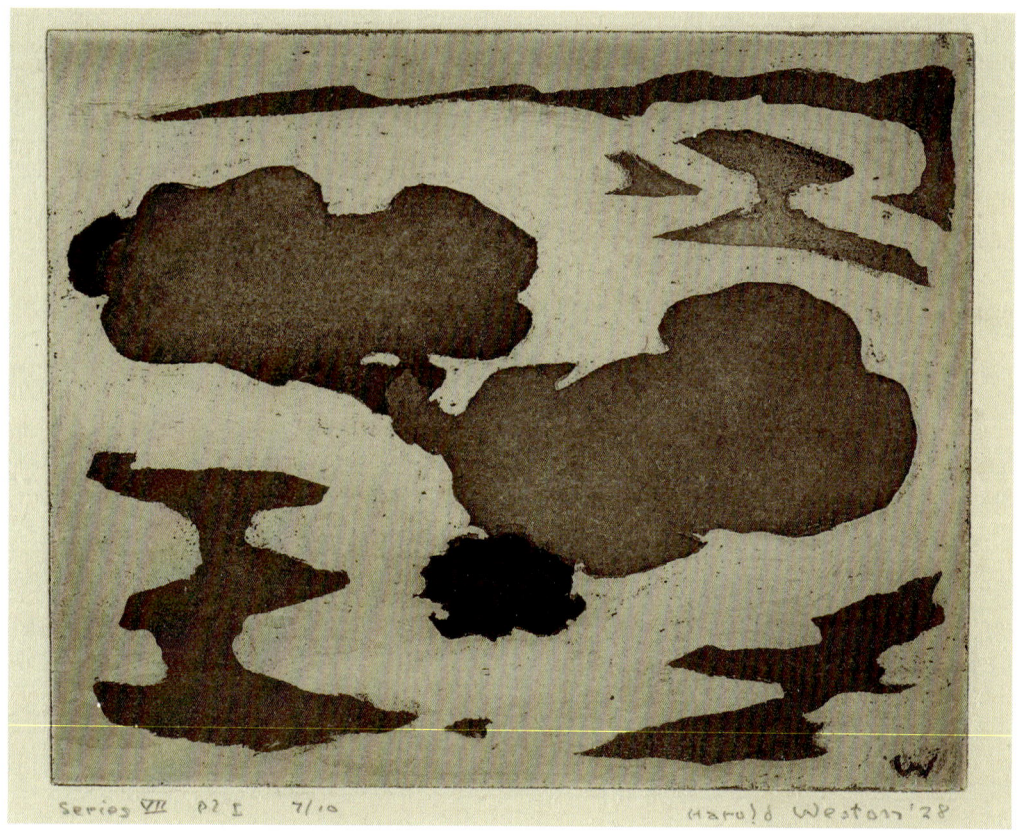

Broadening Our Vision

Had Weston never painted again after the war, he would have left a significant body of work and a humanitarian legacy. But by pushing through the last twenty-four years of his life with repeated attempts and failures, he not only created a coda to round out his career, but also arrived at a singular kind of abstraction. "Into the career of every creative artist must come periods of complete sterility," wrote the artist Charles Burchfield. "Some learn to accept such times and to await with resignation the return of the impulse to paint."[116] Weston was impatient and did not wait. While painting the United Nations series, he started to lose confidence in the realism that had been fundamental to his art, and he wanted to get away from his conservatism, his tightness. It was more difficult than learning how to paint in the first place. He started to focus his compositions more narrowly. With the botanical exactness of the romantics, Weston's leaves and snow-laden pine boughs of this period cover entire canvases. Getting closer to the microcosm, they start to reveal abstract patterns (see figs. 52, 53). Abstract art was already formulaic by the 1950s, but it still provided a valid, new approach to which he was compelled to respond. Or perhaps not so new. Close-up photographs he took of ice in the Alps in 1909 were as abstract

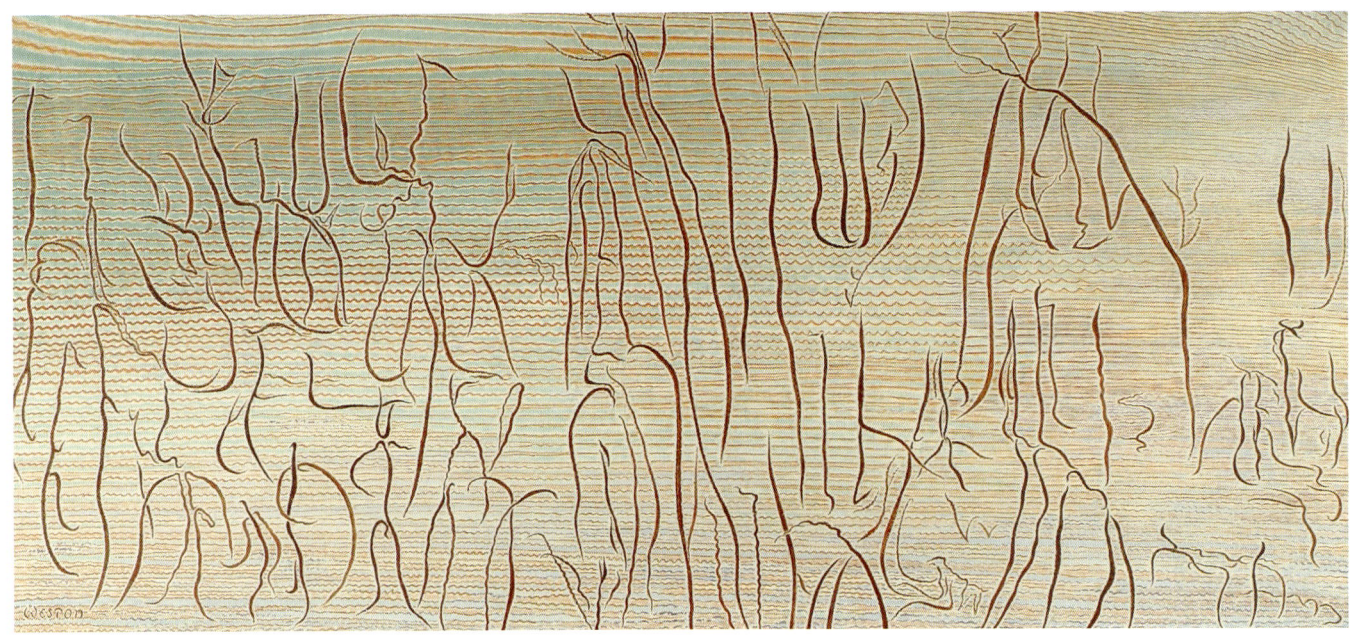

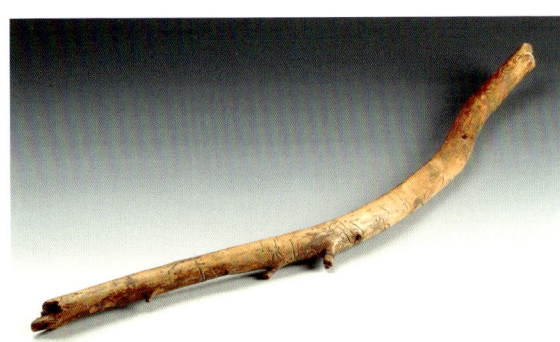

56. Harold Weston, *Wood Script*, 1967. Private Collection.

57. Worm-eaten branch that inspired Weston's *Wood Script* and other paintings. Harold Weston Foundation.

as some of his early Adirondack oil sketches, which were as abstract as his etchings done in France (see fig. 55). As Octavio Paz wrote, nature is the best abstract artist, and nature's forms were embedded in Weston.[117]

On a trip to Rhodes, Greece, in 1958, Weston was again close to the Middle East, and he was reminded of the Islamic preference for the nonrepresentational. The wave motif entered his work, and in 1959 he introduced the image of lichen to his painting. The precise rendering of the folds and intricate shapes of the funguslike plant seemed, like clouds, to suggest objects: craggy hands or distorted, febrile animals. To the wave theme he added ideas that he took from the lined veins on pebbles and nature's other ephemera, such as the worm tracings under the bark of a fallen branch. He started to separate his compositions into two spatial planes of a calligraphic foreground overlaid on a wavelike background that in its most extreme form turned into horizontal bands.

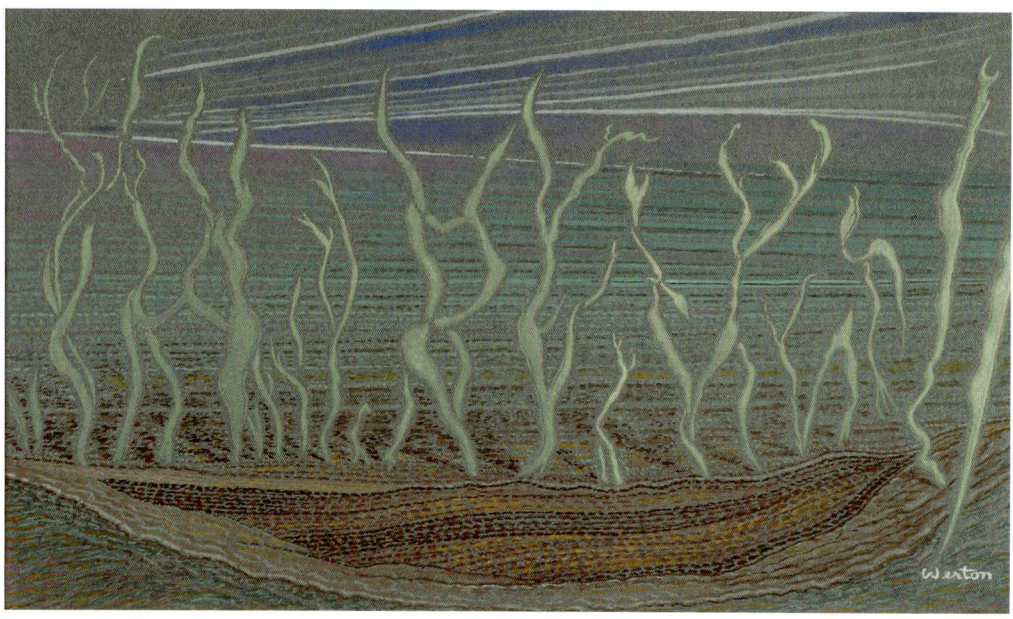

The technique was articulate and exact, and Weston's love of materials—the Belgian linen canvas reinforced with hemp, the prewar American pigments mixed with linseed oil, and turpentine used as binder—was respectful. The precision and lack of surface texture belied the chance involved in determining the compositions, which, he said, unfolded over a period of days or weeks of their own accord. He inverted the early project of rendering established forms in an expressionistic style into a careful rendering of uncalculated forms that suggested themselves through the act of painting. Meanings are no less or more abstruse in these abstract landscapes than in the 1920s work.

For an artist who once thought he might be showing too frequently, it must have been difficult to have only three public solo exhibitions in the last two decades of his life, although his work could be seen privately in the Adirondacks every summer. By the time Babcock Gallery gave him a show in 1961, Weston was so enthusiastic about the new direction of his painting that he hung only the latest, abstract works. Affirming Weston's vision, John Dos Passos perceived in this radical direction paintings that were personal and still clearly "Westons." Yet they were difficult for most people to understand because they did not fit easily into any of contemporary art's major categories. The Babcock show was critically ignored, except by one reviewer who panned it harshly. Weston's Harvard classmate, Theodore Sizer, who was an art professor at Yale, grasped the larger point. "You have seen what others have not," he wrote Weston. "You have broadened our vision and, whether the things are 'good' or 'bad,' bless you for that."[118]

By 1964 most of Weston's art advocacy obligations had concluded, and he experienced a burst of creativity. Much of modernism was about tearing down images and techniques that had been established over centuries, a "going back" to primitivism, a retrospective view that acknowledged and dismissed the present civilization. In his most successful late paintings Weston was like a cave painter who knew nothing of modernity. Carefully, slowly, he built an image out of the primal forces of nature, giving language to thought, like someone who cannot yet understand an image of the whole—the tree, the animal, the rock— before he has understood the part—the branch, the horns, the geologic veins. These paintings were of a vernal tongue, like the infant language that Emerson called more picturesque and poetic because it was tied to natural symbols.[119] Weston believed in beauty and in the eternal rhythms of nature that always had and could still withstand human folly. This was the subject of his paintings, avatars of this faith that now had simple, if far-reaching, titles: *Quest, Maelstrom, Surge.*

Increasingly restricted physically, Weston searched for new ways of expressing an inner landscape. In the summer of 1968 Faith's brother, John Borton, and his wife, Polly, visited the Westons in St. Huberts after a trip to Quebec. Polly had collected smooth, charcoal stones from the beach on the St. Lawrence River that had an infinite variety of patterns in their white veins. Harold saw her precious collection and argued that she should,

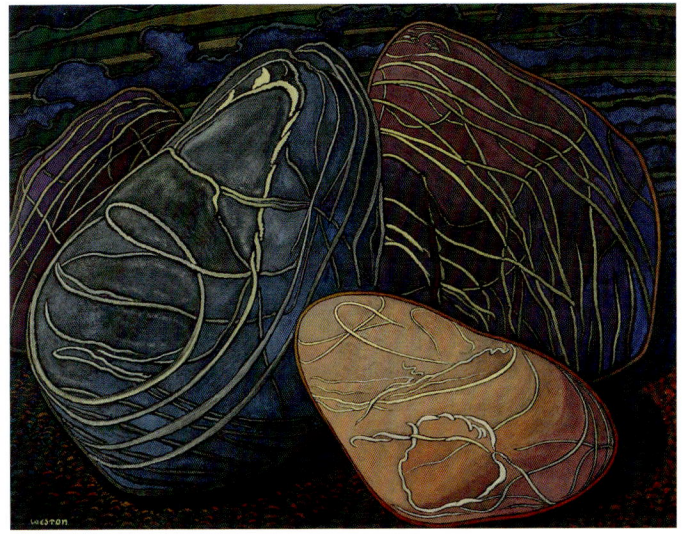

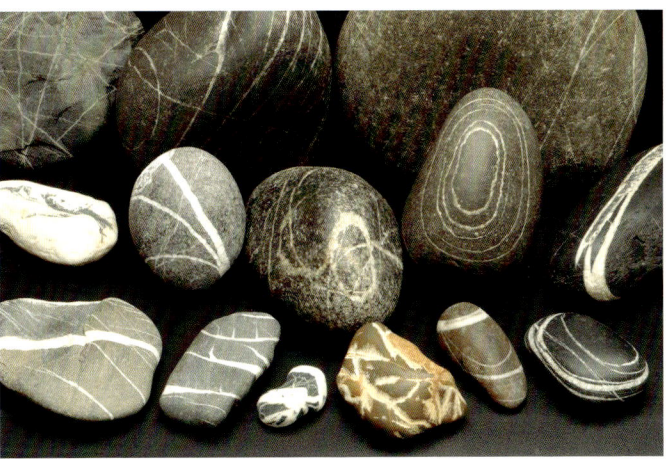

59. Harold Weston, *Conference (Stone Series No. 3)*, 1968. Harold Weston Foundation, courtesy of Atea Ring Gallery, Westport, N.Y.

60. Stones that inspired the Stone Series. Harold Weston Foundation.

for the sake of art, hand them over (fig. 60). Thus, he started the Stone Series, which captivated him until his death in 1972, by which time he had painted seventy-six gouache compositions. This late-blooming resurgence of wild exuberance was uniquely personal, just like earlier phases of his work. When he finally withdrew again and painted for himself, it was like the days that Phillips described, of an artist painting "without any claim that his records are important. And yet important they are because true independence is rare."[120]

The heightened abstraction of the Stone Series invites broad interpretations. *Tibetan Dawn (Stone Series No. 38)*, 1969 (fig. 61), for instance, suggests a cosmic reading that might end up in very much the same place as an early landscape such as *Afternoon Shower*, 1920 (fig. 62). The Stone Series paintings are so inward looking that it is as though Weston could have painted them with his eyes closed, from memory. Even late in life, his memory was acute; he corrected his grandchildren's descriptions of their day's hiking even though he

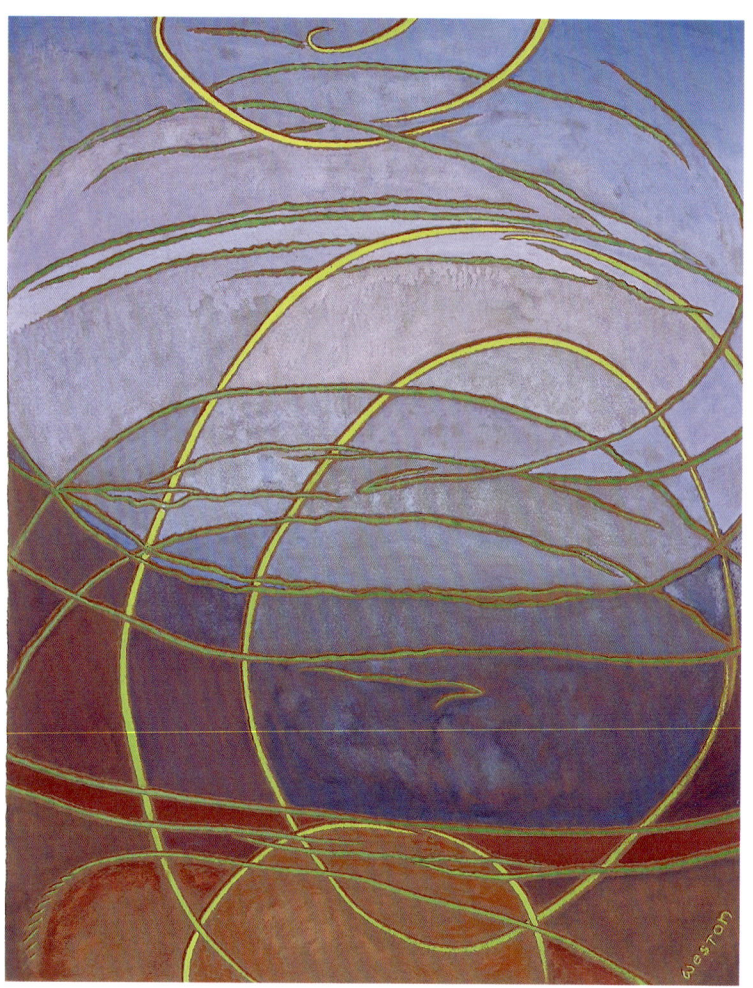

had not been on the trails for twenty or thirty years. At a passionate age he had heaved his spirit into the mountains, where it seemed to be held in a geologic vein for him to tap into ever after. Weston knew that his own inner wildness, which he had worked hard to preserve his whole life, could not be destroyed, but he worried about future generations. In the last few years of his life he wrote a book of reminiscences, *Freedom in the Wilds: A Saga of the Adirondacks*, that championed the preservation of wilderness tracts as well as the preservation of personal freedom. "The forever wild area within us," wrote Weston, "serves as a link to ages past and other spheres." Any creative person, he continued, "can sense from a single fern frond, a leaf, a stone or the song of a bird, the quintessence of the kind of freedom a wilderness tract can convey."[121] He died on 10 April 1972 as the second printing of his book was going to press.

61. Harold Weston, *Tibetan Dawn (Stone Series No. 38)*, 1969. Harold Weston Foundation, courtesy of Platt Fine Art, Chicago.

62. Harold Weston, *Afternoon Shower*, 1920. Donna and Michael O'Rourke.

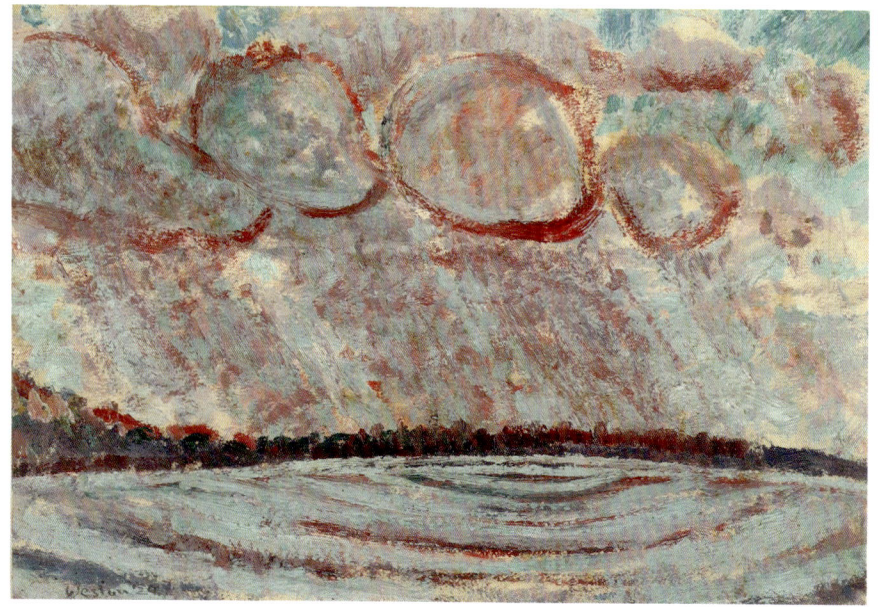

63. Harold Weston, *Spring (Stone Series No. 61)*, 1970. Harold Weston Foundation.

Weston was a modernist in that he sought freedom, but a romantic in that he sought freedom through beauty. For many modernists the social and aesthetic stance was one of disenchantment. Weston was never jaded and never thought he could not make a difference. "I can see how I am often a very difficult person to live with," he told Faith once. "Many women would want more frivolity, but I am serious. My frivolity is more like the rain falling on the fields in the Spring or the wind blowing the flowers."[122] His life was earnest but wildly optimistic, and his painting singularly devoid of cynicism. He refused to concede to the fractures of modern life—or to his own. "The reward is what you do," he said a year before he died. He was talking about his arts advocacy work, but he could have been talking about going to war in Persia, painting unpopular paintings, or any other decision he had made. "If you're looking for other rewards it isn't going to be done in the right spirit. You've got to believe in things before you can have the earnestness and the honesty to overcome opposition and achieve what you're trying to do."[123]

Notes

All letters, journals, and diaries cited in this chapter are from the Harold Weston Manuscript Collection, Harold Weston Foundation, West Chester, Pa., unless otherwise noted. Harold Weston is referred to as "HW."

1. Clive Bell, "Art and Politics," *New Republic*, 10 Nov. 1920, Harold Weston Papers, 1916–72, Archives of American Art, Smithsonian Institution, Washington, D.C. (hereafter AAA).

2. Duncan Phillips, *The Artist Sees Differently: Essays Based upon the Philosophy of a Collection in the Making* 2 vols. (New York: E. Weyhe; Washington, D.C.: Phillips Memorial Gallery, 1931), 1: 137.

3. Harold Weston, "A Painter Speaks," *Magazine of Art* 32 (Jan. 1939), 16.

4. MacLeish quoted in Faith Borton Weston (hereafter FBW), Journal of an Artist's Wife (hereafter Journal), 12 May 1927.

5. Ralph Flint, "Exhibitions in New York: Harold Weston, Montross Gallery," *Art News*, 3 Dec. 1932, 5.

6. Ralph Waldo Emerson, "Nature," in *Ralph Waldo Emerson, "Nature," and Henry David Thoreau, "Walking"* (Boston: Beacon Press, 1991), 28.

7. FBW, Journal, 18 July 1928.

8. HW to his father, 9 Mar. 1931.

9. HW, Diary, 14 Feb. 1911.

10. HW, Diary, 30 Sept. 1910.

11. HW, Diary, 4–20 Aug. 1911. HW, tape recording, 26 Mar. 1971.

12. HW, Diary, 2 Aug. 1911.

13. HW, "Plans for Study," Guggenheim Foundation Application, 1934, AAA.

14. HW to his parents, 27 May 1916.

15. HW, Diary, 24 Nov. 1915.

16. HW to his parents, 27 May 1916.

17. HW, Diary, 7 Sept. 1916.

18. HW to his parents, 18 Sept. 1917, AAA.

19. Ibid.

20. *Exhibition of Paintings by William E. Schumacher, 1912–1931* (Woodstock, N.Y.: Woodstock Art Gallery, 1931). "The Woodstock Art Colony," *The Younger Set*, Sept. 1922.

21. HW, Diary, 8 Apr. 1920, citing Luke 5:16.

22. HW, Diary, 19 May 1920.

23. HW, Diary, 26 May and 4 June 1920.

24. HW to Hamilton Easter Field, transcribed in Diary, 25 Nov. 1920.

25. Walter Pach, "Art. At the Pennsylvania Academy," *Freeman*, 18 May 1921, AAA. HW to his parents, 11 Dec. 1920.

26. James quoted in Daniel L. Schacter, *Searching for Memory: The Brain, the Mind, and the Past* (New York: Basic, 1996), 201–2.

27. James cited in P. L., "Books & Things," *New Republic*, 29 Dec. 1920, AAA.

28. HW to Faith Borton, 28 Oct. 1922.

29. HW, Diary, 12 Nov. 1921.

30. Ibid.

31. Margaret Breuning, "Galleries Show Many Phases of Modern Art," *New York Evening Post*, 18 Nov. 1922, 11.

32. D. H. Lawrence, "Humming-Bird," *New Republic*, ca. 1921, AAA.

33. HW to Faith Borton, 25 June 1922.

34. Mansfield Bascom, curator of Wharton Esherick Museum, interviewed by Rebecca Foster, Paoli, Pa., Dec. 1996.

35. HW to Faith Borton, 5 Nov. 1922. Henry Tyrell, "A Roundabout Modernist," *New York World*, 12 Nov. 1922.

36. Tyrell, "A Roundabout Modernist."

37. Breuning, "Galleries Show Many Phases of Modern Art," 11; "Weston's Persian and American Views," *American Art News*, 11 Nov. 1922, 2, 6; "Harold F. Weston: An Adirondack Painter," *Art Review*, Nov. 1922, 21; Ruth de Rochemont, "Notes on Painting and Sculpture: Comments on the Current Exhibitions in New York," *Vanity Fair* 19, no. 3 (Nov. 1922): 29.

38. Henry McBride, "Art News and Reviews: Attractive Shows in Many Galleries," *New York Herald*, 12 Nov. 1922, sec. 7, 7.

39. Christian Brinton to Mrs. Joseph Hill Brinton, n.d.

40. R[alph] F[lint], "Adirondack Hills and Persian Vales Painted by Harold F. Weston," *Christian Science Monitor*, 17 Nov. 1922, 8.

41. HW to Faith Borton, 11 Dec. 1922.

42. Faith Borton to John Borton, 1 Jan. 1920, John Borton Papers, Terry Borton, Haddam, Conn.

43. Faith Borton Weston, *Newsletter* (Federated Garden Clubs of New York State, Inc.) 22, nos. 7–8 (July–Aug. 1950), 9.

44. HW to Faith Borton, 21 June 1922.

45. HW to James B. Munn, 20 May 1923, Harold Weston Papers, Harvard Univ. Archives, Cambridge, Mass.

46. FBW to her mother, 1 July 1923, AAA.

47. FBW, Journal, 10 Dec. 1925.

48. Moholy-Nagy quoted in Anna Moszynska, *Abstract Art* (London: Thames and Hudson, 1990), 93.

49. FBW, Journal, 5 Feb. 1925.

50. FBW to her mother, 21 Nov. 1924, AAA.

51. HW, Diary, 19 Nov. 1925.

52. O'Keeffe quoted in Harold Weston, "Interlude in the Adirondacks," in *Paul Rosenfeld: Voyager in the Arts*, edited by Jerome Mellquist and Lucie Wiese (New York: Creative Age Press, 1948), 184.

53. Gertrude R. Herdle to HW, 14 Jan. 1925, AAA.

54. Ernest A. Weiss, "Art in Rochester," *Rochester (N.Y.) Herald*, 25 Jan. 1925, 11.

55. Ernest A. Weiss, "Art in Rochester," *Rochester (N.Y.) Herald*, 18 Jan. 1925, 9.

56. Alexander Booth to HW, 1 May 1925.

57. J. O. H. Cosgrave to HW, 13 Apr. 1925, AAA.

58. FBW, Journal, Mar.–Apr. 1925. This story is told in *Freedom in the Wilds*, published forty-six years later, but I use the version written contemporaneously.

59. FBW, Journal, 5 Feb. 1925, emphasis in original.

60. HW to Faith Borton, 27 Mar. 1923.

61. FBW, Journal, 19 Mar. 1926.

62. FBW, Journal, 25 Mar. 1926.

63. FBW, Journal, 10 Apr. 1927.

64. FBW, Journal, 26 Feb. 1927, emphasis in original.

65. HW quoted in "Around the Studios," *New York Herald*, 29 Aug. 1927, 9.

66. FBW, Journal, 20 May 1927.

67. Montross quoted in FBW, Journal, 18 July 1928.

68. "Weston," *La Semaine à Paris*, 25 July–3 Aug. 1927, 51.

69. FBW, Journal, 28 Oct. 1927.

70. "Paintings in Oils Like Mosaics," *New York World*, 23 Oct. 1927.

71. FBW, Journal, 9 Aug. 1928.

72. Mary Hartshorne Weston quoted in FBW, Journal, 12 July 1928.

73. Harold Weston, "Paul Looks at Paintings," unedited draft for essay in *Paul Rosenfeld: Voyager in the Arts*, AAA.

74. Paul Rosenfeld, "Harold Weston's Adventure," *New Republic*, 31 Dec. 1930, 190–91.

75. Margaret Breuning, "Other Shows," *New York Evening Post*, 15 Dec. 1928, M11.

76. HW to Boyer Galleries, 1 Feb. 1934, AAA.

77. Duncan Phillips to HW, 12 Jan. 1931, AAA.

78. Margaret Bourke-White to HW, 20 Sept. (ca. 1933), AAA.

79. Edward Alden Jewell, "Art in Review: Exhibition of Recent Paintings by Harold Weston Opens at the Montross Gallery," *New York Times*, 2 Dec. 1932, 24.

80. Phillips, *The Artist Sees Differently*, 1: 138.

81. HW quoted in FBW, Journal, 1 Jan. 1928.

82. "Solid, Rugged Things Make Up Weston's World," *Art Digest*, 15 Mar. 1935, 23.

83. HW, notes for lecture at Phillips Memorial Gallery, ca. early 1930s, AAA.

84. Phillips, *The Artist Sees Differently*, 1: 139.

85. Lewis Mumford, "Goings On about Town: Weston," *New Yorker*, 23 Mar. 1935, 6.

86. Leila Mechlin, "Inspiration Marks Etchings by World Leader in Art. Harold Weston's Virile Paintings," *Washington, D.C., Evening Star*, 29 Feb. 1936, B3. "Solid, Rugged Things," 23. Phillips, *The Artist Sees Differently*, 1: 138.

87. "Harold Weston at Montross's: Artist Exhibits His Late Work in Varied Fields," *New York Sun*, 30 Nov. 1932, 16.

88. FBW, Journal, 16 Feb. 1926.

89. Malcolm Vaughan, "Current Events in the Realm of Art, Antiques: In the Parade of New York Art Shows This Week," *New York American*, 3 Dec. 1932, 32.

90. Peppino Mangravite to HW, 27 Apr. 1937, AAA.

91. Carpenter quoted in Weston, "A Painter Speaks," 21.

92. Lewis Mumford, "The Art Galleries: The Treasury's Murals," *New Yorker*, 17 Oct. 1936, 70–71.

93. Duncan Phillips to HW, 19 Nov. 1937, AAA.

94. HW, tape recording, 28 Mar. 1971.

95. Phillips, *The Artist Sees Differently*, 1: 139.

96. "Harold Weston," n.d., AAA.

97. "[Weston], more than anyone else—as Mrs. Eleanor Roosevelt has written me—was responsible for the original conception and carrying through of UNRRA." Lewis Mumford, statement of support, 5 June 1952, AAA.

98. Harold Weston, "Battle of Bread," 1948, 46.

99. Fried quoted in "Artists' Reactions to No. IV of U.N. Series," AAA.

100. See, for example, *Reality: A Journal of Artists' Opinions* 1, no. 1 (spring 1953).

101. FBW to HW, 18 Oct. 1952, AAA.

102. HW to Bruce Weston, 12 Dec. 1952.

103. HW, tape recording, 26 Mar. 1971.

104. Richard Carline to William Smith, 14 May 1972.

105. HW, "Proposal for the Organization of an Advisory Commission for Government and Art," Jan. 1955, Harold Weston Manuscript Collection, George Arents Research Library, Syracuse University, Syracuse, N.Y.

106. "[Weston] had a unique combination of an acceptance of different viewpoints, an extraordinary grasp of details, tireless energy, and a complete devotion to any cause that he undertook. These were the qualities that made all of us follow his banner, and that made him our ideal leader." Lloyd Goodrich, *Congressional Record: Proceedings and Debates of the 92d Congress, Second Session*, vol. 118, no. 101 (21 June 1972), S9850. This statement is in reference to Weston's work with arts legislation, but the characteristics it lists could be applied to Weston in other areas of his work.

107. HW to Lloyd Goodrich, 30 July 1956, Harold Weston Manuscript Collection, George Arents Research Library.

108. HW, tape recording, 28 Mar. 1971.

109. *NCAG Interim Report*, 12 Nov. 1962, 3, AAA.

110. Goodrich, *Congressional Record*, S9850.

111. Helen Treadwell to HW, 25 Apr. 1965, AAA.

112. Lloyd Goodrich to Dr. Joshua C. Taylor, 30 Apr. 1974, AAA.

113. Edward Steichen to HW, 12 Jan. 1966, AAA.

114. Helen Treadwell to HW, 25 Apr. 1965, AAA.

115. Translation of news clipping "Neues Österreich," ca. 5 Oct. 1960.

116. Charles Burchfield, "Hopper: Career of Silent Poetry," *Art News* 49 (Mar. 1950), 63, quoted in Gail Levin, *Edward Hopper: An Intimate Biography* (New York: Knopf, 1995), 424.

117. Octavio Paz, "Three Notes on Painting," 1973, reprinted in *Writers on Artists*, edited by Daniel Halpern (San Francisco: North Point Press, 1988), 347.

118. Theodore Sizer to HW, 8 Mar. 1961, AAA.

119. Emerson, "Nature," 26.

120. Phillips, *The Artist Sees Differently*, 1: 139.

121. Harold Weston, *Freedom in the Wilds: A Saga of the Adirondacks* (St. Huberts, N.Y.: Adirondack Trail Improvement Society, 1971), 216–17.

122. FBW, Journal, 3 Dec. 1926.

123. HW, tape recording, 28 Mar. 1971.

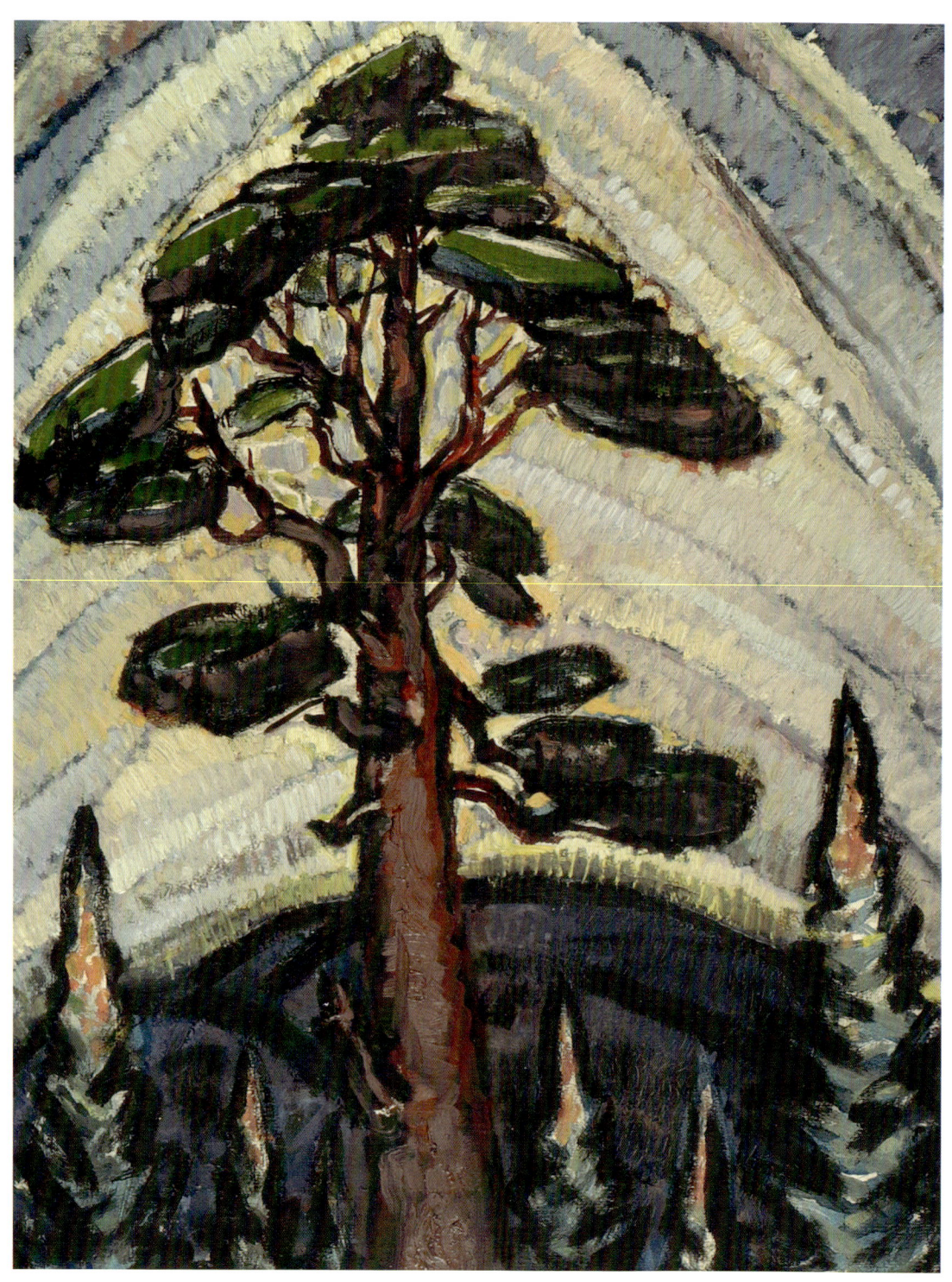

HAROLD WESTON
Rugged Painter of the Adirondacks

Stephen Bennett Phillips

There is a young American painter who stirs in me the hope for a rebirth on this new soil of something that was not lost to the art of painting with the passing of Vincent Van Gogh. It is something earthy and rugged and at the same time of a lyric poignancy, something unguardedly and tactlessly frank yet tenderly humane. I am thinking of Harold Weston.

—Duncan Phillips, *The Artist Sees Differently* (1931)

FACING PAGE
64. Harold Weston, *Pine Tree,* 1920. Collection of Katherine Merle-Smith.

RUGGEDNESS WAS A TERM that critics consistently applied to Harold Weston's work in the 1930s.[1] Nevertheless, Weston's style changed several times during his career, demonstrating an original and personal response to current trends in art. Perhaps critics were responding as much to his biography as to the works themselves, for many of the paintings, in particular those of the 1930s, range between the precise distillations of precisionism and the detailed realism of American regionalists. Certainly Weston always chose a life of hard asceticism that is reflected in much of his subject matter, and, like any good artist, he painted what he knew and loved. His repertoire included the human form, especially the nude, and still life, but his real subject was always the rugged landscape of the Adirondacks. The critic and collector Duncan Phillips observed that "Weston must live his pictures before he paints them. . . . He adapts his style to his subject and his subjects to his choice of medium—his water colors have sensuous charm while his oils are rough hewn and vibrant with broken tones, patterned with vigorous colored contours."[2] Weston chose to approach painting in a personal fashion, skipping formal academic training. As he said, "Felt it more important to train the mind before the hand."[3] His work carried none of the staid convention of nineteenth-century academicism.

Weston's first style developed in Mesopotamia (now Iraq) and Persia (now Iran) during World War I. The Persian views were rapidly sketched and display a reductive approach to information. They are characterized by a fauvist palette of oranges and violets, with a stylized approach to the receding layers of hills, which Weston sometimes captured as colored scallops, much like those found in Persian and Indian miniatures, bordered by the heavy dark outlines of modernist painting.

Returning to the United States, Weston built a studio in the Adirondacks in 1920, and for three years he worked outdoors on hundreds of landscape sketches. They became the basis for finished paintings that he created in his studio. Weston made it clear that the paintings were not done outside. He wanted to paint what he felt rather than what he saw. As he said, "If I felt the mood of a certain landscape was akin to the music of some composer, I would play my Victor records of it over and over while I painted."[4]

In expressive brush strokes, *Self-Portrait*, 1923 (Foster chap., fig. 6), reveals the essence of Weston's Adirondack personality. With his chiseled cheeks and elongated, pronounced chin, pipe, and oversize hand, he is a ruggedly handsome man. Using artistic license, he has increased the scale of his hand in the foreground, drawing the viewer's attention to its powerful mass with crisp strokes of white paint on the knuckles. With the black outlines, crooked shoulder, and off-center three-quarter profile, Weston has given the painting visual variety, a modern feeling, and a contemporary dynamism. With its short brush strokes and juxtaposition of warm and cool colors, the painting is full of energy and life. A Japanese print in the background speaks to the importance of Asian art and aesthetics to the artist and his work. Compositionally and stylistically there is much in this self-portrait that is reminiscent of self-portraits by Vincent van Gogh.

The landscapes of the early 1920s are painted in a predominantly blue palette with touches of warm violet, salmon, red, and yellow. Forms, delineated with dark lines, become increasingly patterned. The familiar scalloping of the Persian mountains is translated to the Adirondack setting, where Weston now applies it to trees and skies. He later referred to his style at this time as "my early 1922 stylized landscape period."[5]

Pine Tree, 1920 (fig. 64), is Weston's first great Adirondack painting. It shows his understanding of early modernism with the use of a distorted perspective, the simplified form in the larger-than-life tree, and the stylized sky. The radiant bands of light in the

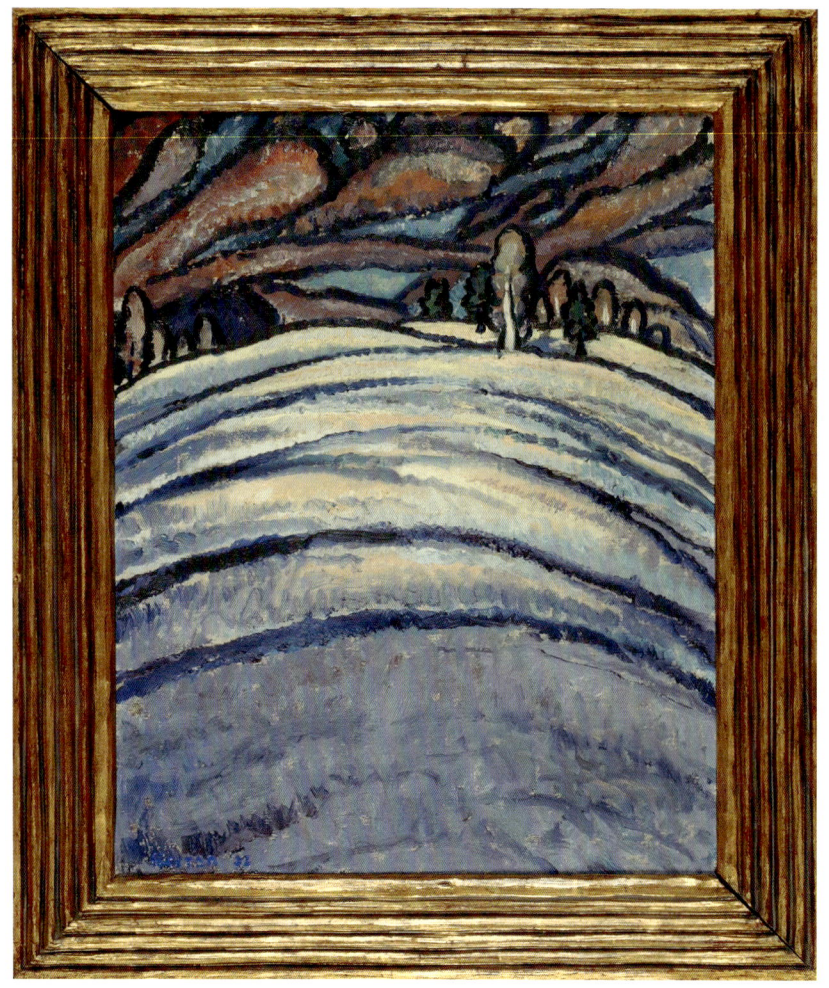

65. Harold Weston, *Winter Hill*, 1922. Private Collection.

sky, like those in works by Charles Burchfield, Arthur Dove, and John Marin, are at once suggestive of his awareness of contemporary art moderne patterning and of a nod to the physics of light. If Weston's handling of paint in the sky is still a little awkward, *Pine Tree* gives a foretaste of where he would go with his early, stylized landscapes. More simplified than *Pine Tree* in its composition is *Winter Hill*, 1922 (fig. 65). It demonstrates Weston's continued interest in perfecting the distorted perspective of the landscape. Again he outlines his stylized forms with dark lines. The painting is notable for the way it approaches abstraction, with its focus more on shapes and lines than on the objective reality of the landscape.

Weston continued to perfect his modernist style of simplifying forms. In *Giant Mountain from Windy Brow*, 1922 (Foster chap., fig. 22), the landscape is pared down to a series of curves, and the palette is reduced to white and blue, suggesting a winter evening with snow on the ground. The dark sky, lit with arcs of white light, mirrors the white ground with its dark scallops of boulders and hills. The mountain to the left is Giant Mountain, which Weston could see from his studio and painted often. Here it appears to be a foreshortened human head, its crown close to the picture plane, with the forehead receding into the distance. In *From Studio Window*, 1922 (fig. 66), Giant Mountain again looks like a foreshortened sleeping figure, with its head, shoulders, and back visible. There is snow on the ground, and the trees cast long, hard-edged triangular shadows in the moonlight. The night sky is painted in short brush strokes of pure color in bands that echo the silhouette of the mountain's bulk. In the middle distance a tree lit by the moonlight moves in the wind. In its simplified form the painting is at once reminiscent of early Persian art and of the art moderne work of Paul Manship.

The tree becomes the focus in *Birch Tree*, 1922 (fig. 67), one of the most stylized paintings from this early period, but the subject is movement. Weston's composition shows the birch tree flanked by two diminutive pines that tilt toward it like

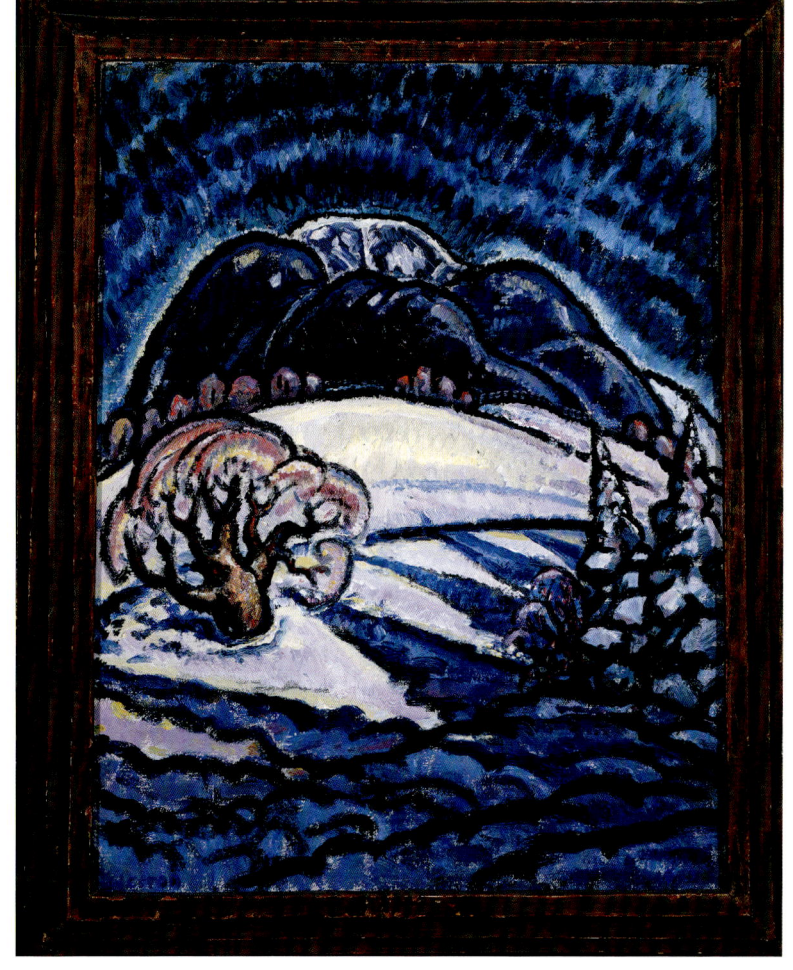

66. Harold Weston, *From Studio Window*, 1922. Collection of Stephen Bennett Phillips.

67. Harold Weston, *Birch Tree*, 1922. Baird and Nancy Edmonds.

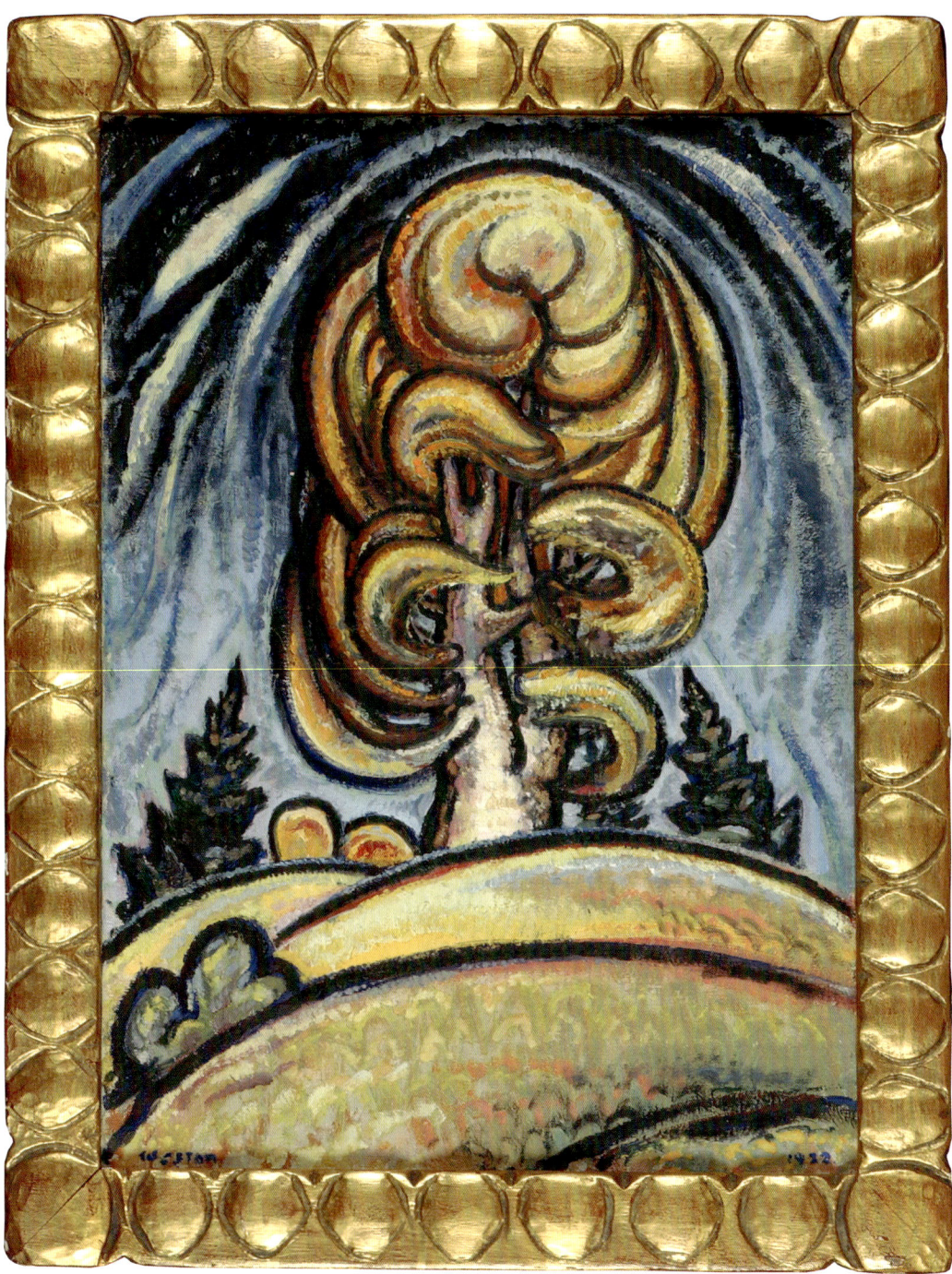

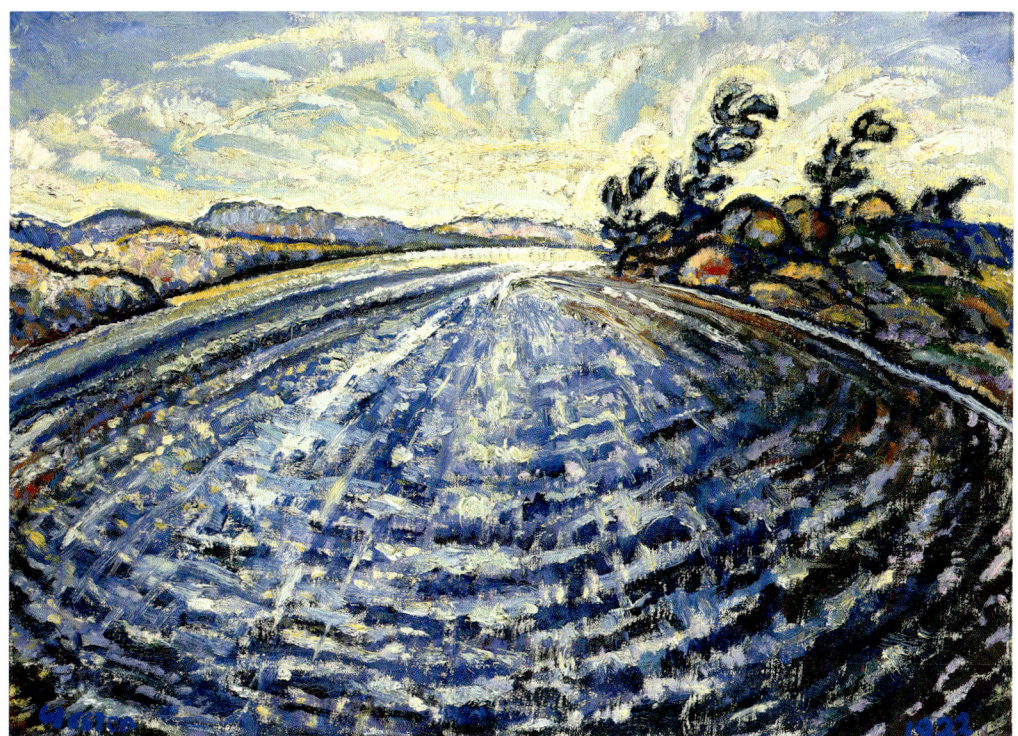

chorus dancers. Birchlike qualities are sacrificed to a sense of movement: the branches are shown as whorls, and the sky is a series of sweeping lines around the tree. In the foreground four hills echo the sweep of the tree branches.

Weston's control of light is apparent in *Forest Winter No. 2,* 1922 (Foster chap., fig. 21), one of the most visually engaging of his works of the early 1920s. The painting glows as light emanates from the back of the composition, hitting each stylized tree. Weston makes light dance through the painting. Unlike in *Birch Tree,* where the realism of the tree was lost in the effort to capture movement, in *Forest Winter No. 2* Weston produces believable trees. In the fish-eye perspective of *Winds—Upper Ausable Lake,* 1922 (fig. 68), one of Weston's greatest paintings of the 1920s, he demonstrates his mastery, capturing the essence of a sunny day by a northern lake. The composition is filled with a large radiant oval, the lake appearing as a giant blue clamshell concentrically ridged with light, its hinge a distant mountain, its upper shell the sky. Quirky trees to the right of the composition and the lines of ripples on the lake show the effect of the wind. The dominant blues of the palette are highlighted with touches of yellows, pinks, oranges, and greens.

In November 1922 Weston had the first of six solo exhibitions at the Montross Galleries in New York.[6] Weston was fortunate to have such a prominent gallery to represent him. Newman Emerson Montross (fig. 69), like Alfred Stieglitz and Charles Daniel, often showed the work of avant-garde artists. Among the artists Montross showed were Henri

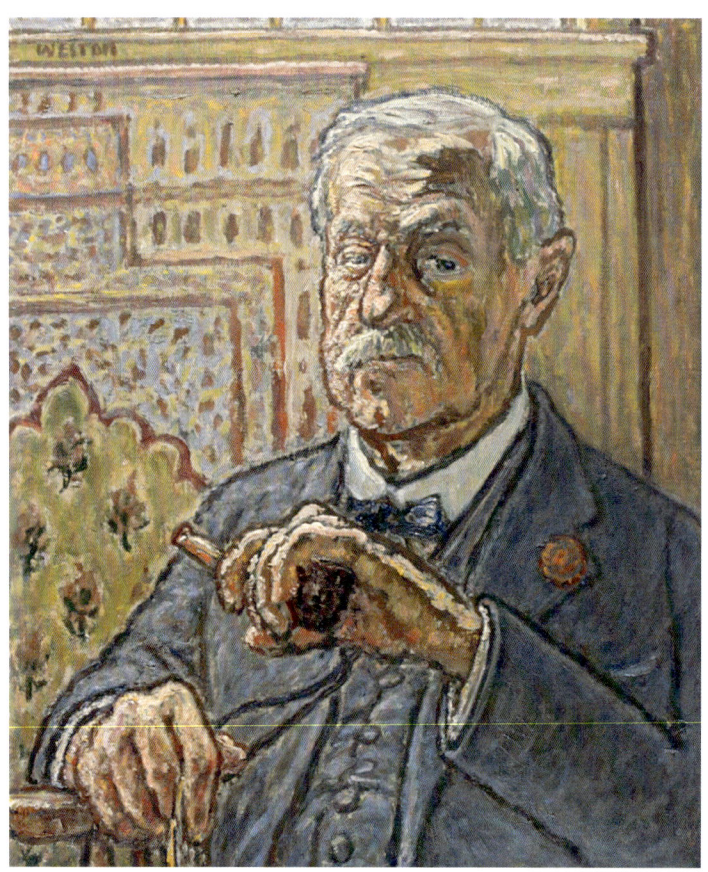

69. Harold Weston, *Portrait of N. E. Montross*, n.d. The Phillips Collection, Washington, D.C. Gift of Mrs. N. E. Montross, 1933.

Matisse (whose exhibition was organized by the critic Walter Pach),[7] Max Weber, Henry Varnum Poor, Philip Evergood, Charles Burchfield, Bradley Walker Tomlin, Charles Demuth, and George Bellows.

Weston's Montross exhibition, featuring sixty-three paintings and seventy sketches of the Adirondack landscape, as well as twenty Persian sketches, was a financial success, but the artist regretted not waiting another year before exhibiting. "The success of the exhibition made me self-conscious about the stylization and the attitude."[8] The exhibition was well reviewed, and several of the reviewers were struck by Weston's individualism.[9]

After Weston's marriage in 1923 he began to paint nudes. They were more than just figure studies. Where his renderings of Giant Mountain (Foster chap., fig. 22) invoked slumbering human forms, his paintings of his wife recalled Adirondack landscapes. When the painter John Marin saw Weston's paintings of nudes, he thought the works conveyed woods and mountains in a very American, primitive way.[10] *Torso*, 1924 (fig. 70), with its close-up view and earthy palette, presents stomach, thighs, shoulder, and breast as a topographic map of hills, valleys, and river. The paint is applied in visible brush strokes, angled to form the contours of the body. The bird's-eye view of *Sleeping Nude*, 1925 (Foster chap., fig. 30), typifies the artist's approach to the subject. Weston shows his understanding of the modern compositional device of cropping the image to create an abstracted form. Until Marin pointed it out, Weston might not have been aware that his nudes looked so much like landscape paintings. Weston had a habit of retitling paintings, so he certainly approved of the correlation when he gave the paintings titles such as *Mountain Nude*, 1924 (Foster chap., fig. 31), and *Headland*, 1925, 1931 (fig. 71).[11]

In 1926 Weston and his wife moved to France. It seems typical of his taste for hardship and life in the wild that he should have chosen to spend most of his time in the Pyrenees rather than in Paris or the Riviera. In the French mountains the Westons roughed it, living in a primitive farmhouse, where Faith cooked over the open hearth.[12] Periodically they spent time in Paris, where he painted and had a gallery exhibition. There he also would have been exposed to modern French art.

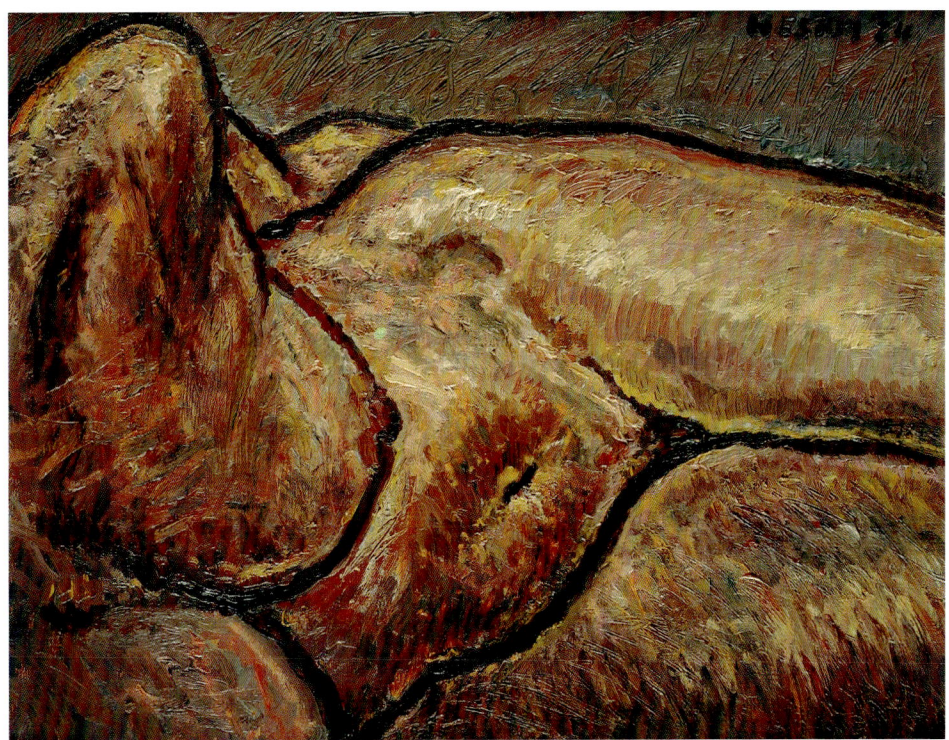

70. Harold Weston, *Torso*, 1924.
Collection of Burns H. and
Marta C. Weston.

71. Harold Weston, *Headland*,
1925, 1931. Private Collection.

During the 1930s, when Weston and his family were again in the Adirondacks, the artist continued to experiment with his style, combining aspects of French modernism with American realism. He described the impact of French art on his work after 1930: "My work became higher keyed in color, more staccato in rhythm and more complex in composition. There was more emphasis on the decorative and less on the emotional. Workmanship became more thorough."[13] As an artist, he was hitting his stride and entering the most important decade of his career, when critics and patrons would take notice of his work. Among them were Archibald MacLeish, Lewis Mumford, Paul Rosenfeld, and Duncan Phillips. Weston's work *Purple Hat*, 1932 (fig. 72), appeared in the first Whitney Biennial in 1932 and was noted by the *New Yorker*'s reviewer as one of the top twenty canvases in the exhibition.[14]

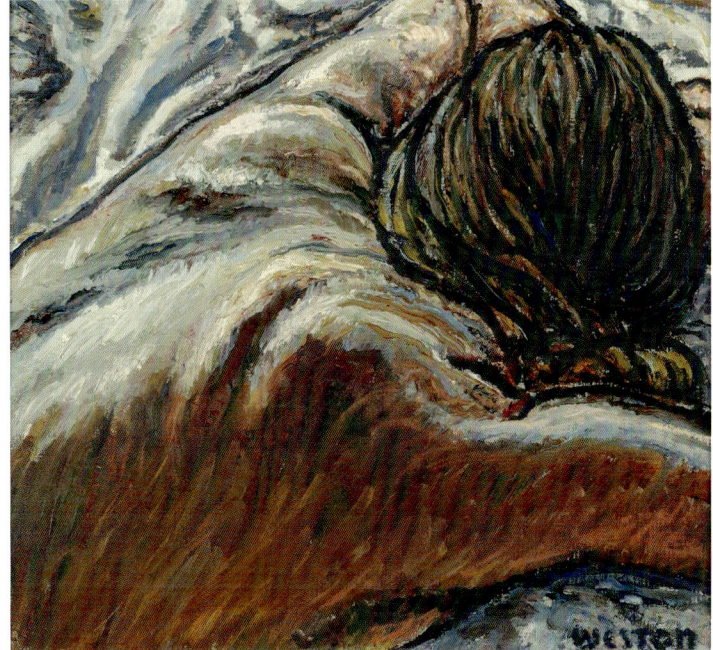

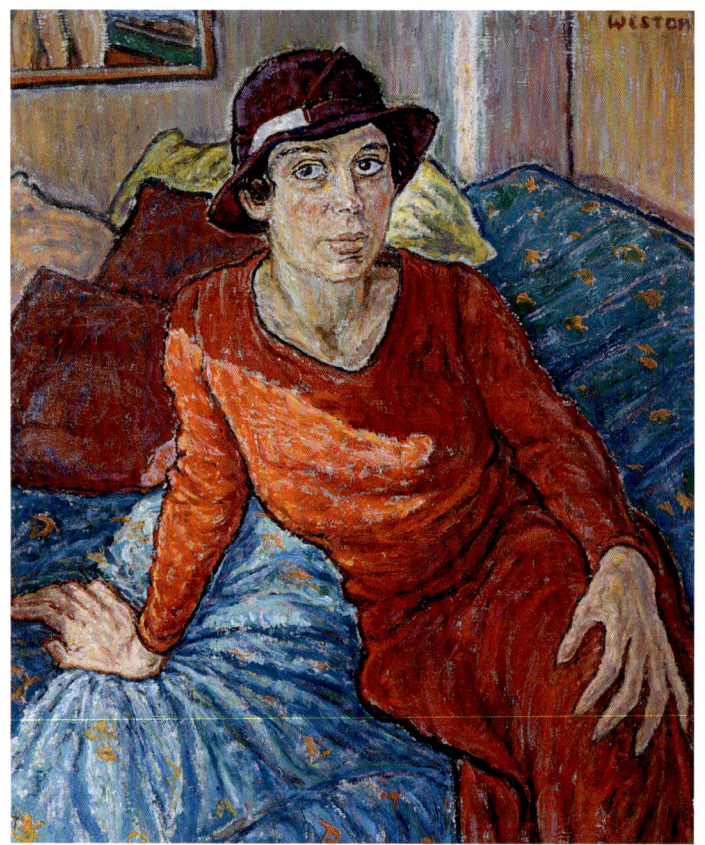

Phillips, the director of the Phillips Memorial Gallery, had founded his museum in 1921 as a museum of modern art and its sources. He was always on the lookout for young artists who showed an independent spirit and skill with a paintbrush. He first purchased Weston's work in 1928 and quickly became an active promoter of it in the 1930s, helping to place it in museum exhibitions and in public and private collections.[15] Phillips also supported Weston financially, giving him large amounts of money on several occasions to alleviate difficult circumstances.[16] He bought several paintings from Weston's 1930 exhibition at the Montross Galleries and went on buying his work, eventually acquiring twenty-five works for the museum and giving the artist five solo exhibitions. One of the paintings, *The Arena*, 1930 (fig. 73), nominally a close-up of a cat in the artist's studio patiently waiting for a mouse, has a narrative title suggesting an ancient Roman arena in which a lion awaits its next victim. The painting demonstrates Weston's increasingly realist approach. This impression

72. Harold Weston, *Purple Hat*, 1932. Robert Fisher.

73. Harold Weston, *The Arena*, 1930. The Phillips Collection, Washington, D.C.

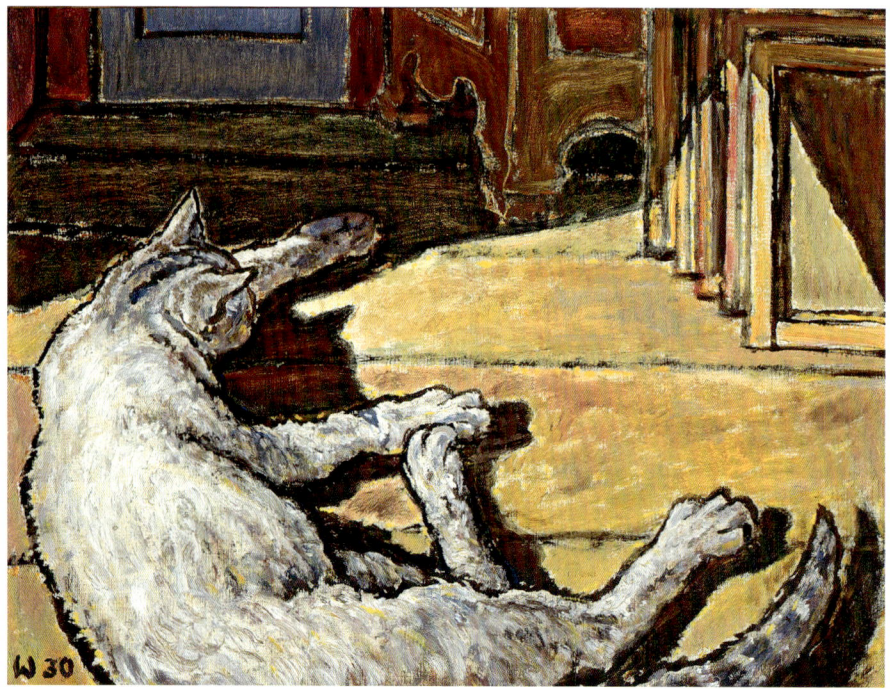

is borne out by his written remarks on the working methods he used in the 1930s: "The process sometimes followed in my oils is: draw the design roughly in charcoal, paint in some of the outline in light key (to be obliterated or strengthened later), remove all charcoal, then begin painting the most important areas, but keep the whole canvas moving. Don't finish one part before the rest is well established. Don't follow any fixed rules or set ideas; adjust color and form emphasis by what the mood and subject dictate as the whole canvas begins to take on a character of its own."[17]

Weston continued to paint passionate nudes in this period. Mumford's comment on the sexual charge of Weston's nudes of the 1920s also applied to the ones he created in the 1930s: "When he presents a woman, one does not think of her to rest presently and be paid off at the end of the day; she is a creature who swells responsively to one's admiration, and will not be dismissed into a state of aesthetic neutrality."[18] In *Seated Back Nude*, 1932 (fig. 74), the expressive brushwork and a slightly

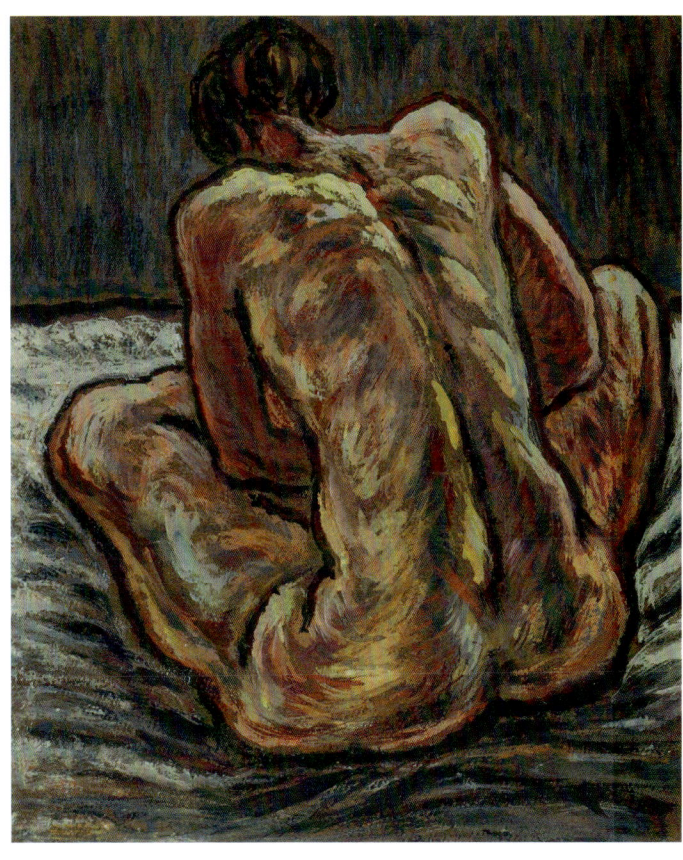

74. Harold Weston, *Seated Back Nude*, 1932. Harold Weston Foundation.

unfinished quality transmit a feeling of sexual urgency. Weston himself wrote, "My wife had a beautiful body, and I wanted to express in paint some of the deep emotions it aroused in me."[19] Indeed, the painting of the back and thighs suggests an artist hurrying to finish the work in order to enjoy the sitter in a less abstract fashion.

Squash Enthroned, 1932 (fig. 75), shows Weston tightening up his brush strokes and working in a more realist vein. The large squash in the center of the painting is clearly the subject matter, but, like Matisse, Weston plays with pattern and color in the Indian fabric in the background and in the loose weave of the leather chair seat. Instead of being a traditional still life, the painting is really a portrait of a squash, which must have been a treasured item during the depression. He approaches the object as he would a portrait of a friend or family member. By focusing on such an atypical subject, Weston was creating a unique painting that had a very earthy, American feeling. *My Snow Shoes*, 1934 (fig. 76), one of Weston's great paintings of the 1930s, is simultaneously a studio still life and self-portrait. Weston's snowshoes—the work's focal point—were a crucial part of his winter life in the Adirondacks. The autobiographical details include a favorite pipe and matches on the wedge of tabletop in the foreground. Near them a bottle of linseed oil or varnish speaks of his life as an artist. The bottle on the ledge above appears to be filled with liquor, necessary

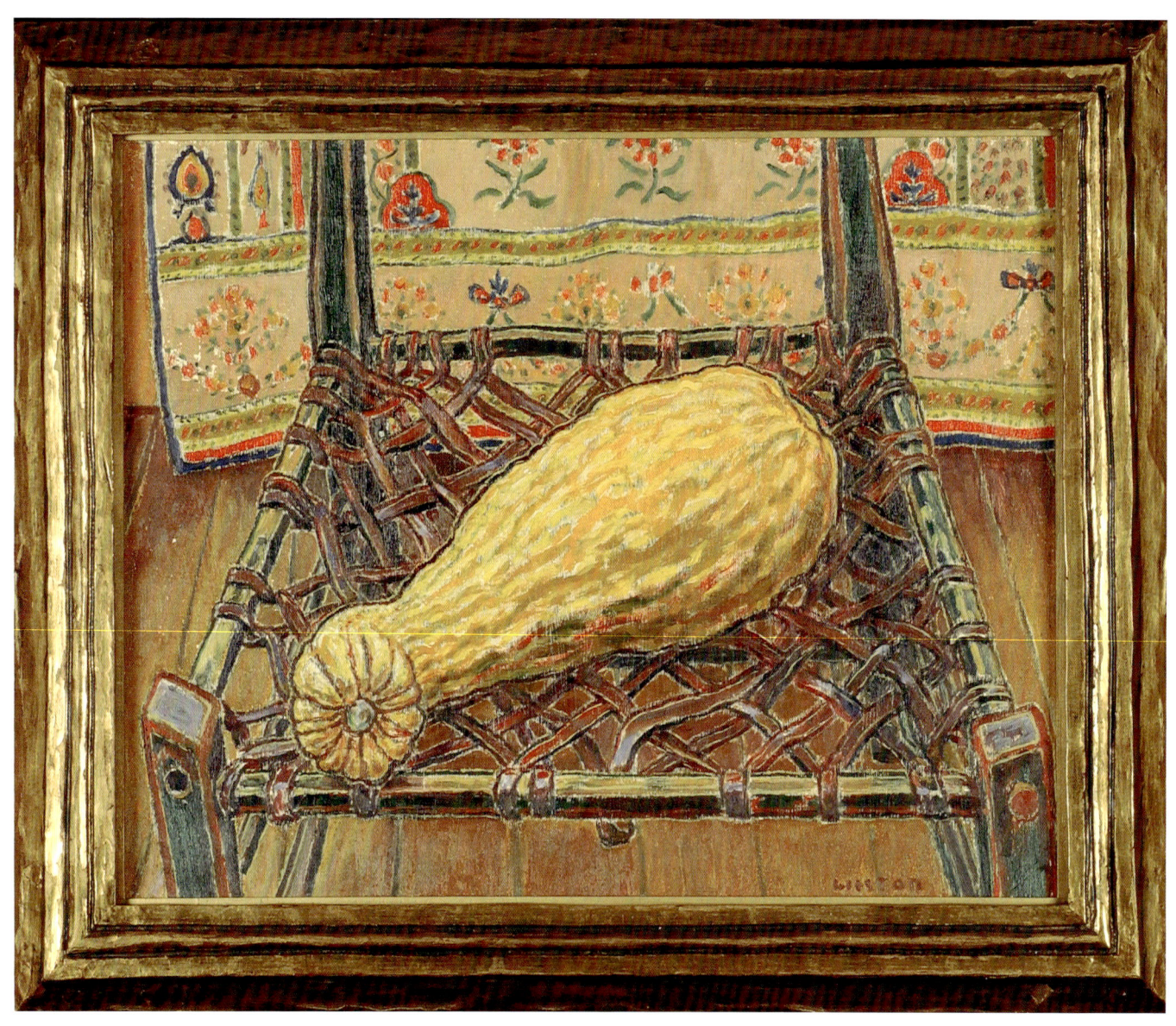

75. Harold Weston, *Squash Enthroned,* 1932. Private Collection.

medicine in the cold Adirondack winters. *My Snow Shoes* is tightly painted and more cool and calculated than the pictures of the 1920s. Aspects of the painting, in particular the architectural quality of the composition, show the artist's awareness of contemporary precisionism. Weston has drawn attention to the vertical and horizontal boards of the corner depicted, slotting together the planes so coolly that the curtain visible in the upper left could be carved of mahogany. Phillips purchased *My Snow Shoes* in 1939, writing to Weston, "I am delighted to add your 'Snow Shoes' to our collection of your paintings. It is certainly one of your finest canvases, strong, sensitive and original, a very personal expression of your point of view and your feeling about things."[20]

From 1936 to 1938 Weston worked on a mural ensemble for the lobby of the General Services Administration Building in Washington, D.C. This experience surely had an impact on his easel paintings, pushing him to increasingly realist expressions. His landscapes and still lifes in the late 1930s and early 1940s, such as *Pheasant*, 1940 (fig. 77), less painterly and more linear than those painted earlier, suggest illustrations. During World War II Weston gave up painting for humanitarian work. For many artists such a sacrifice would have been unthinkable. During this period Weston occasionally created small-scale works, but the overall cost of his self-imposed exile to his facility as an artist must have been tremendous. He did not paint again in earnest until the late 1940s, when he was able to combine his art making with his interest in world peace by enthusiastically painting a series of six paintings titled *Building the United Nations*.[21] During this time he also returned to painting the landscape of his favorite haunt, the Adirondacks. As *Chapel Pond—Autumn*, 1949 (fig. 78), shows, Weston was able to reclaim his skills and continued to evolve as a realist artist. Painted in tight strokes, the landscape in the foreground shows sumac and a rhythmic screen of birch trunks. The emphatic separation of

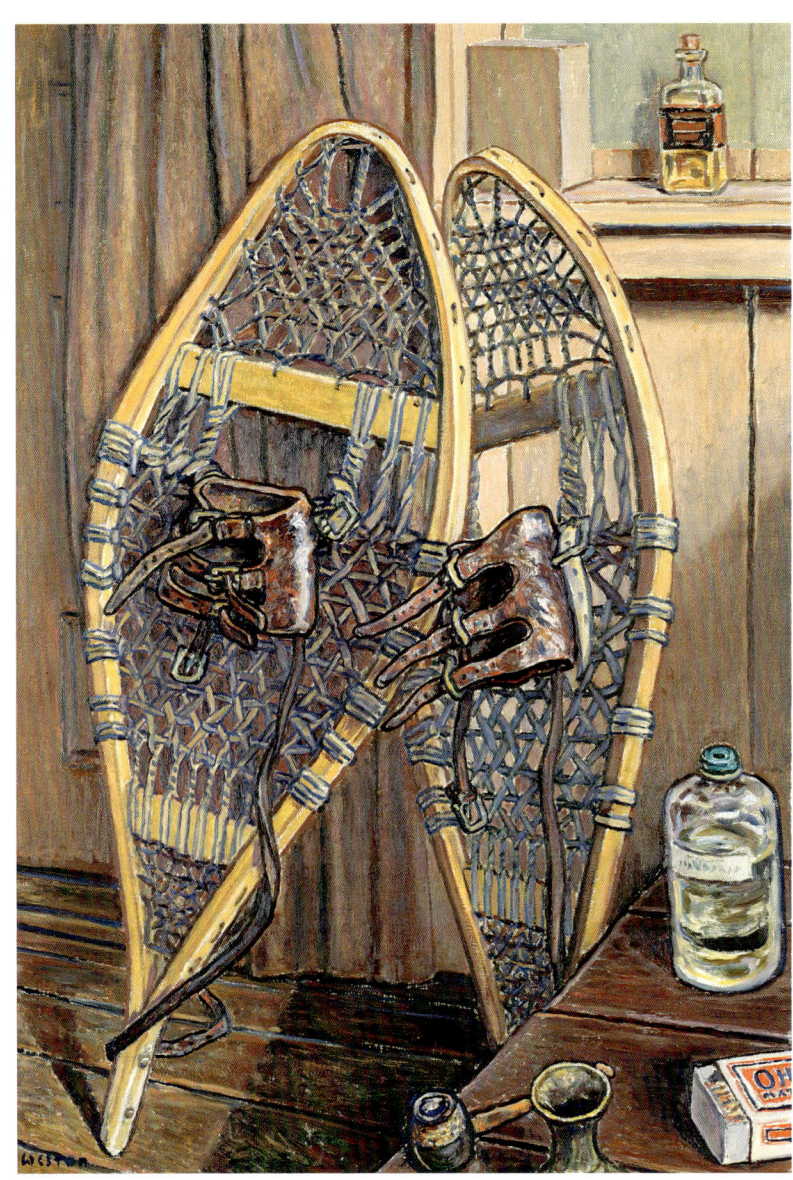

76. Harold Weston, *My Snow Shoes*, 1934. The Phillips Collection, Washington, D.C.

77. Harold Weston, *Pheasant,* 1940. Collection of Jonathan and Jennifer Ring.

BELOW LEFT
78. Harold Weston, *Chapel Pond—Autumn,* 1949. Private Collection.

BELOW RIGHT
79. Harold Weston, *Morning Wind,* 1964. Harold Weston Foundation.

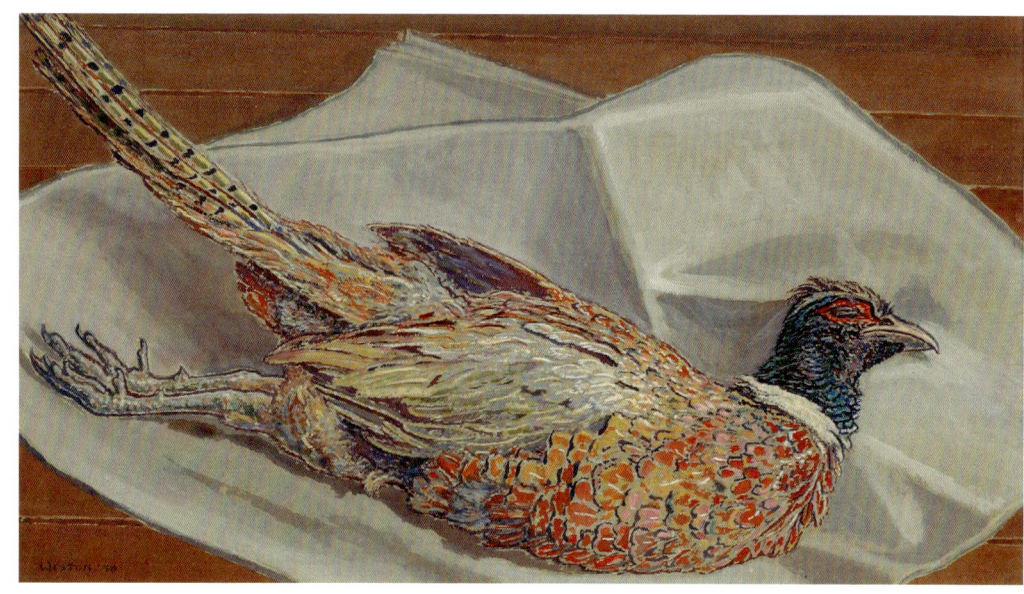

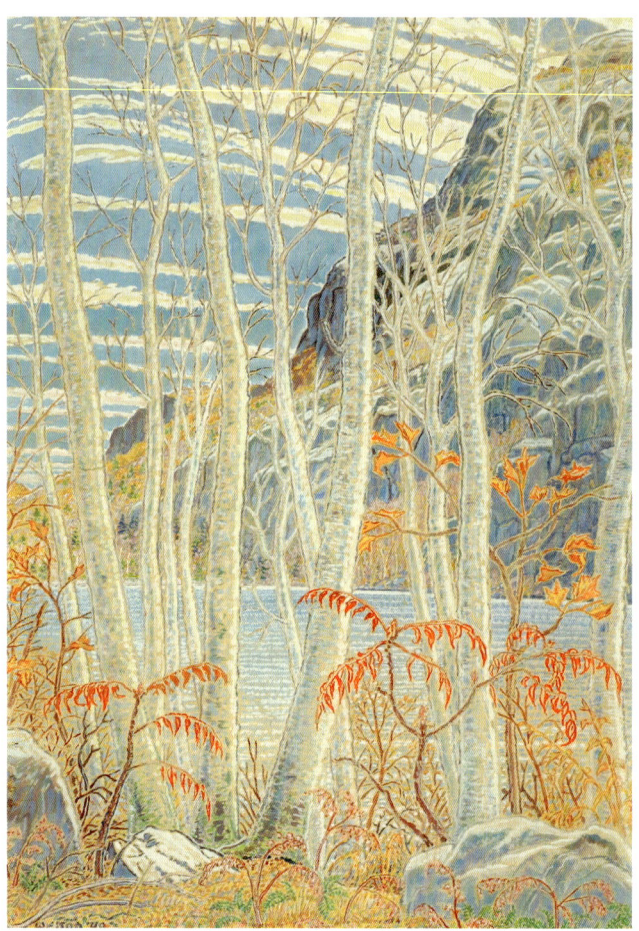

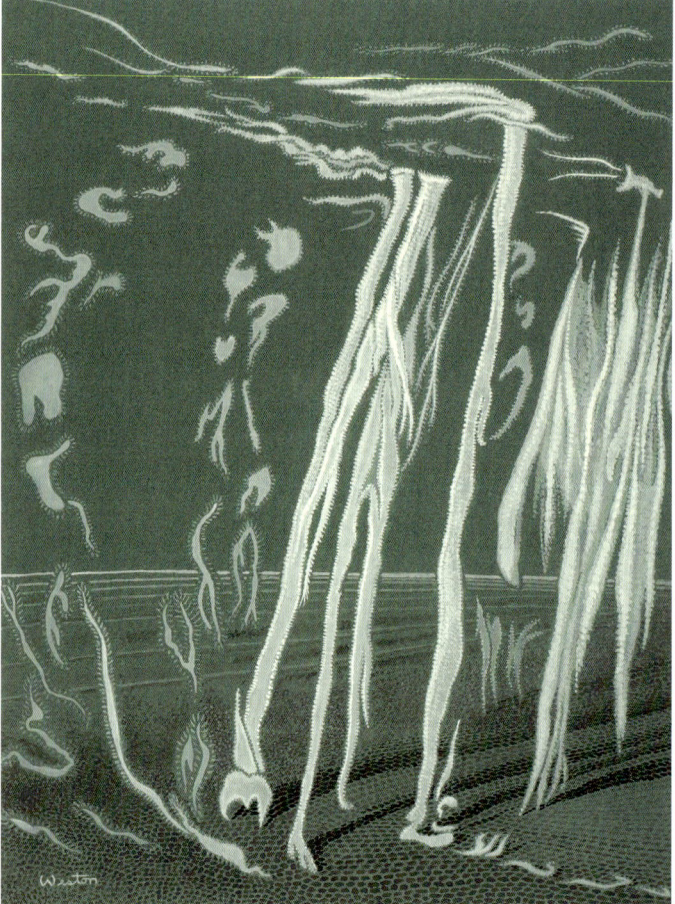

foreground and background is new to Weston's work, while the stylized sky, a pattern of arcs, is characteristic of his work from the early 1920s. The trees and sky produce an abstract pattern, an early sign of his nonobjective art of the 1960s.

In the 1950s and 1960s Weston created work that responded to contemporary nonobjective trends in art. *Silent Barriers*, 1961 (Foster chap., fig. 53), reads like a landscape, with large mountain forms creating a horizon line in the bottom half of the painting. The dark, flat forms create a solid mass in the foreground. Lyrical lines on the surface give it a nonobjective quality. *Morning Wind*, 1964 (fig. 79), and *Wind-Swept*, 1964 (fig. 80), show Weston's experimentation with biomorphic surrealism. By giving both paintings realist titles, the artist grounded the works in nature. With a horizon line and walking limbs, *Morning Wind* approaches an otherworldly landscape. Although *Wind-Swept* looks less like a landscape, it is based in the real world, probably inspired by a photograph the artist took forty years earlier of the silhouette of a dead pine against a winter sky.[22] The white curving forms in the background might be wind howling through the canvas, but the rendering of the dead pine trees as dark stick forms gives the painting a surreal quality, grounding it more in the imagination than in the real world.

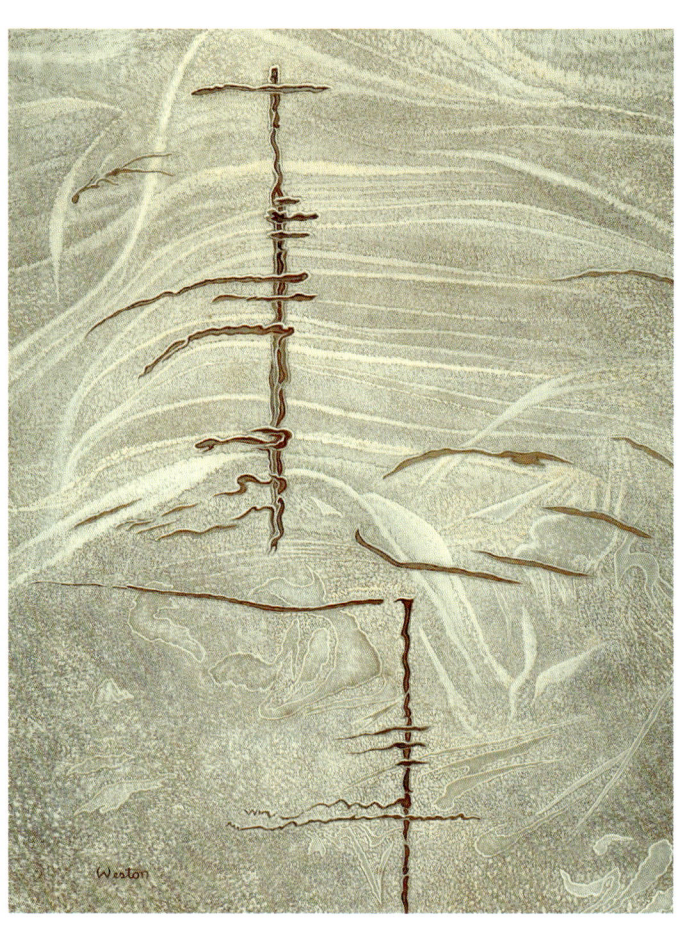

80. Harold Weston, *Wind-Swept*, 1964. C. Corscaden Galbraith.

At the end of his life Weston abandoned realism for an abstract style. Abstraction was in vogue at the time, but, as always when responding to current artistic trends, Weston made it personal, creating some of the most original works of his career. Inspired by stones from the Gaspé Peninsula, he made a series of seventy-six gouaches on colored paper, called the Stone Series.[23] These paintings combine the linear elements that he played with during the 1960s and the circular forms that are a constant in his work from the beginning. The results are enchantingly quirky, abstract paintings. *Conference (Stone Series No. 3)*, 1968 (Foster chap., fig. 59), has an amazing quality of light. With the light, lyrical lines on dark forms, the painting appears to glow from within in much the same way as the four decades older *Forest Winter No. 2*, 1922 (Foster chap., fig. 21). The stones are readily apparent in this work and are positioned on a representational ground of pebbles. The sky is noted by a band of stylized clouds across the background. Instead of giving the work a landscape title, Weston personified the inanimate objects in the title *Conference*, suggesting the stones are

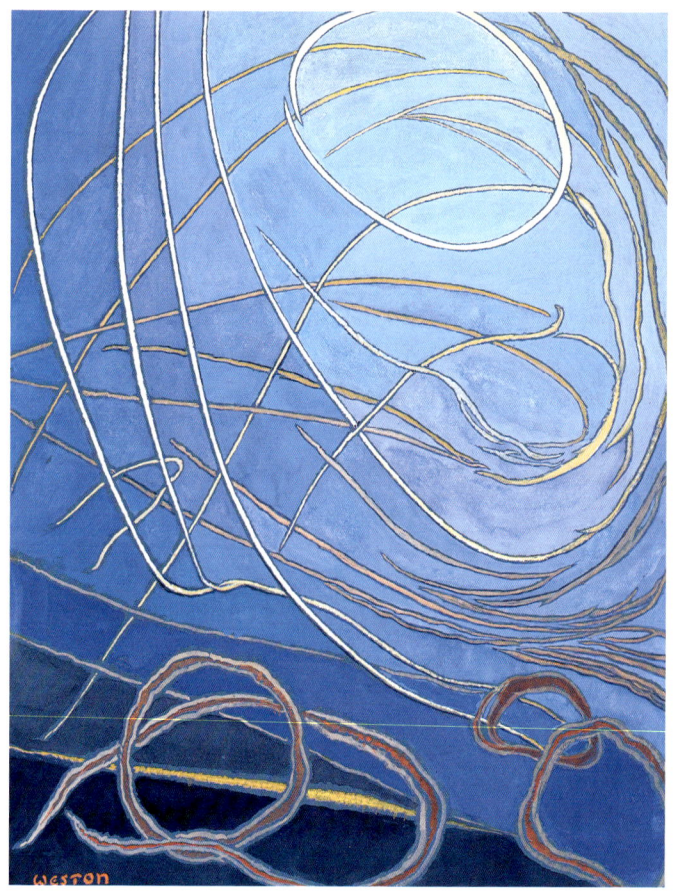

in conversation. In both title and form *Blue Beyond Blues (Stone Series No. 17)*, 1968 (fig. 81), pushes toward pure abstraction, using the same palette and linear forms as *Conference*. This work also appears to glow from within. With the same compositional devices, *Suspense (Stone Series No. 62)*, 1970 (fig. 82), carries abstraction further with the kinetic white lines, creating a circular pattern, while the 1970s palette of brown, harvest gold, turquoise, and avocado is less harmonious than the color combinations in *Blue Beyond Blues* and *Conference*.

Whether Weston was embracing American modernism, adopting realism, or making plans to feed the hungry, he was of his time. He was always responding to new directions in art and to current events in his own way. Over time his work shed the rugged characteristics that so many critics had insisted on, "the rugged force that the painter finds in the more solid things that make up his world,"[24] giving way to a lyrical abstraction at the end of the artist's life. Although Weston relinquished the rugged style, he maintained a rugged individuality, which, in the end, was perhaps more important.

81. Harold Weston, *Blue Beyond Blues (Stone Series No. 17)*, 1968. The Phillips Collection, Washington, D.C.

82. Harold Weston, *Suspense (Stone Series No. 62)*, 1970. Harold Weston Foundation.

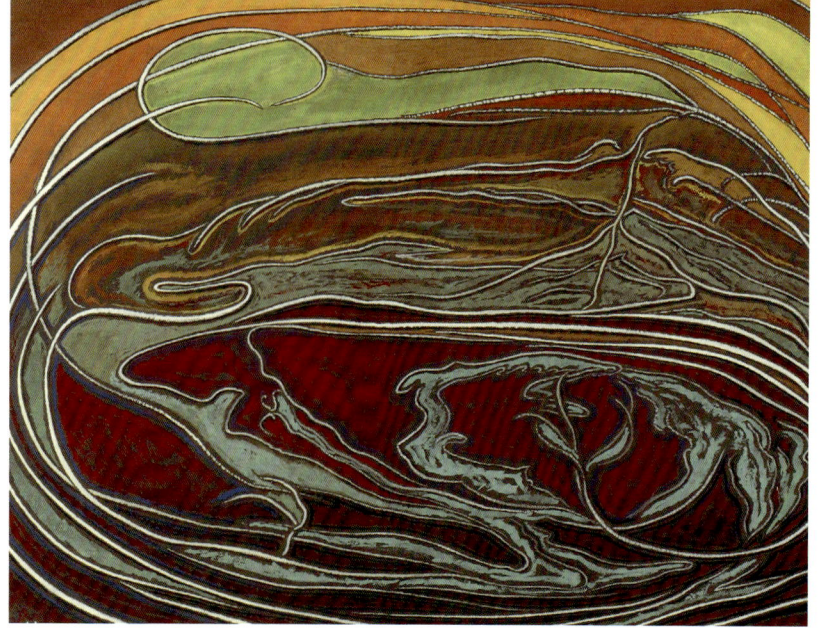

Notes

1. Weldon Bailey, "Weston's Oils Show Rugged, Bold Strength," *Philadelphia Record*, 19 Nov. 1933, sec. 4, 4: "boldly rugged"; C. H. Bonte, "In Gallery and Studio," *Philadelphia Inquirer*, 19 Nov. 1933, Society sec., 10: "rugged individualists in art" and "rugged and vigorous"; Emily Genauer, "Weston Paintings Rugged and Pure," *New York World-Telegram*, 23 Mar. 1935, 27; and the essay for the exhibition catalogue *Exhibition: Recent Work, 1935. Harold Weston*, text by Paul Rosenfeld (New York: Eighth Street Gallery, 1935), n.p.: "lean and rugged character of the shapes, and the fine roughness and Puritanic sobriety of much of the rich color, reveal their American roots."

2. Phillips, statement in support of application for a Guggenheim Fellowship, n.d., Harold Weston Papers, 1916–72, Archives of American Art, Smithsonian Institution, Washington, D.C. (hereafter AAA).

3. Schrafft Restaurant (1216 Chestnut St., Philadelphia) sponsored a radio interview conducted by Lucy Grey Black with Harold Weston on Monday, 4 Dec. 1933, AAA.

4. Harold Weston, "A Painter Speaks," *Magazine of Art* 32 (Jan. 1939), 19.

5. Weston to Phillips, 9 Dec. 1941, the Phillips Collection Papers, AAA.

6. Other solo exhibitions took place in 1927, 1928, 1930, 1931, and 1932.

7. Walter Pach, an important writer, critic, and champion of modern art, traveled to Paris in 1914 to secure works by Matisse for an exhibition at the Montross Gallery that was to run from 20 January to 27 February 1915. Walter Pach Papers, AAA.

8. Weston, "A Painter Speaks," 19.

9. One reviewer wrote, "A very individual note is struck in the work of Harold F. Weston, who is showing paintings of the Adirondack Mountains and of Persia. . . . It is not alone a division of subjects in Mr. Weston's exhibition, but there is a division of interest and method in his approach" (Margaret Breuning, "Galleries Show Many Phases of Modern Art," *New York Evening Post*, 18 Nov. 1922, 11). In "Art and Artists," *New York Globe and Commercial Advertiser*, 13 Nov. 1922, H. C. Nelson wrote, "The Montross Galleries are introducing to us a new talent, that of Harold F. Weston, who fills two rooms with 150 sketches and paintings, largely of marked individuality. To the sketches one may apply the adjective individual without the least hesitation."

10. Weston, "A Painter Speaks," 19.

11. This information was pointed out to me by Rebecca Foster.

12. Weston, "A Painter Speaks," 19.

13. Ibid., 20.

14. Lewis Mumford, "The Art Galleries: Assorted Americana," *New Yorker*, 17 Dec. 1932, 62.

15. As Phillips wrote in 1932, "Being one of your most enthusiastic patrons, I have counted it not only a pleasure but a privilege to be able to add to our group of your canvases." Phillips to Weston, 13 Dec. 1932, the Phillips Collection Papers, AAA. Weston appreciated Duncan and Marjorie Phillips' support. Twenty years later he wrote, "through these many years, your belief in me as a painter and as a person have [*sic*] been a source of constant stimulus and strength-giving inspiration at all-too-frequent times of discouragement." Weston to Phillips, 14 Oct. 1952, the Phillips Collection Papers, AAA.

16. Phillips gave Weston one thousand dollars each time to help with trips to Europe, where Weston rented a studio to paint, and to help after an accident in Paris. Phillips to Weston, 24 Apr. and 29 July 1954, the Phillips Collection Papers, AAA. Phillips sent one thousand dollars to Weston in support of his United Nations series and reported that he was giving *Hand Holding Bowl of Fruit* (also known as *Fruit Bowl*) to the Corcoran Gallery of Art. Phillips to Weston, 1 May 1956, the Phillips Collection Papers, AAA.

17. Weston, "A Painter Speaks," 20.

18. Mumford, "The Art Galleries," 62.

19. Quoted in Anne Mackinnon, "A Passionate Nature: The Consummate Art of Harold Weston," *Adirondack Life* 25, no. 1 (Jan.–Feb. 1994), 33.

20. Phillips to Weston, 29 Mar. 1939, AAA.

21. Jean C. Harris, "Harold Weston: The Man and His Art," in *A Retrospective Exhibition of Paintings by Harold Weston (1894–1972)*, exhibition catalogue, (South Hadley, Mass.: John and Norah Warbeke Gallery, Mount Holyoke College, 1975), 8.

22. Insight provided by the artist's daughter, Nina Weston Foster.

23. Mackinnon, "A Passionate Nature," 66.

24. "Solid, Rugged Things Make Up Weston's World," *Art Digest*, 15 Mar. 1935, 23.

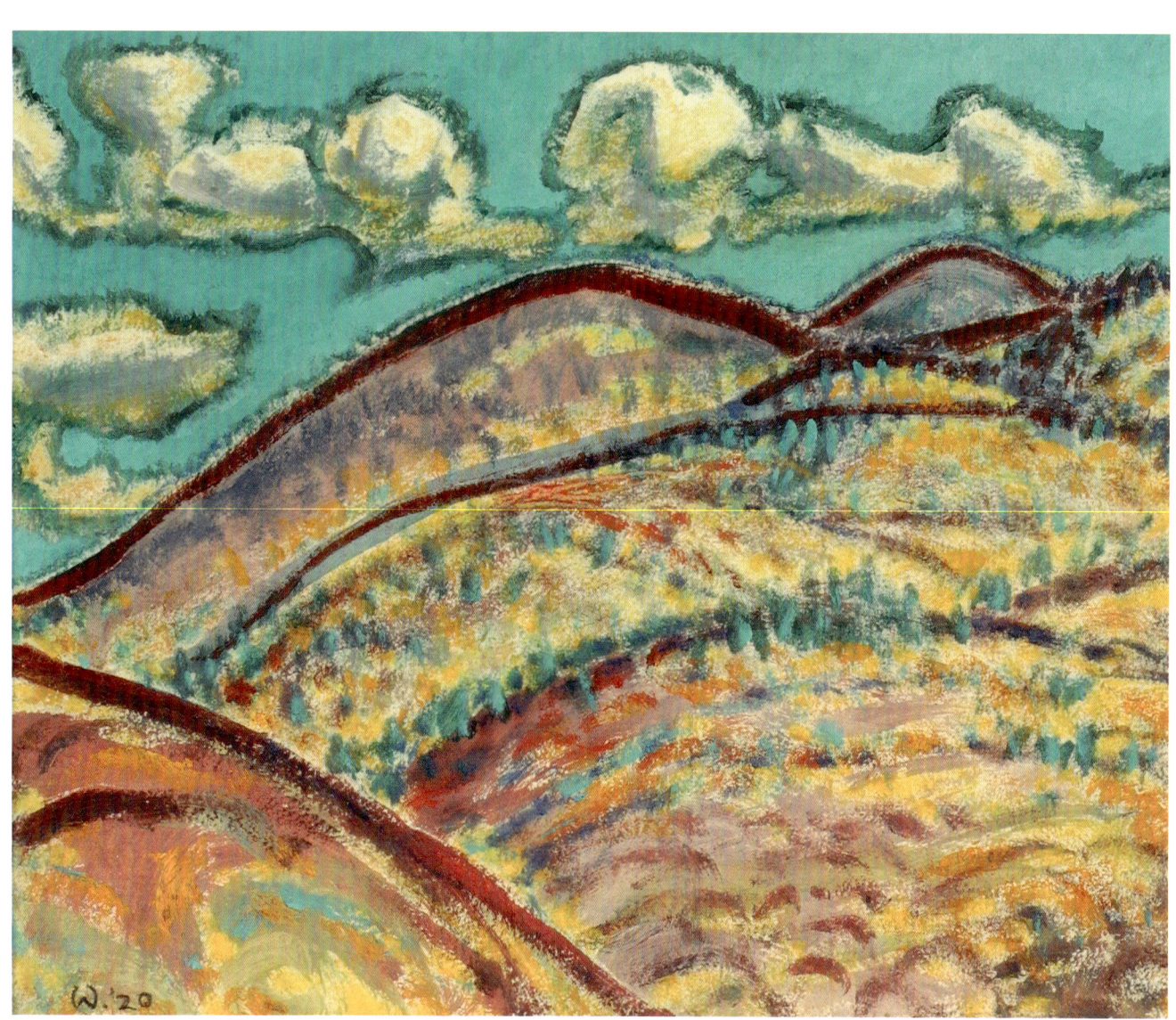

THE RICH REWARDS OF WILDERNESS
Adirondack Art, 1900–1970

Caroline M. Welsh

One of the rich rewards of living in the wilderness . . . has been the opportunity provided to experience rare moments of nature and to absorb its basic rhythms into my blood.

—Harold Weston, *Freedom in the Wilds* (1971)

FACING PAGE

83. Harold Weston, *Afternoon's Glory*, 1920. St. Huberts Trust.

NOWHERE ARE MOUNTAINS AND VALLEYS, forests and lakes so dramatically juxtaposed as they are in the Adirondacks. Artists of national and regional renown have painted Adirondack wilderness scenery and tramped its trails and mountains to capture nature's vistas and rare moments (fig. 83). In so doing they have helped define a national landscape vision and in the process have provoked awareness of the landscape's vulnerability and the need to preserve the natural world. The art of the Adirondacks is part of the American landscape canon, illuminating the centrality of nature to the American experience.

The vast, sparsely settled Adirondack Mountain region of upstate New York is composed of close to three thousand lakes and ponds, some of the highest peaks in the Northeast, and the largest wilderness east of the Mississippi River. The Adirondack Park encompasses 6 million acres of public, state-owned land guaranteed by the state constitution to "be forever kept as wild forest lands" and of private lands ranging from huge tracts held by timber companies or private preserves to land owned by homeowners, towns, and villages. This unusual landscape of public and private lands has made the park a living laboratory for wilderness preservation in a world where wild places must coexist with human communities. Art has played a key role in promoting and preserving the Adirondacks. The paintings in the collection of the Adirondack Museum, the largest single repository of images of the region, are an index to the art inspired by the area. This essay focuses on the artistic activities of some of the artists working in the Adirondacks during the time that Harold Weston painted there.

A Wild Sort of Beauty

The first images of the Adirondacks were made by explorers and mapmakers led by Samuel de Champlain in 1609. Naturalists and scientists followed, detailing the region's flora and

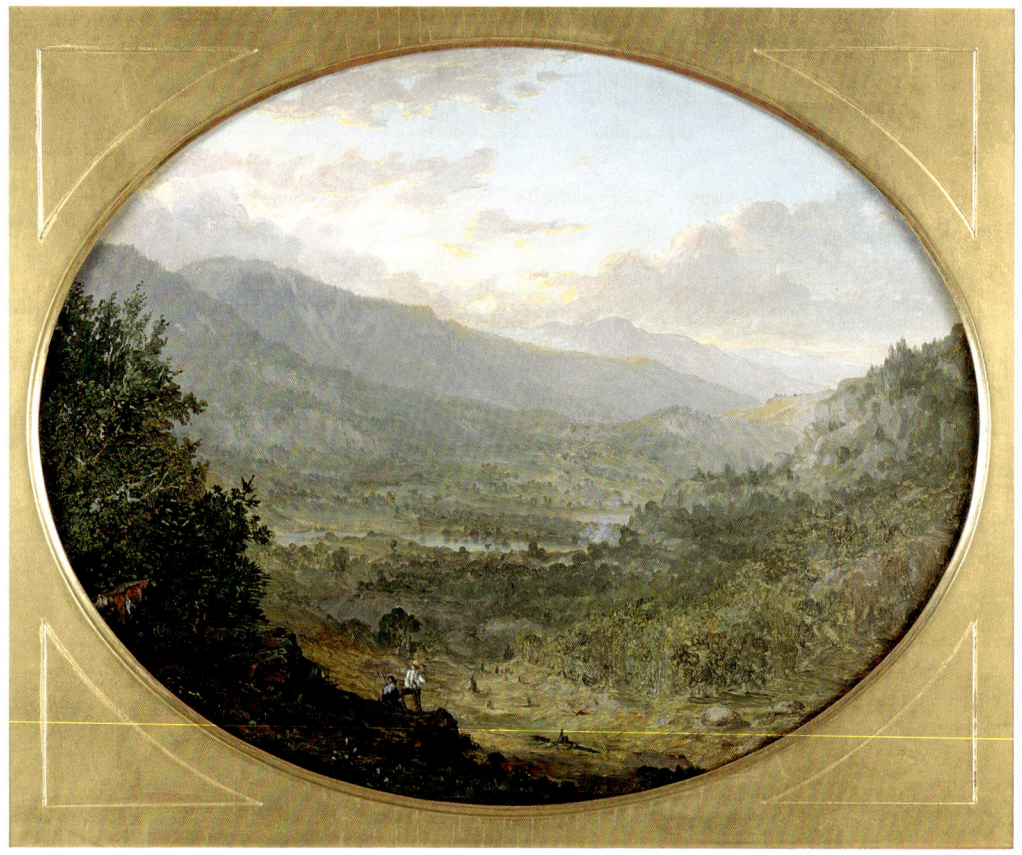

fauna. It was not until the early nineteenth century, however, that artists influenced by European romanticism found a source of spiritual values and affirmation of nationhood in New York's northern mountains (fig. 84). "The scenery is not grand but has a wild sort of beauty," wrote Thomas Cole in 1837.[1] Led by Cole and Asher B. Durand, who painted the Hudson River and its scenery from New York City to its headwaters in the Adirondacks, artists came to the area and were captivated by the lake and mountain vistas. Many paintings were reproduced as prints for the popular press and chromolithographs for middle-class parlors, thus broadening the exposure of the region's picturesque qualities.

For centuries few people other than artists regarded mountains as anything other than serious geologic and geographic obstacles to travel and communication. In the fourteenth century the Italian poet and humanist Petrarch climbed a mountain and wrote that he enjoyed the view from the top. Four hundred years passed, however, before the scenic wonders of mountains began to lure European travelers in search of the "picturesque."[2] The Swiss built a tourist industry on the charms of Alpine lakes and mountains. Soon people flocked to see the natural wonders touted by artists and poets. In the America of the late 1860s, the Adirondack Mountains became such a destination.

Artists' depictions of the Adirondack wilderness mirrored the often contradictory images of wilderness that prevailed in nineteenth-century popular imagination and literature. Travelers saw the wilderness as desolate and forbidding. Artists saw the romantic sublime in the exquisite compositions of mountains, woods, and waters. Upper-class urban sportsmen saw a genteel hunting and fishing preserve (fig. 85). Homesteaders saw a landscape in which it was difficult to eke out a living and raise families. Businessmen saw a seemingly infinite supply of trees and minerals to harvest. Artists' pictures of an exploited Adirondacks provided powerful aesthetic arguments for conserving the wilderness, however. As early as 1835 Thomas Cole decried destruction of the landscape: "We feed ten-thousand fires! In one short day / The woodland growth of centuries is consumed."[3] Cole's imagery, both written and visual, framed the terms of the national debate over the use of land and natural resources that has preoccupied Americans ever since.[4] On the one hand, the land and its bounty was property, commodity, and resource given by a providential God to sustain humanity; on the other, it was a vale to be kept sacrosanct as the dwelling place of God.

Cole's concern was echoed later by other wilderness advocates such as George Perkins Marsh, Verplanck Colvin, John Muir, and the artist Julian Rix, whose 1885 images of a Hudson River feeder stream before and after logging dramatized the threats to the land-

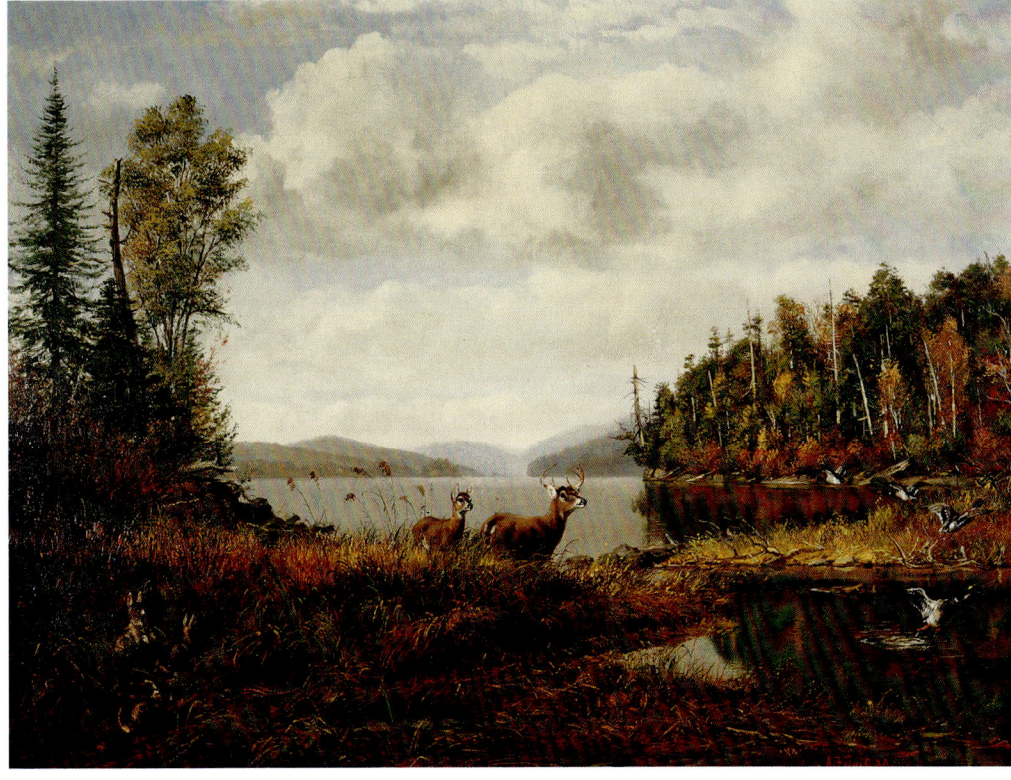

85. A. F. Tait, *Good Hunting Ground*, 1881. The Adirondack Museum, Blue Mountain Lake, N.Y., 1974.293.

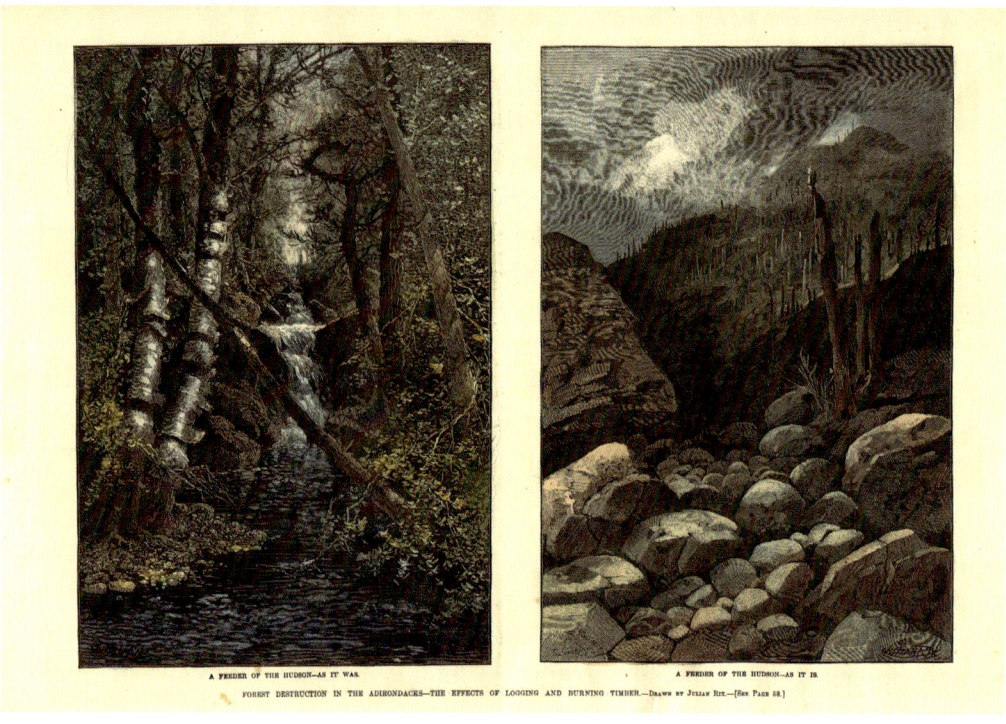

A FEEDER OF THE HUDSON—AS IT WAS.   A FEEDER OF THE HUDSON—AS IT IS.

FOREST DESTRUCTION IN THE ADIRONDACKS—THE EFFECTS OF LOGGING AND BURNING TIMBER.—Drawn by Julian Rix.—[See Page 52.]

scape (fig. 86). New York businessmen joined the complaint when diminished Adirondack and Catskill watersheds impinged on downstate water supplies and canal interests. Seneca Ray Stoddard, landscape photographer, painter, and guidebook writer, made an eloquent presentation to the New York State Assembly in February 1892. His lantern slides of dammed rivers and drowned lands graphically illustrated the damage done to the landscape by uncontrolled logging. He made a passionate plea to save the landscape and to create the Adirondack Park. All of these efforts combined to establish the Forest Preserve (1885) and the Adirondack Park (1892) as public places of wilderness.[5]

Twentieth-century landscapes of the Adirondacks continue their nineteenth-century counterparts' preoccupation with nature. Realism is the dominant aesthetic. The grandeur of High Peak vistas, the purity of light, and iconic sites such as Whiteface Mountain sustain changing aesthetics over time. Paintings are imaginative renderings of individual artists' experiences of nature often conditioned by prevailing pictorial conventions. Modernist styles include impressionism and expressionism, but abstract and nonobjective art is rare (fig. 87).

Keene Valley

Weston's Adirondacks were rich with artistic tradition. Although artists painted in Lake George, Lake Placid, Saranac Lake, Elizabethtown, Pleasant Valley, Canada Lake, and many other places in the Adirondacks, no one place attracted a sustained artistic and intellectual colony on the scale of Keene Valley. Established in 1797, Keene Flats was one of the earliest settlements in the Adirondacks. The first hotel opened in 1823. Artists discovered the valley around 1850 during summer sketching trips to the Hudson River Valley, the Catskills, and Lake George. After the Civil War they came for longer stays and built studios. By the 1880s the area was such a magnet for painters and their students that the popular magazines of the day called Keene Valley an "Artist's Mecca" and a "Haunt for Landscape Painters." Orson Phelps, a local guide and entrepreneur, claimed "Keene Flats . . . was discovered by the artist. With pencil he made pictures and sent them back to the cities, to be noticed in the drawing rooms and public halls. Visitors began to arrive. Each one brought three next year. . . . [The artists] are quiet people, who see more beauty in a summer cloud hanging for a moment on the mountain summit than others" (fig. 88).[6]

The abundance of landscape vistas in and around Keene Valley was irresistible; artists captured mountain ranges, forest interiors, the Ausable River roaring through a gorge or meandering tranquilly through the valley, and the Upper and Lower Ausable Lakes lying between lofty peaks. Landscape painters celebrated the valley's beauty in all its moods and seasons and, in the process, helped to stimulate a boom in tourism and wilderness appreciation. "I shall never forget my first glimpse of Keene Valley," wrote artist Roswell Morse Shurtleff in 1868. "As we reached the top of Spruce Hill and began the descent, the valley hardly yet touched by the morning sun, the mountains beyond flecking with cloud shadows, the luxuriant foliage of early summer seen through the morning mists made it seem

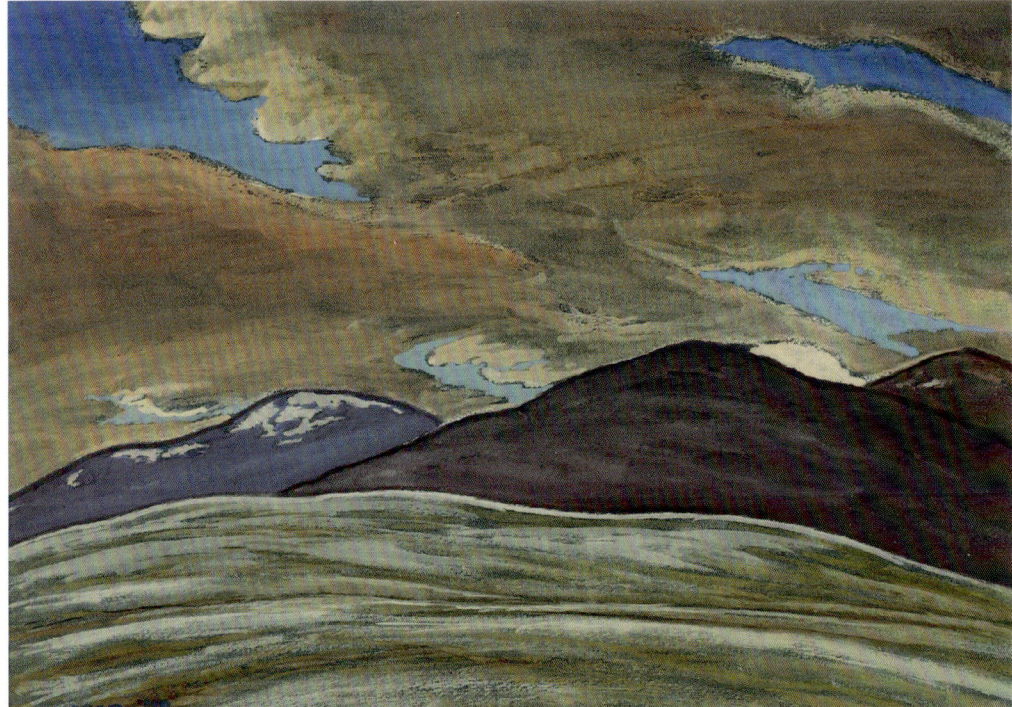

87. Harold Weston, *Adirondacks in Winter*, 1940. Private Collection.

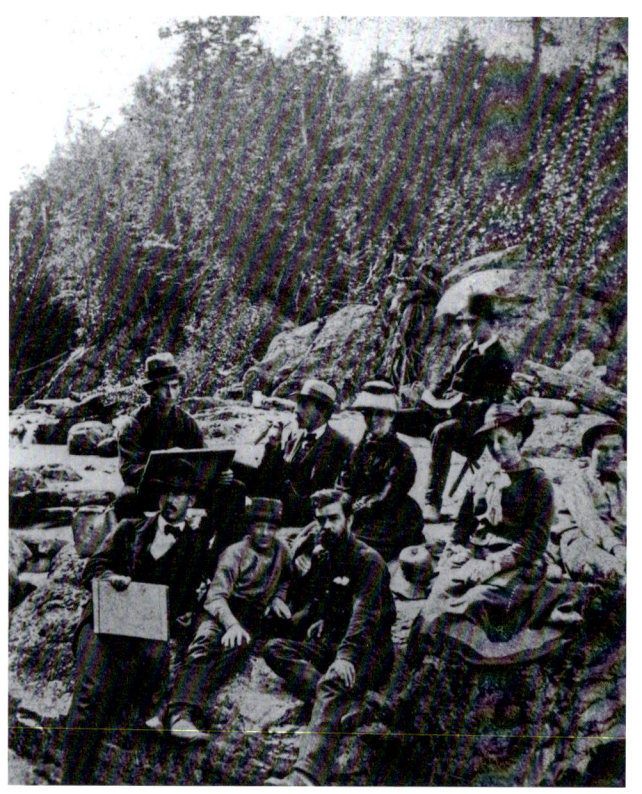

like the fairy land it was."[7] The artists shared a reverence for nature communicated by their works of art and demonstrated by their devotion to mountain climbing, hiking, fishing, hunting, and camping. More than seventy prominent artists either summered in or visited Keene Valley between 1870 and 1910 (fig. 89).[8]

Nineteenth-century artists interpreted the landscape as a dynamic panorama of changing effects of light and shadow, reflections and movements affected by weather, time of day, and season. As artists moved from their studios out of doors to paint, nature's many moods and brilliant palette were revealed, either veiled by shadows or accentuated by light. Weston continued this tradition in his wilderness studies. Whether depicting rolling mountain vistas or the cat by the fire, his art is personal, intense, and exuberant. His love of nature and of the act of painting is palpable in the Adirondack oils of the 1920s.

88. J. F. Murphy, *Artists at the Ausable River*, 1874. The Adirondack Museum, Blue Mountain Lake, N.Y., P047500.

89. Roswell Morse Shurtleff, *Day Before the Storm*, ca. 1889. The Adirondack Museum, Blue Mountain Lake, N.Y., 1998.51.

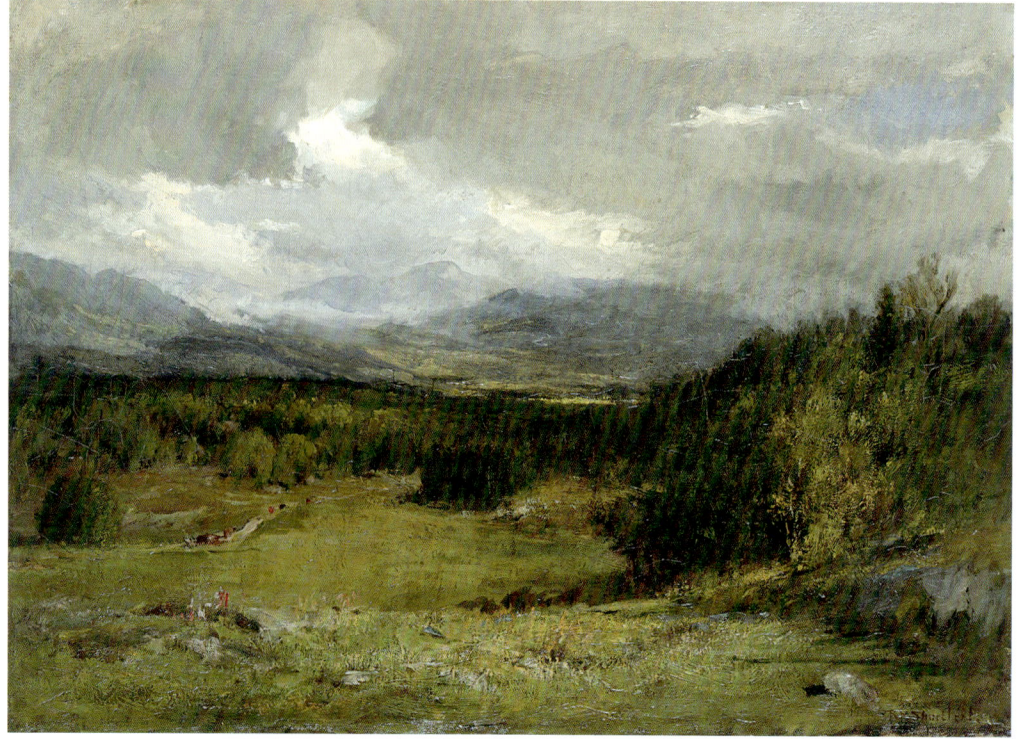

Harold Weston's Wilderness Muse

Few artists were as deeply rooted in the Adirondack wilderness as Harold Weston (1894–1972). Weston came to his family's summer home in the Adirondacks from earliest childhood. There he was imbued with a passionate love of nature. He climbed mountains, walked the woods, rowed the lakes, and committed his life to painting (fig. 90). At sixteen Weston was preoccupied by the study of nature and his need to express what he saw and felt. He wrote in 1910, "If one could but seize the reality of the beauty of nature and preserve it longer—that is the object of painting."[9] In 1932 Duncan Phillips, art collector and Weston's patron and friend, affirmed the artist's methodology: "he keeps before his mind's eye as he paints an ideal of expression which not only starts from nature as its source but returns to nature as its goal."[10] Throughout the artist's long and multifaceted life, the Adirondack wilderness remained one of his most important subjects and creative catalysts.

The artist's maternal grandfather, Charles Hartshorne, along with two other men purchased the forest land comprising the High Peaks in the east central Adirondacks around St. Huberts in Keene Valley to form the Adirondack Mountain Reserve in 1887. The purpose of the Adirondack Mountain Reserve, to preserve "the forever wild character of this forest land…in a manner appropriate to the enjoyment of [its] wilderness beauty,"[11] remains to this day. Such large landholdings have played a central role in preserving the region's open space. Weston continued the family commitment through his work with the Adirondack Mountain Reserve and the Adirondack Trail Improvement Society, organizations charged with maintaining the preserve. In addition to guiding policy and promoting innovative ideas, he inspired generations of children to protect the landscape through his

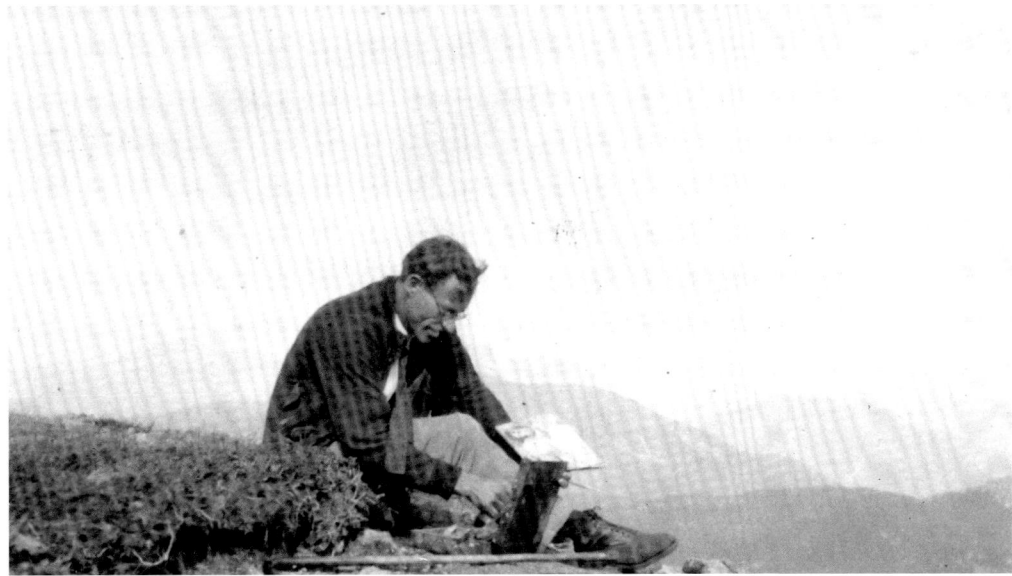

90. Harold Weston sketching on Mount Marcy, 1922. Photograph by Esther Weston King. Harold Weston Foundation.

leadership in the Adirondack Trail Improvement Society's youth program.[12] "The children of the early summer residents of Keene Valley and St. Huberts," observed Weston, "got to know intimately the lay of the land, the feel of the mountains, the spots of rare beauty, and they became aware of the rich range of forest growth in an area kept forever wild."[13]

Academics, philosophers, philanthropists, theologians, and physicians also summered in the valley in the late nineteenth and early twentieth centuries. This high-powered mix of artists and intellectuals, many of whom were influenced by the transcendentalists, shaped the valley's social and creative life. The Weston family energetically entered into and became central to this life in the 1880s. Harold Weston spent considerable time as a child in the company of people whose observations on the philosophical aspects of natural beauty made a lasting impression on him.[14]

Weston began to paint full-time in 1920. He shunned formal training, preferring to retreat alone to the mountains and woods of the Adirondacks in the belief that "the techniques of how to paint would work out"[15] in the presence of nature (fig. 91). "I did a lot of wandering in the woods, up streams and mountain climbing, always with my sketchbox. A great many small oil paintings on cardboard were done on the spot. A semi-pantheism permeated my reactions: the tree, cloud, mountain life and the eternal seen through the incandescence of the moment."[16]

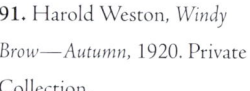

91. Harold Weston, *Windy Brow—Autumn*, 1920. Private Collection.

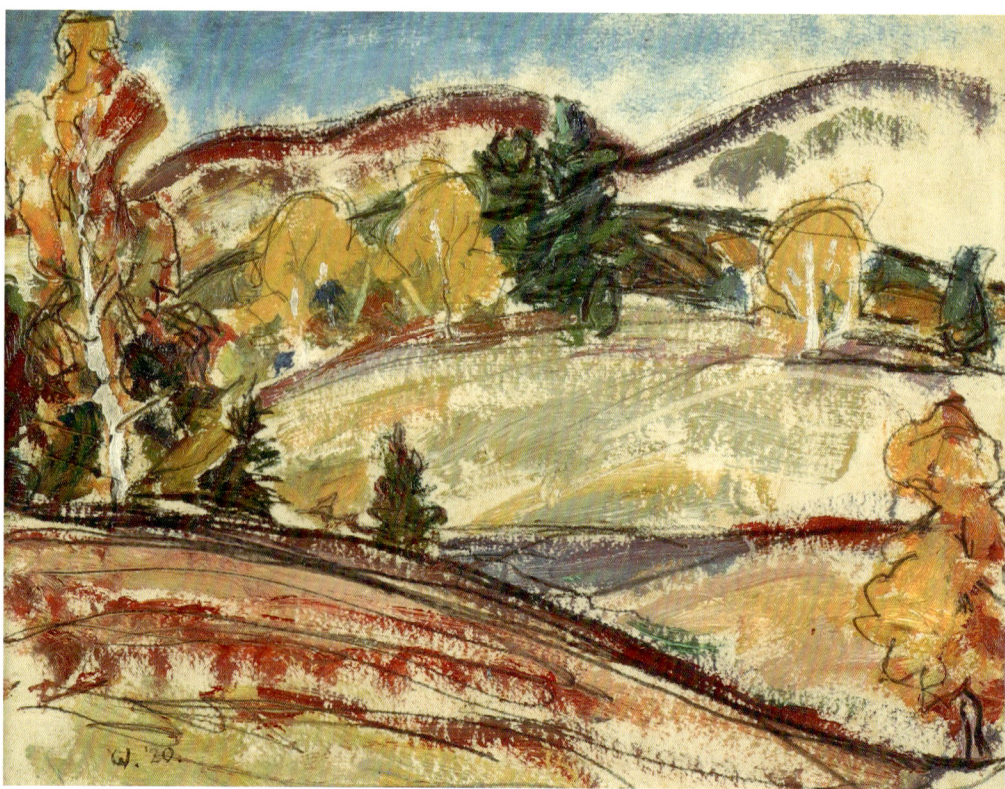

Thousands of artists have made the Adirondacks their subject. Few artists, however, have painted abstract images of Adirondack scenery, nor did the region attract modernist painters in numbers equal to the Hudson River School landscapists. It seems that the landscape itself compels its delineators to capture it in recognizable interpretations. Weston stands apart from other twentieth-century transcribers of the region because his art was distinctly and ultimately his own, singularly uninfluenced by trends or schools. His Adirondack art evolved over fifty years as an intellectual and personal quest: from the immediate expressionism of the 1920s, stimulated by the direct and deeply felt experience of nature, to the expressive realism in the 1930s and 1940s and then to the mystical abstractions in the Stone Series of the 1960s. No other artist who worked in the region shows a similar exploration of style while remaining true to his or her subject.

Turn-of-the-Century Adirondack Impressionism

The Adirondacks at the beginning of the twentieth century was no longer the forbidding wilderness it was perceived to be as late as the 1850s. By the 1890s the region was a fashionable destination for pleasure seekers; hotels, resorts, clubs, and private preserves dotted the forests and mountainsides. Between 1890 and World War I, railroads and automobiles began to supplant horse-drawn wagons and steamboats in the region, expanding business, tourism, and development opportunities. Logging and mining operations multiplied; affordable passenger travel by railroad brought new visitors. Telegraph and telephone wires followed railroad rights of way, enhancing communication to and within the region. The magnificent scenery continued to attract professional artists to visit, some returning year after year. Their ranks expanded to include photographers and amateurs.

In the early 1900s Keene Valley's landscape was changed by extensive logging, drought, and forest fires.[17] A 1903 typhoid epidemic resulted from the drought that provoked the fires. Tourism declined, and most of the professional artists relocated to Newport in Rhode Island, the coast of Maine, and the Catskills. Avocational artists, however, continued the art tradition in the valley. Among them were Lillian Haines Crittenden (1858–1919) and Nancy Bowditch (1890–1979), who documented much-loved Adirondack vacation retreats. Crittenden had studied with the noted American impressionist and landscape painter William Merritt Chase. She first came to the Adirondacks in 1908 and spent much of every summer there until 1917. Staying at the Ausable Club in St. Huberts, she found unending subject matter in the valley's dramatic vistas. *Partley* [sic] *Cloudy* (fig. 92), a pastel she created around 1910, is a radiant, sapphire-hued celebration of mountain scenery. Bowditch's father, George DeForest Brush, was one of the most distinguished academic figure painters in nineteenth-century America. She and her family summered at Putnam

92. Lillian Haines Crittenden, *Partley* [sic] *Cloudy*, ca. 1910. The Adirondack Museum, Blue Mountain Lake, N.Y., 1983.68.

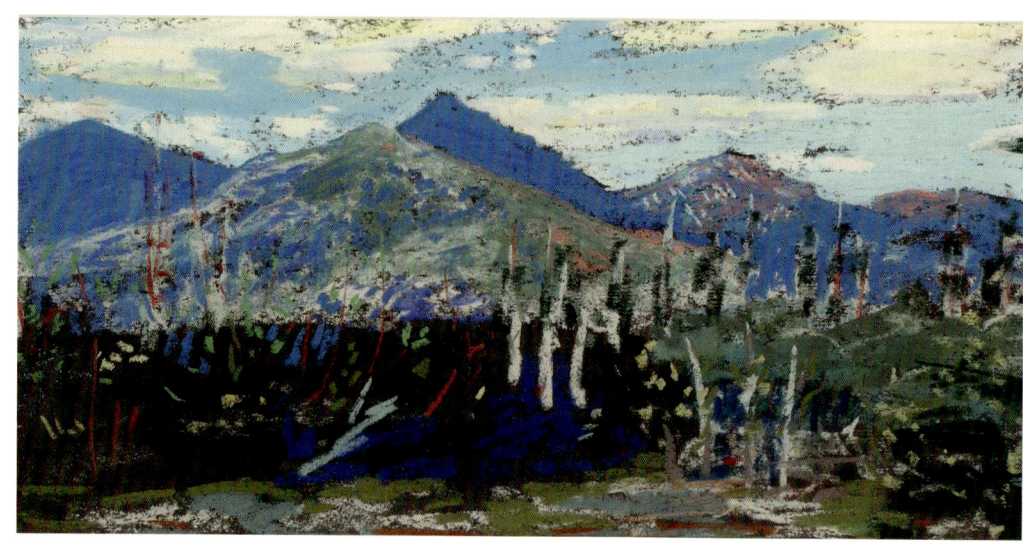

93. Nancy Douglas Bowditch, *Morning Mist Rising from the Woods, Keene Valley, Adirondacks, N.Y.*, 1941. The Adirondack Museum, Blue Mountain Lake, N.Y., 1967.114.2.

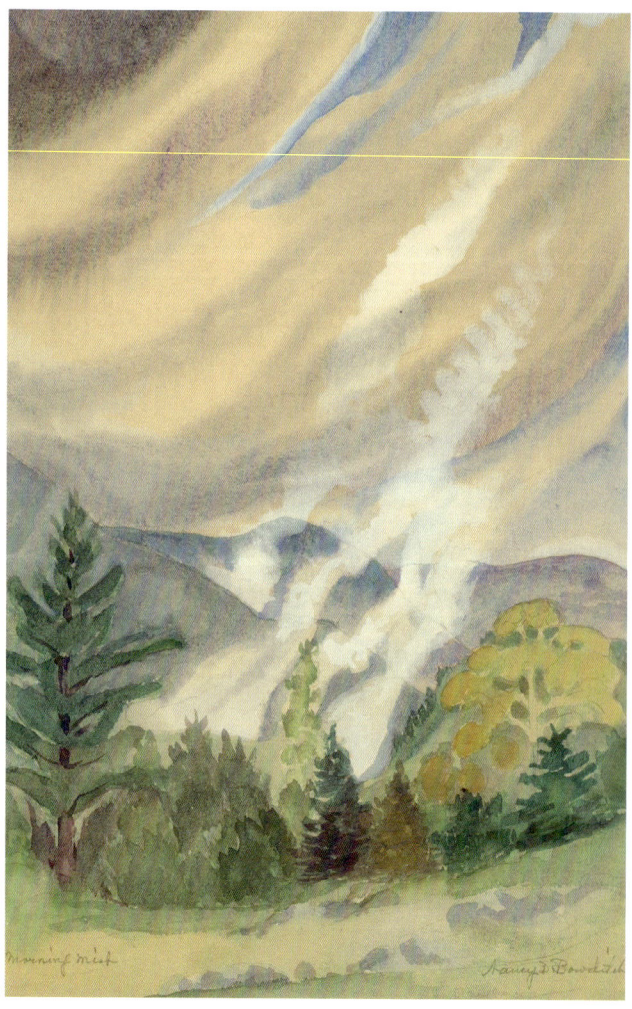

Camp, a retreat on the banks of the Ausable River near St. Huberts that attracted their intellectual and physician friends. Harold Weston observed in his memoir *Freedom in the Wilds* that the Putnams, Bowditches, and their relatives always came in September. Bowditch preserved Adirondack light, atmosphere, and color with graceful brushwork, usually in watercolor. She captured a moment in nature impressionistically in *Morning Mist Rising from the Woods, Keene Valley, Adirondacks, N.Y.*, 1941 (fig. 93). Like Weston, she used pencil beneath the paint to outline the mountains.

James Rosenberg (1874–1970) fell in love with the Adirondacks in the 1880s, when he spent his childhood summers near Keene Valley. In 1923, after becoming a successful lawyer in New York City, he built a summer home close to his favorite trout stream on Hurricane Mountain Road, not far from Elizabethtown. Rosenberg painted seriously most of his life and full-time after retiring in 1947; the Adirondack landscape was his chief subject. Charles C. Cunningham, director of Hartford's Wadsworth Atheneum, wrote in 1947: "In the Adirondacks, where he [Rosenberg] spends much time, he is constantly alert to the ever-changing landscape, the swirl and drive of great rain clouds, the changing light upon the hills, the intricate pattern of great trees, the

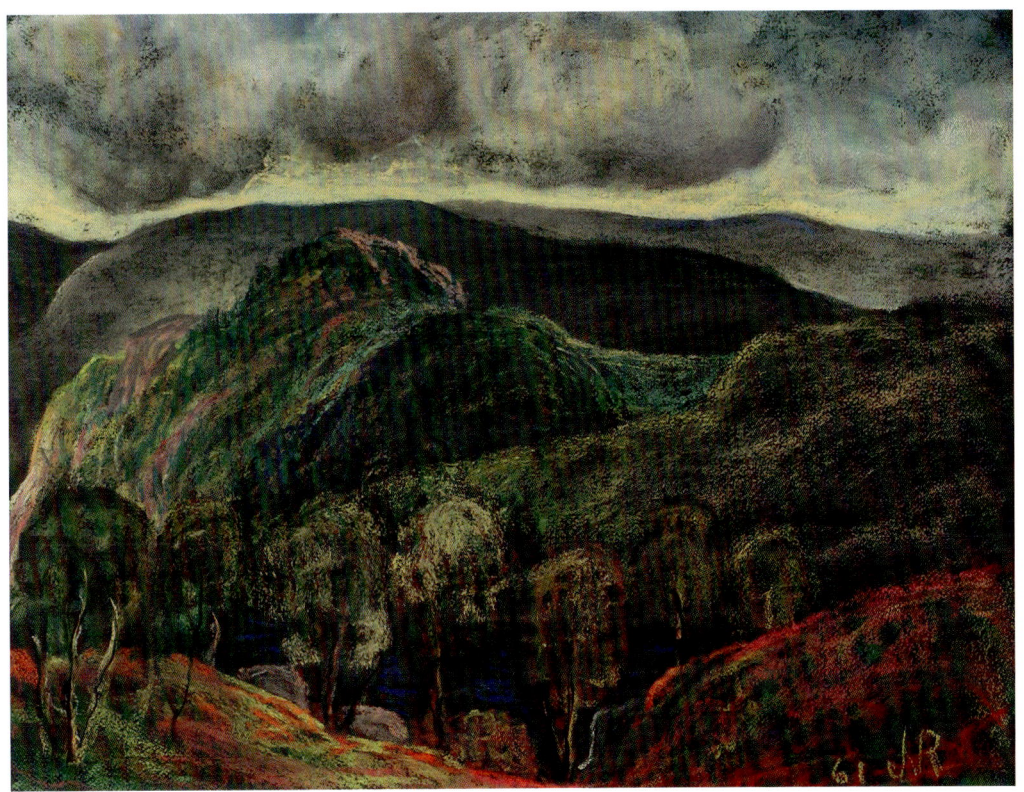

shimmer of a trout brook. . . . Rich broken colors are placed on the canvas with a palette knife or heavily loaded brush, giving form and luminosity to his work. These paintings . . . reveal man's joy in elemental forces" (fig. 94).[18]

A native of Bremen, Germany, Gustave Adolf Wiegand (1869–1957) immigrated to the United States in 1883. He studied at the Brooklyn Art School with the American impressionist William Merritt Chase and later returned to the Dresden Royal Academy in Germany to complete his academic training with Eugen Bracht. Wiegand was introduced to the region by Roswell Morse Shurtleff. Around the turn of the century Wiegand discovered Blue Mountain Lake, where he spent twenty summers and the winters of 1912 and 1913. While there, Wiegand, his wife, and daughter stayed at the Blue Mountain House, now the site of the Adirondack Museum. Wiegand maintained a studio at the hotel and offered painting lessons to other guests. His Adirondack scenes document the environs of Blue Mountain Lake and the Blue Mountain House hotel; many were sold to patrons eager to preserve memories of their holiday visit. The atmospheric light and harmonious tonalities of Wiegand's many on-the-spot scenes of Blue Mountain Lake and Blue Mountain capture impressionistic moments in nature at different times of day and in different seasons. His plein air sketches have immediacy and spontaneity resulting from his painterly brushwork and emphasis on light and color (fig. 95).

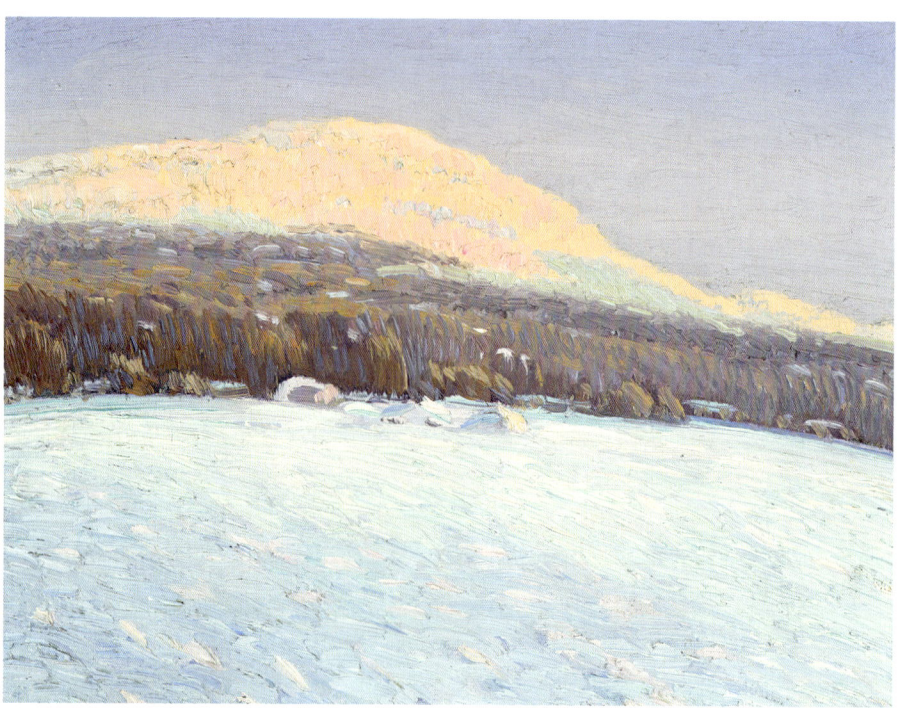

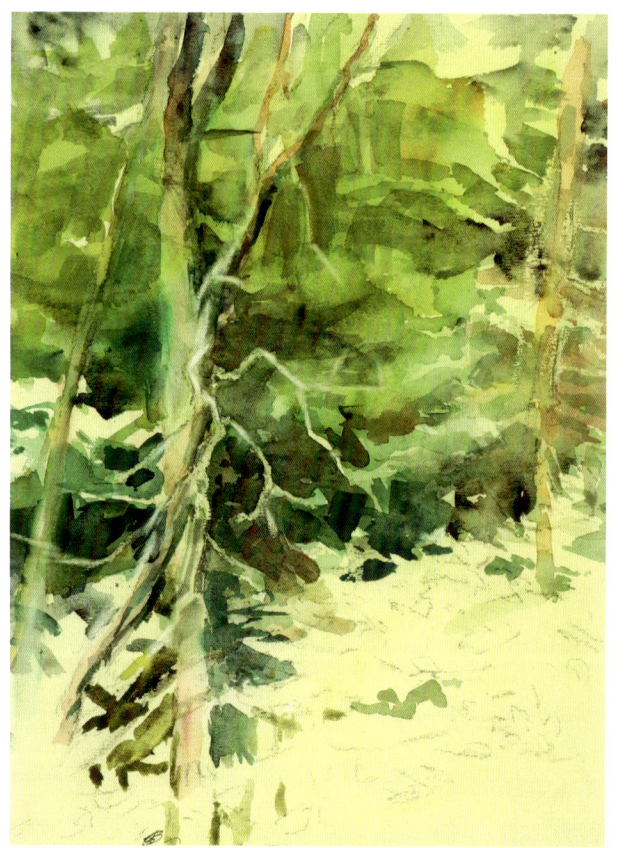

Several well-known American illustrators and writers congregated on Canada Lake in the southern Adirondacks. Paul Bransom (1885–1979) was a world-famous wildlife artist. Over his sixty-year career he illustrated magazines and nearly fifty books, including Jack London's *The Call of the Wild* and Kenneth Graham's *The Wind in the Willows*. Bransom's illustrations were singularly evocative of real-life situations. The key to his success, he said, was his love of nature and animal subjects. Bransom first came to the Adirondacks in 1908, when he and his wife rented a cottage on Canada Lake for the summer. In 1917 he built his own camp on the lake near other artists and writers, including Charles Nicholas Sarka (1879–1960). At this retreat Bransom produced much of his best professional work as well as lyrical and impressionistic Adirondack landscapes in watercolor (fig. 96).

Sarka's bold, quick strokes in watercolor or pen and ink captured nuances of people and impressions of places with vivid insight. This made him one of the most popular illustrators of the early twentieth century. He was born in Chicago, where he studied with his father, a frame maker, and at the Art Institute

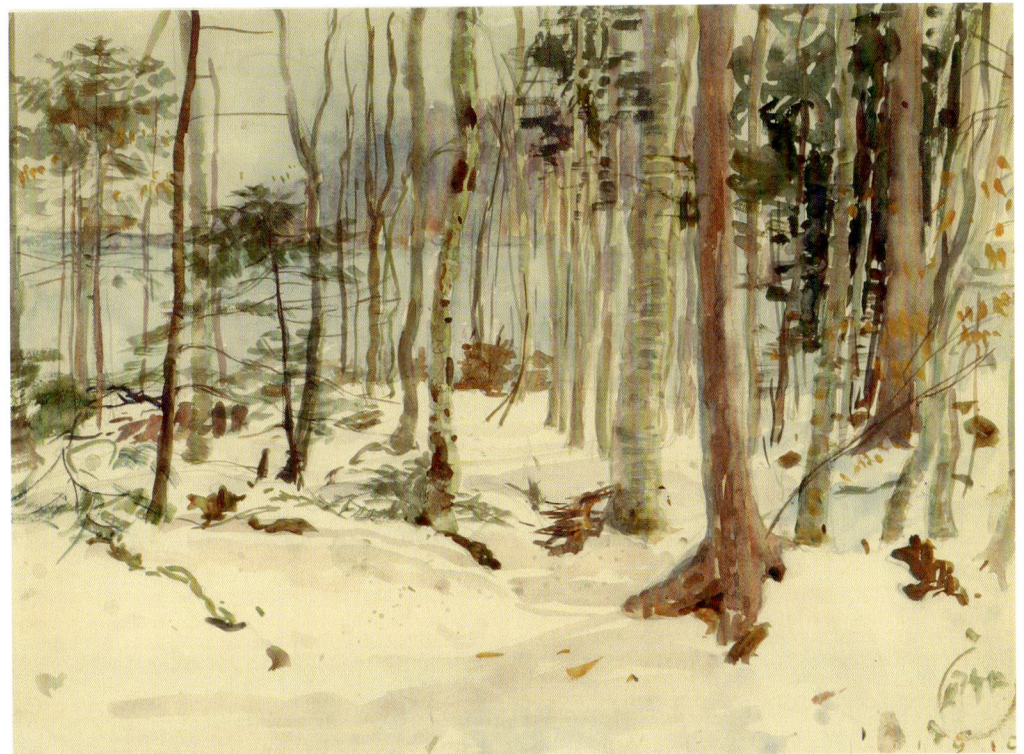

97. Charles Nicholas Sarka, *Untitled: Winter Landscape*, 1910. The Adirondack Museum, Blue Mountain Lake, N.Y., 1963.76.4.

of Chicago. At twenty he went to New York, where he soon became an illustrator much in demand for the *New York Herald, Harper's, Collier's,* and other prominent newspapers and magazines. Between 1900 and 1910 he traveled widely, financing his trips by selling his lively depictions of people in their native habitats. In 1910 Sarka married a fellow artist's daughter and bought a large property on Canada Lake. He spent the next fifty summers there, inspired by the lake's endlessly changing light and its effects on foliage and animals, and by the water and mountains. People were central to Sarka's paintings of foreign lands; nature was central to his views of the Adirondacks (fig. 97).

Modernism in the Adirondacks

Between 1910 and 1930 American painting was influenced by a rapid succession of modern innovations that affected painting techniques, articulation of forms, and subject matter. Some artists rejected academic art and turned to the activities of modern life for subject matter. American democracy and ingenuity were mirrored in the new urban landscape of steel, skyscrapers, and electric lights. Other artists experimented with new responses to nature. Some American painters studied European modernism in Paris and returned home to find their own expression and artistic direction. Their concern with nature derived from traditional American aesthetics and New England transcendentalist beliefs, according to which the natural world was the manifestation of divine or spiritual force. When early modern painters such as John Marin (1870–1953) and Georgia O'Keeffe (1887–1986) came to the Adirondacks, they focused not on nature's panoramic vistas, but on its form and texture, color and light, pattern and movement (fig. 98). They used paints and brush strokes in new ways to picture the dynamics they saw in nature in terms of pure form, energy, and color while retaining a vestige of objective reality. "Art," wrote Marin, "is produced by the wedding of man and nature. When man loves material and will not under any circumstances destroy its own inherent beauty then and only then can that wonderful thing we call art be created."[19] Weston's Adirondack paintings of the 1920s are a fusion of new expressive techniques and traditional landscape formats suffused with his own intense and personal response to wilderness (fig. 99).

Alfred Stieglitz (1864–1946), photographer, dealer, critic, and theorist, was important in fostering the modern spirit. In his gallery at 291 Fifth Avenue, New York, known as Gallery 291 or the Little Galleries of the Photo-Secession, he showed the works of European pioneers and championed American experimentalists. In the Intimate Gallery on Park Avenue, which was in operation from 1925 to 1929, he focused on Americans— including Marin and O'Keeffe, whom he had introduced to the Adirondacks—and promoted a "unique, homegrown school" of national art.[20] He nurtured and supported painters and photographers, encouraging them to be original, fresh, and honest rather than rhetorical, stale, and unfeeling, as he felt most contemporary art was. The gallery thus became a center for artistic and intellectual stimulation. Weston's art possessed purity and freshness, hallmarks that Stieglitz believed American modernism needed to have to be authentically American.

Stieglitz had a long connection to the Adirondacks through his family summer home at Lake George.[21] There he entertained American modernists and photographed the buildings on his farm; his family, servants, and friends; and the landscape and objects of everyday life. In the late 1910s he began experimenting with subject matter, theorizing that photographs did not have to be about something. For fifteen years, beginning in 1922, he

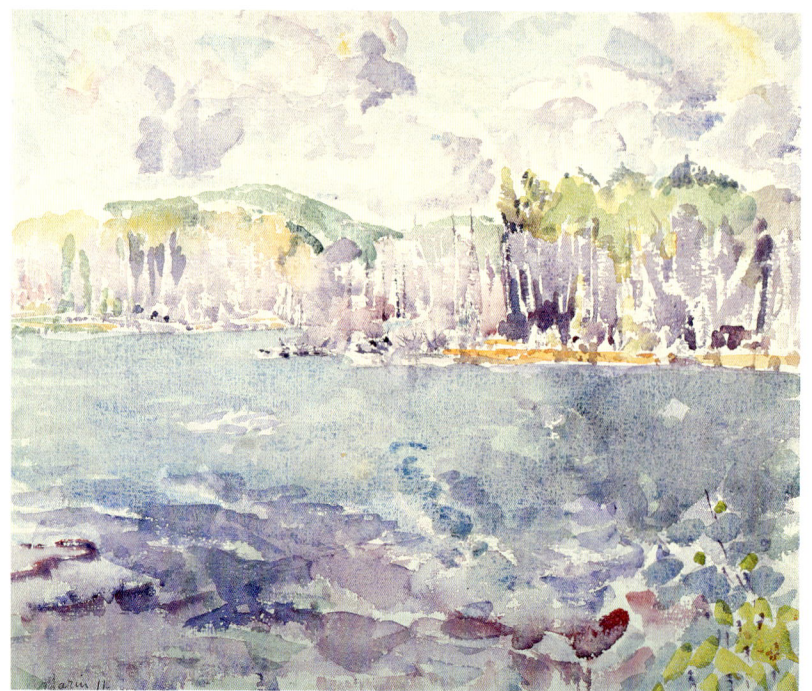

98. John Marin, *Adarondack* [sic] *Lake*, 1911. The Adirondack Museum, Blue Mountain Lake, N.Y., 1969.142.

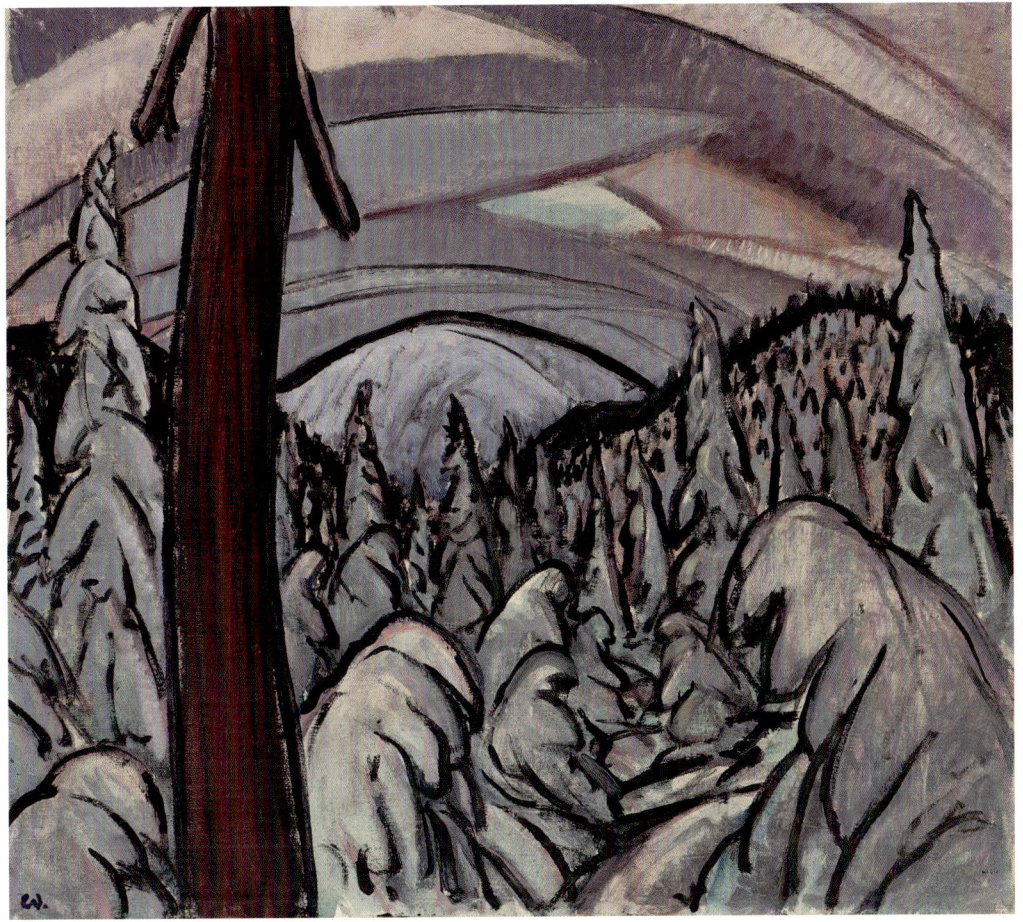

99. Harold Weston, *Wilderness—Marcy, Dvôrák New World Symphony, Largo*, 1922. Museum of Fine Arts, Boston. Robert Jordan Fund, 1999.504.

produced hundreds of four-by-five-inch images of clouds, sky, and sun above Lake George. He called these pictures *Equivalents* because his intent was to visualize his thoughts and feelings, not the actuality of the subject, and to suspend reality in order to achieve spiritual awareness of the vastness of the cosmos. Through their focus on the essential aspects of existence these works referenced the transcendentalists Ralph Waldo Emerson and Henry David Thoreau, but without their sense that God was present in nature. Duncan Phillips called the photographs "miracles of sensitized individual perception and interpretation while remaining true to the medium's...concern with objective truth." The artist called them "my most profound life experiences" (fig. 100).[22]

From 1918 until 1934 O'Keeffe joined Stieglitz (her husband from 1924) at Lake George. She produced a large number of paintings during her time there, including her first flower and leaf paintings as well as landscapes of the lake and surrounding countryside. She and Stieglitz depicted similar subjects at Lake George, but with very different interpretations. In 1923 O'Keeffe wrote to the American playwright Sherwood Anderson, "There is

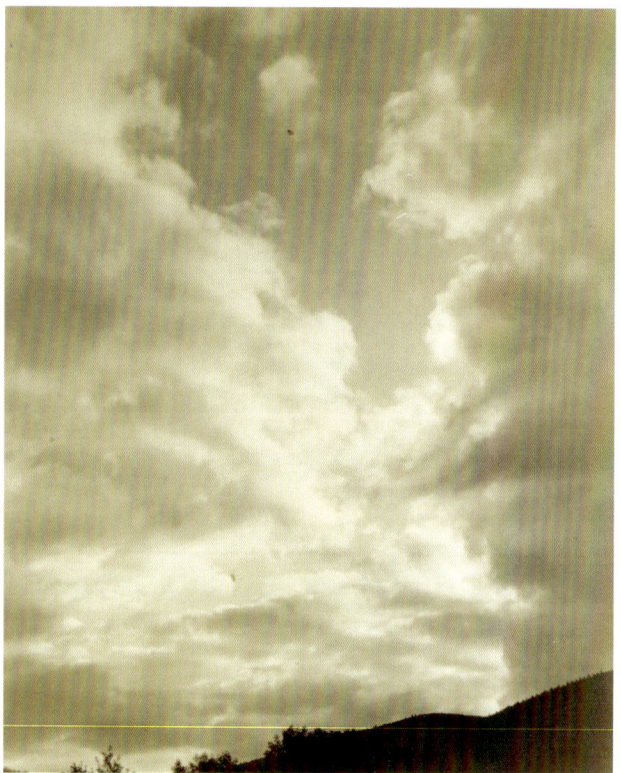

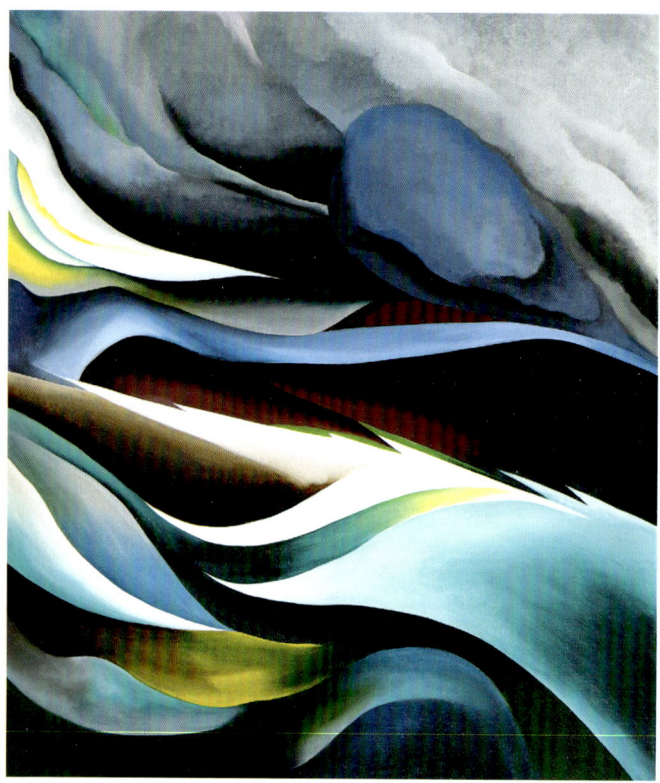

something so perfect about the mountains and the lake and the trees—sometimes I want to tear it all to pieces."[23] She did just that in *From the Lake No. 1*, 1924 (fig. 101). O'Keeffe abstracted the landscape of the region's storied lake with stylized profiles and interweaving lines to portray a roiling sky above the mountains and lake. The strong sense of design derives from undulating forms, sensual masses, bold contrasts between light and dark, and bright colors.[24] After 1934 O'Keeffe went to Taos, New Mexico, for the summer and did not return to Lake George until 1946, when she came to bury Stieglitz's ashes under a tree near the lakeshore.

John Marin, also closely associated with Stieglitz, found many subjects in the region. Works of art document his visits to Lake Placid in 1911 and 1947, to the Fulton Chain lakes in 1912, to the southern Adirondacks and Watertown area in 1913, to Lake Champlain in 1927 and 1931, to Lake George in 1928, and to Keene Valley in 1931 and 1947 (fig. 102).[25] Eight watercolors document his time at Lake George, inspired by a visit to Stieglitz's summer home. Marin divided his life between three loves—the man-made dynamism of New York City, the elemental power of the sea on the Maine coast, and the mountains in the Adirondacks. In his words, "Seems to me the true artist must perforce go from time to time to the elemental big forms—Sky Sea Mountain Plain . . . to sort of retrue himself up. . . . For these big forms have everything. But to express these you have to love these . . . to enfold too the relatively little things that grow on the mountains' back. Which if you don't recognize you don't recognize the mountain."[26] "John Marin once said to me," said Weston, "'If a man wants to paint a mountain, let him fish its streams first.'"[27] Both Weston and Marin immersed themselves in nature to know it so they could paint it.

Marin's diaphanous washes of brilliant color, atmospheric light, and expressive brushwork animate his 1912 scene of Fourth Lake, Fulton Chain, in a way not seen before in Adirondack art (fig. 103). His art synthesizes elements of cubism, abstraction, and objective realism with references to James McNeill Whistler. Marin's pantheism and Gothic fear of the unknown converge in vibrant color and angular design. Like Weston's, Marin's color was an explosive graphic language that expressed the light and movement he saw in nature. Trees and woods as definers of nature's elemental power and mystery figure prominently in his paintings and writings, as they do in Weston's art of the 1920s (see Foster chap., figs. 18, 21; Phillips chap., figs. 64, 67). Marin wrote:

> The woods are wonderful
> The WOODS—Can one think of them without
> Picturing wild beasts and wild men—The Element
> Of fear—and is it not that which makes them
> Alluring and can one thoroughly Enjoy without
> This mixture of fear.[28]

The inner vision informed the artist's response to the visual experience.

102. John Marin, *Adirondacks near Owl's Head*, 1947. Private Collection.

103. John Marin, *Fulton Chain, Adirondacks No. 2*, 1911. The Adirondack Museum, Blue Mountain Lake, N.Y., 1991.23.

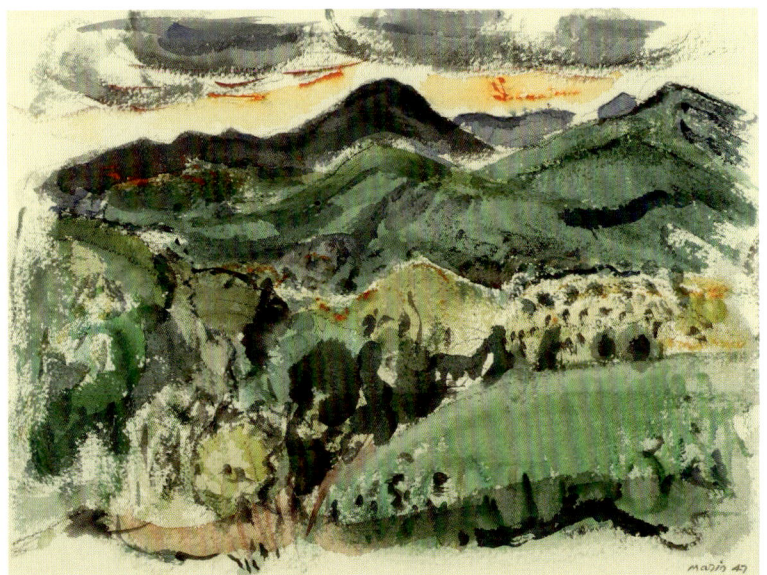

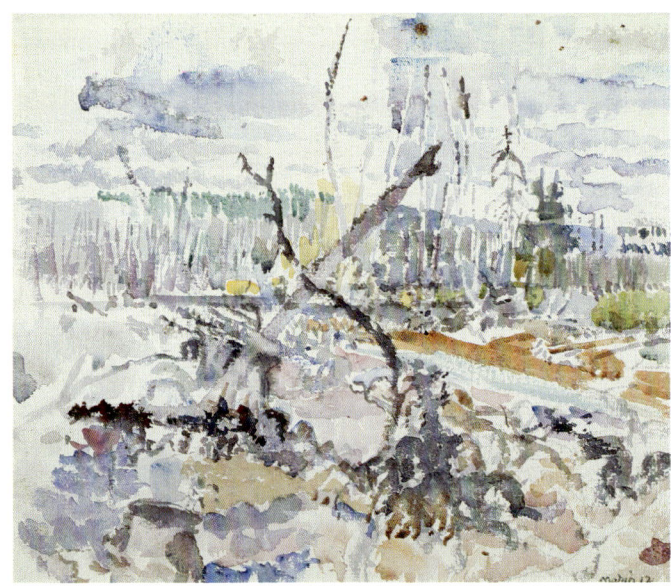

Adirondack Realism in the 1930s

The economic upheaval and social dislocation of the Great Depression stimulated a resurgence of realism in art. Regionalism in the 1930s was more than an artistic style; it embodied a set of values that became widespread and was, in fact, a reaction to the icons of modernization—industrialization, urbanization, and the standardization resulting from a mass culture. It envisioned an America in the natural landscape, where rural communities were thought to be more stable than urban ones, and the virtues of an agrarian past were seen as the key to building a new American society. The resulting art was occasionally chauvinistic and sentimentalized, but it often revealed tangible realities and details of actual life as opposed to esoteric concerns with aesthetics.

Artists painting the Adirondacks at this time were primarily realists. Rockwell Kent (1882–1971) strongly defended his approach as the only artistic truth, believing that realism alone recognized and revealed the inherent beauty of the universe.[29] The mountainous landscape of the Adirondacks was his muse for the second half of his life. "Mountains, dipping again to rise again as farther, higher, steeper, bare-ridged mountain walls to heaven, wave after mountain wave," were his catalyst to convey on canvas the much deeper meanings he saw in nature.[30] Kent saw his paintings as unions of his own imagination and nature. This sense of reciprocity with nature was key to his creative life. "I'm not trying to make people love my art," he said at Bowdoin College in 1969. "Through my art, I'm trying to make people love nature."[31] His mentor, Robert Henri, summarized Kent's credo: "The very things that he portrays on his canvas are the things that he sees in the great organization of life; and his painting is a proclamation of the rights of man, of the dignity of man, of the dignity of creation. It is his belief in God. It is what art should mean."[32] Kent's Adirondack art continued the distinctively austere style he developed on Monhegan Island, Maine, in 1910. He reduced the details of nature to large, flat planes and rhythmic, grand shapes. His approach was modern in its reductive simplicity but realistic in style (fig. 104).

Both Harold Weston and Rockwell Kent found their muse in the Adirondack wilderness from the 1920s to their deaths in the early 1970s. Weston lived year-round in St. Huberts from 1920 to 1925, then went to France for a few years. Kent bought property in Ausable Forks, twenty some miles to the north, in 1927. He used his Asgaard Farm as his home, his studio, and the base from which he traveled for inspiration or to maintain his commercial art business until his death in 1971. Weston returned to the Adirondacks in 1930 with a growing family (two children were born in France and one in St. Huberts) to live and paint full-time until 1942 and thereafter for summers until his death. According to family, Weston referred to Kent's political stances with a certain wariness. He did not socialize or work with Kent while in the Adirondacks, New York, or Washington.[33] Nonetheless, Kent's and Weston's paintings of the 1930s and 1940s share similar fascina-

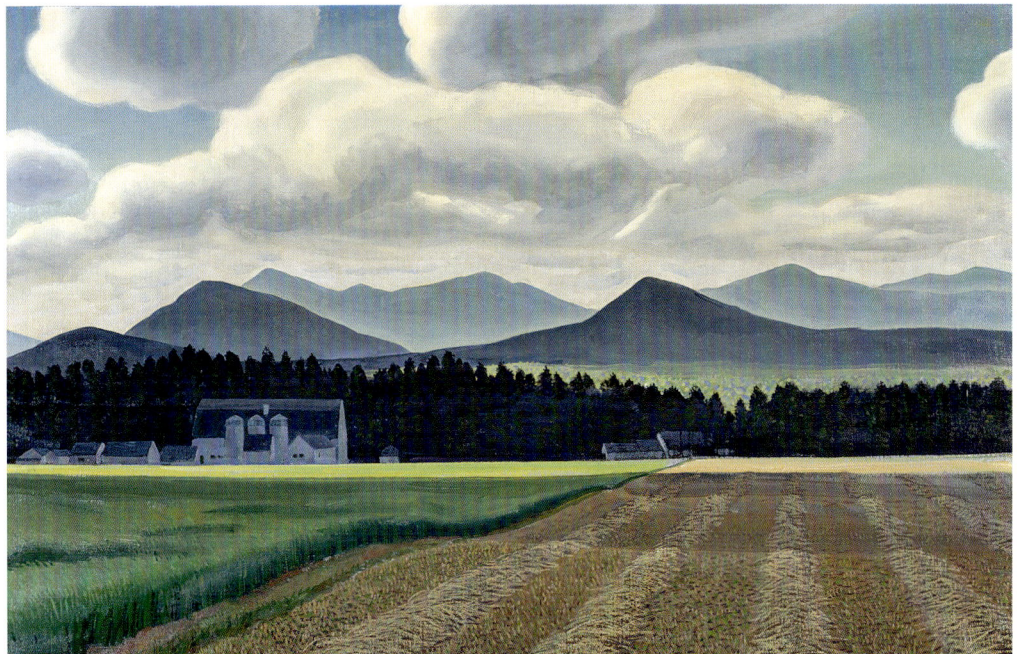

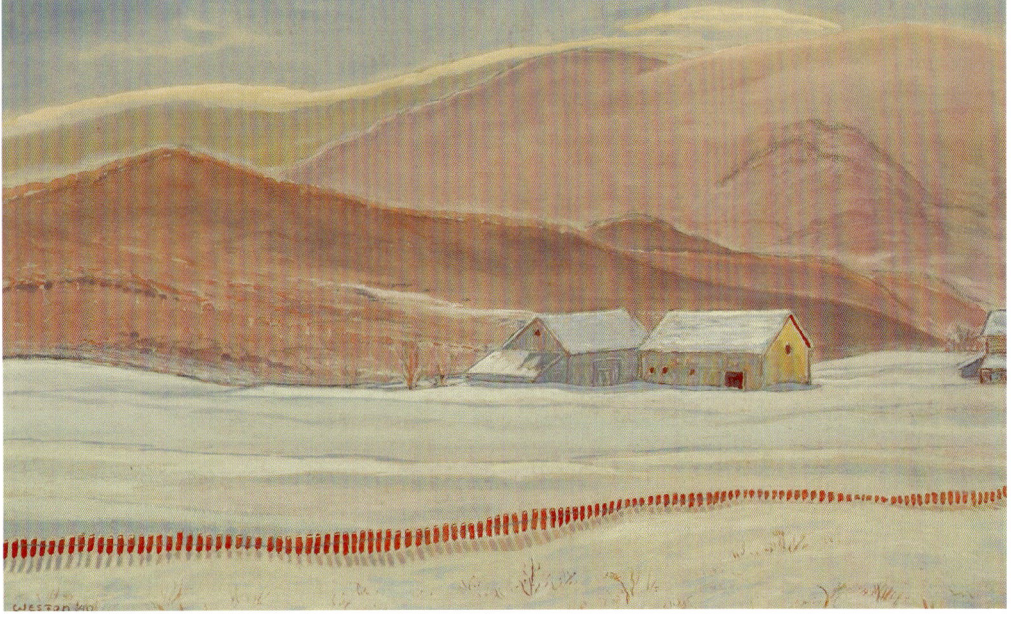

tions with light, patterns made by snow on trees or light on grass, bold and simple shapes, clear colors, and the stark, elemental loneliness of winter in the Adirondacks (figs. 105 and see fig. 129).

In the 1930s in Keene Valley Weston rooted his art in the everyday subjects around his home. These paintings were intimate records of treasured people, places, and objects. Not only did he know his beloved Adirondack Mountains, but he also knew the people

106. Harold Weston, *The Lumberman*, 1922. Private Collection.

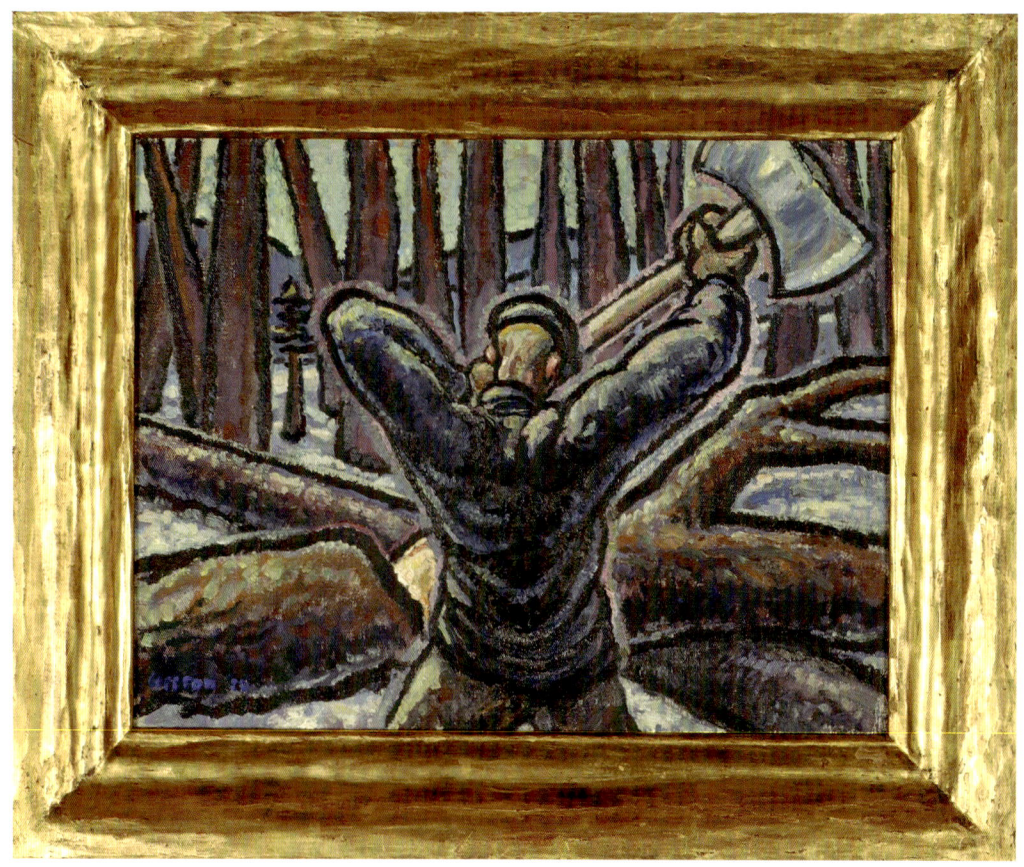

who shaped and were shaped by the land as they rowed the lakes, cut the forests, fought the fires, built their homes, and told their stories. Men like the one in *The Lumberman*, 1922 (fig. 106), worked the woods for the region's primary industry. This Bunyanesque figure forges his way through the wild forest, perhaps symbolizing the heroic aspect of the native Adirondacker living on the land. Even though the region remains the poorest in the state, many communities in the Adirondacks did not experience the full weight of the depression: the Winter Olympics came to Lake Placid in 1932; treating tuberculosis was a thriving industry for Saranac Lake; and lumbering was big business throughout the region. Adirondackers have always clung to self-sufficiency.

Nearby in Elizabethtown and Saranac Lake, Wayman Adams (1883–1959) and Jonas Lie (1880–1940) also made the Adirondack people and landscape their subjects. The nationally renowned portraitist Adams first came to the region in 1920 to make portraits of the guests at the Lake Placid Club. He bought an abandoned farm in Elizabethtown and founded a summer art school, operating the Old Mill Art School in the 1930s as its only teacher. He soon attracted major artists to teach a growing number of students coming from all over the country.[34] Adams painted Adirondack people who posed for his portrait classes. *Lovitt and Son*, circa 1935 (fig. 107), is a compelling image of an Adirondacker and his son. The father holds a scythe and the son an ax, tools emblematic of their work. Adams's brushwork is bold and expressionistic. Students and colleagues remarked on his dexterity with a paint-laden brush and the speed with which he painted, usually finishing a portrait in one sitting. Contemporary reviews of Adams's work called his style "brutally frank" and his insights penetrating but kind. Weston achieved similarly keen insights in his portraits, especially the one of Dr. Felix Adler (fig. 108), founder of the Society for Ethical Culture and Weston's father's mentor and colleague as well as a longtime summer resident of Keene Valley. When Mrs. Adler saw the portrait, she told the artist that she "felt a sense of his [her husband's] presence more keenly than at any time since his death."[35]

Son of a Norwegian civil engineer and an American mother, Jonas Lie was a popular painter of landscapes, cityscapes, and contemporary engineering marvels such as the Panama Canal. His Norwegian family had included many artistic personalities, such as his

107. Wayman Adams, *Lovitt and Son*, ca. 1935. The Adirondack Museum, Blue Mountain Lake, N.Y., 1996.5.

108. Harold Weston, *Dr. Felix Adler*, 1934. Private Collection.

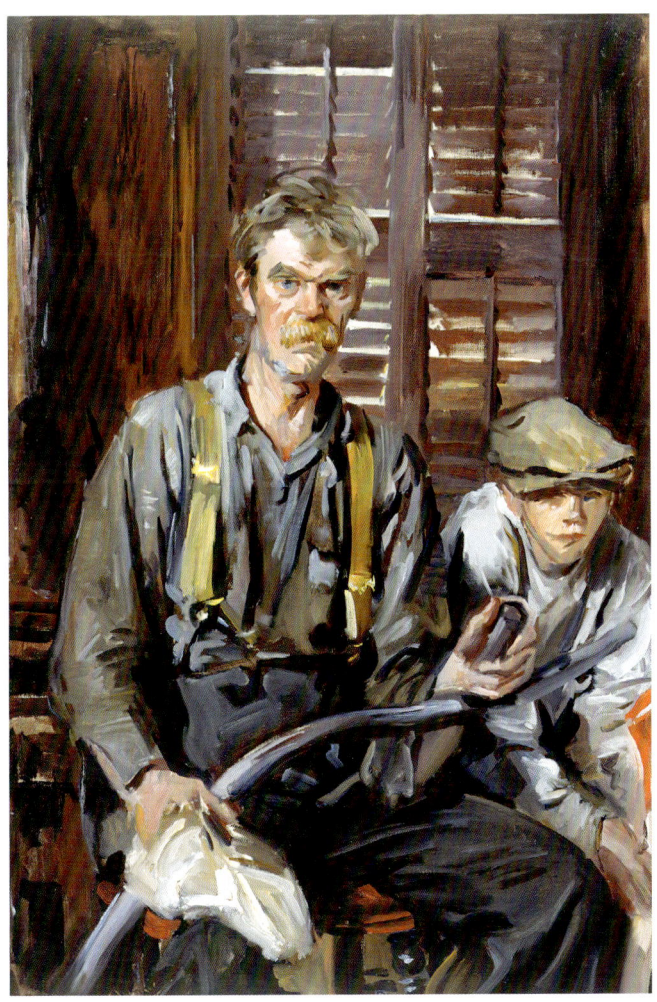

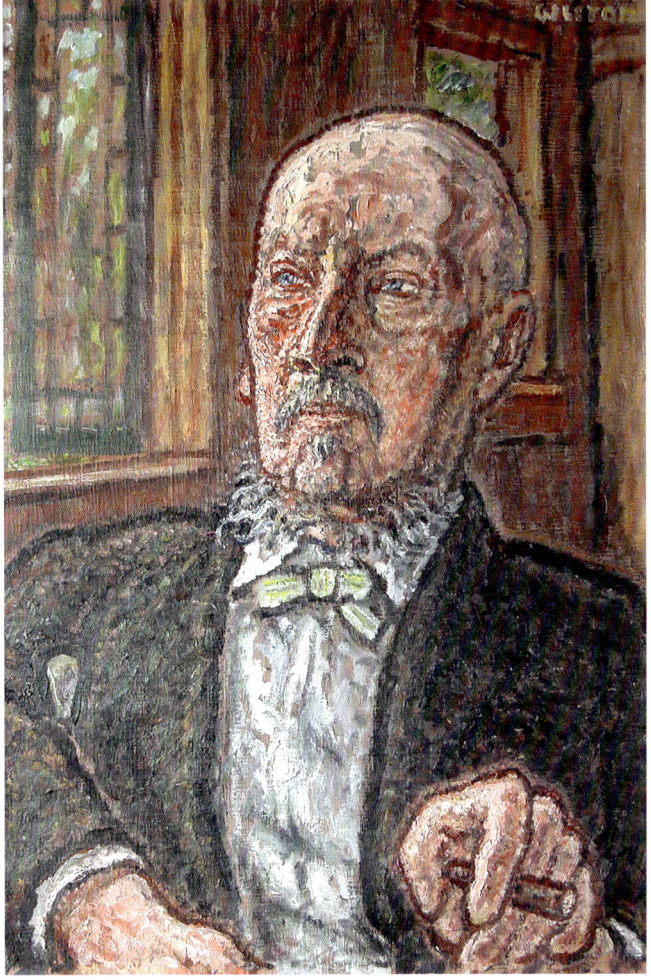

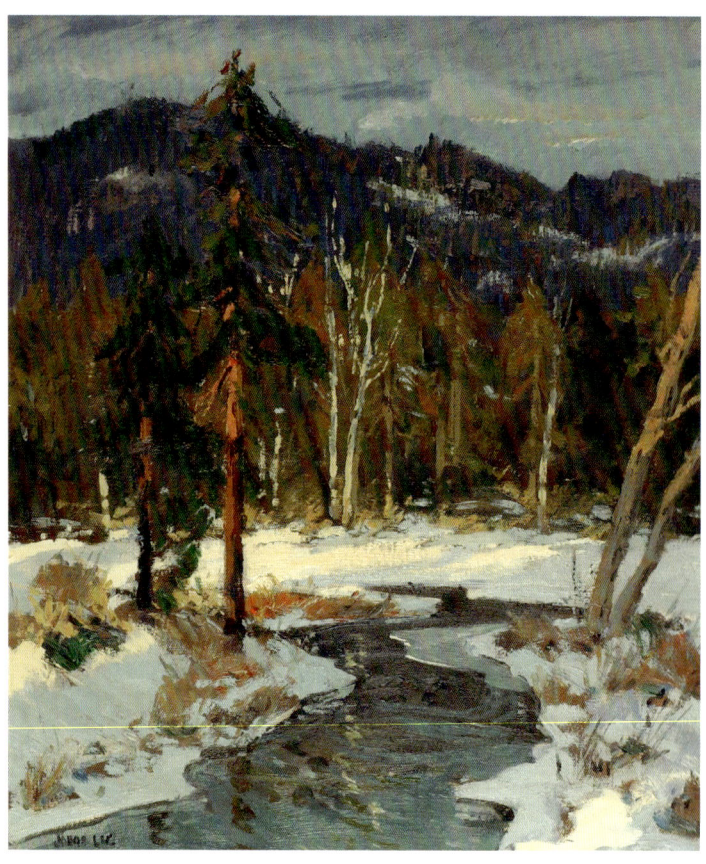

109. Jonas Lie, *Home Pond*, 1930. The Adirondack Museum, Blue Mountain Lake, N.Y., 1976.217.2.

uncle, a noted poet and novelist, for whom he was named. Lie came to America in 1893, at age thirteen, after his father died. His mother enrolled him in Dr. Felix Adler's Ethical Culture School in New York City, where his budding artistic talents were nurtured. He went on to study at the National Academy of Design and the Art Students League.

Lie came to the Adirondacks in the 1920s so his wife could be treated for tuberculosis at Trudeau Sanatorium in Saranac Lake. Nature was Lie's chief inspiration, and he depicted its explicit realities and inherent meanings in a highly personal manner. "I do not attempt," he said, "voluntarily to symbolize nature, but in portraying nature to impart to my work a suggestion of that which is within, and that which is beyond." The Adirondack wilderness and villages afforded him a host of subjects. In 1930 he was commissioned to paint Patrick Garvan's great camp Kill Kare. In the manner of Marin and Weston, Lie used color as an expressive language and focused on the effects of light and shadow on natural and man-made forms. "Colour is the chief medium through which we attain pictorial expression, but colour must be suggestive and interpretive, not imitative. In order to achieve enduring work the actual, visual impression we receive from nature should be even less forceful, less vivid, than the accompanying mental impression."[36] *Home Pond*, 1930 (fig. 109), is one of the series of the Garvan camp.

Photographer-artists came to the region at the invitation of friends and colleagues to document nature and vacation retreats. This was the case for Margaret Bourke-White (1904–71), who had a personal and professional relationship with the Westons in the 1930s. The letters between her and Weston detail projects, experiments with new techniques such as color photography, a new studio, her expanding business and staff, their anticipation of seeing each other in the Adirondacks, her eagerness to learn from him, and the pleasure of recounting conversations with mutual friends, such as Archibald MacLeish, about Weston and his work.[37] She referred at one point to a photomural that the American Broadcasting Corporation (ABC) commissioned from her, on which Weston helped: "They will treat the photomural … the one you helped me lay out … with the same respect that they would a painting … a great victory for photography I think."[38] As a young staff

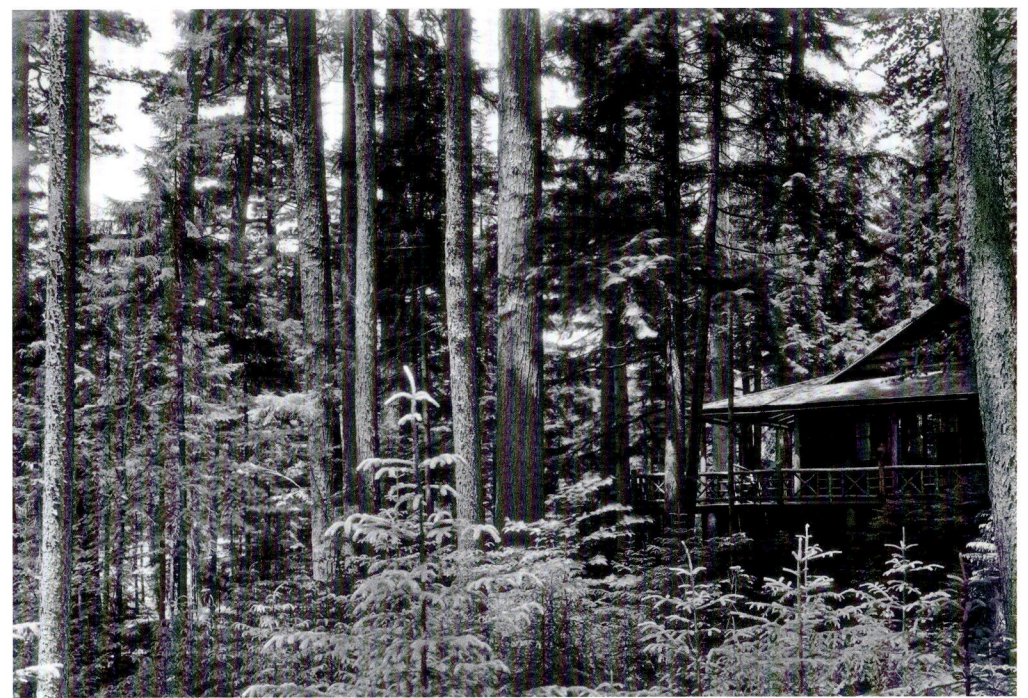

110. Margaret Bourke-White, *Camp Cedars*, 1933. The Adirondack Museum, Blue Mountain Lake, N.Y., P010988.

photographer for *Fortune* magazine in the early 1930s, Bourke-White traveled to the Soviet Union to document its industrial progress. There she met Kenneth Durant, manager of the American bureau of Tass, the Soviet press agency. He invited her to Camp Cedars, the

111. Jacob Asanger, *Adirondack Mountains, New York*, ca. 1920. The Adirondack Museum, Blue Mountain Lake, N.Y., 2002.66.

Adirondack great camp designed by his great-uncle William West Durant for Frederick Clark Durant. She photographed the camp as a thank-you for her July 1933 visit (fig. 110).

Twentieth-century artists, like their nineteenth-century predecessors, played a role in luring tourists to the region. Jacob Asanger's painting *Adirondack Mountains, New York*, circa 1920 (fig. 111), was commissioned by the Los Angeles advertising firm Foster and Kleiser. The artist was sent to the nation's great natural wonders to capture them in paint, and then the firm produced posters from the paintings to promote the sites to tourists. Born in Bavaria, Jacob Asanger (1887–1941) immigrated with his family to the United States in the late 1800s and soon settled in Los Angeles. He studied art at the Los Angeles School of Art and Design and honed his skills in the forums provided by an abundance

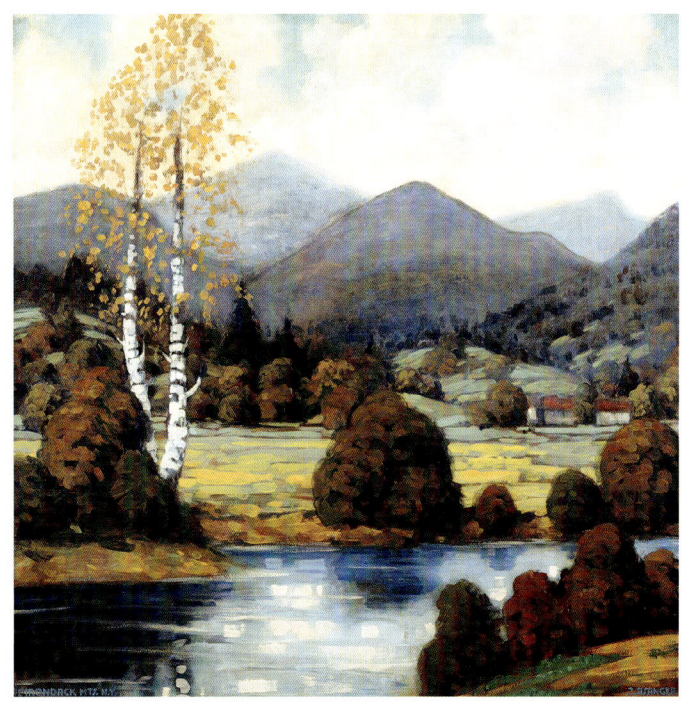

of art clubs that flourished in southern California. Asanger became a landscape painter, poster artist, etcher, craftsman, and art teacher.

Dale Nichols (1904–1995)—artist, printmaker, illustrator, watercolorist, designer, writer, and lecturer—was one of the most significant figures in American regionalist painting. He was born in David City, Nebraska, and his rural upbringing had a major influence on his interpretations of the American landscape. He studied art at the Chicago Academy of Fine Arts and the Art Institute of Chicago, and in Vienna with Joseph Binder. Between 1930 and 1940 he served as Carnegie Visiting Professor at the University of Illinois, and he succeeded the American artist Grant Wood as art editor of the *Encyclopedia Britannica* from 1942 to 1948. He was also an early champion of good art in advertising and illustration, creating artwork for direct-mail industrial advertising in the 1930s and 1940s.

Nebraska was the primary inspiration for his rural landscapes. His precise technique and crisp application of paint complemented the stark subject matter of his farmscapes. *Lake Saranac*, 1934 (fig. 112), has the same sense of monumentality that can be seen in those farm scenes. The bold dark purple of the lake, the deep green of the mountains, and the serene clarity of the sky highlighted in yellows and lilacs overwhelm the tiny red cabin and suggest the limited presence of people in this vast wilderness. Nichols's treatment is mod-

112. Dale Nichols, *Lake Saranac*, 1934. The Adirondack Museum, Blue Mountain Lake, N.Y., 2003.26.

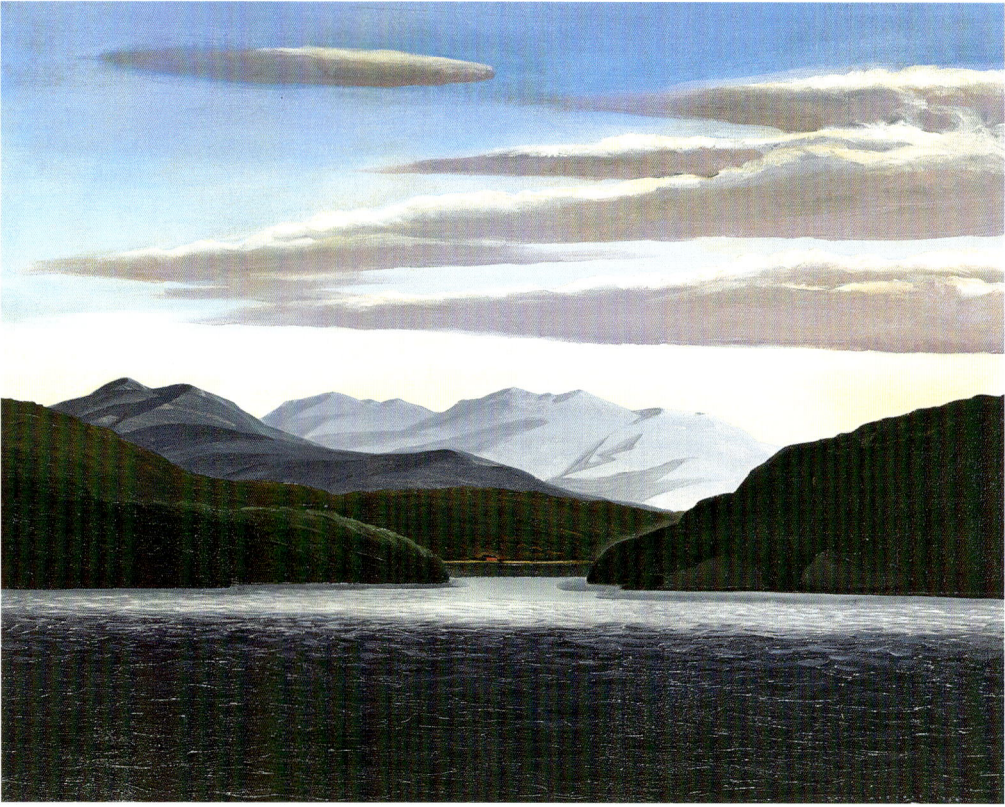

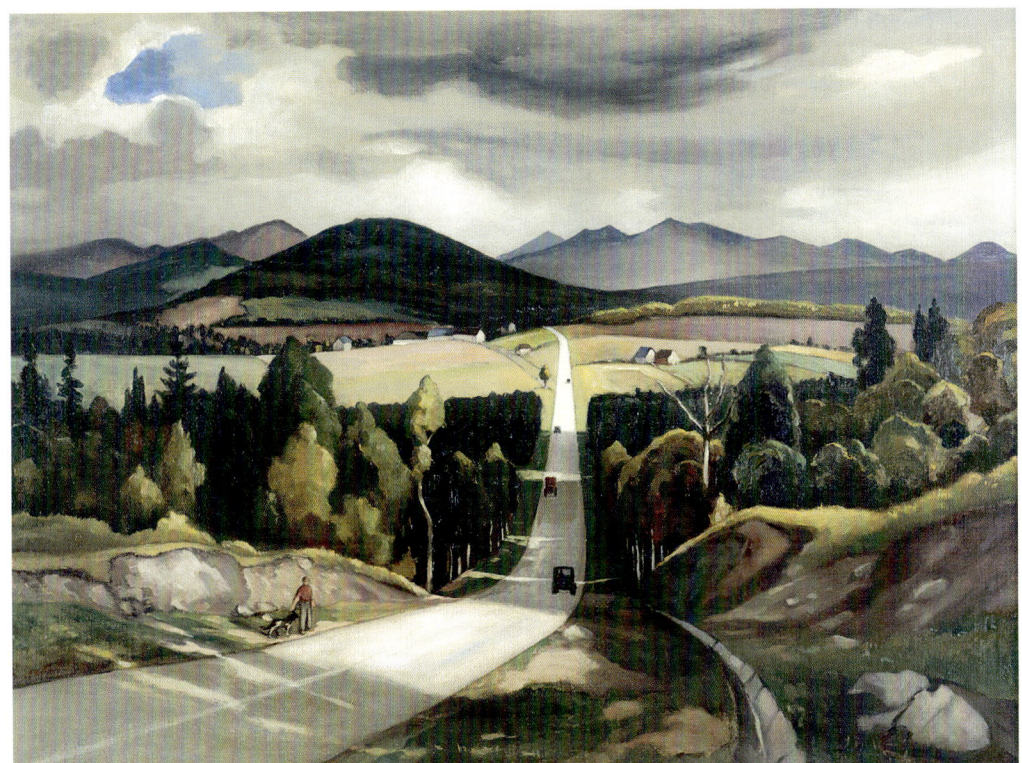

113. Julius Delbos, *The Road from Tupper Lake to Saranac Lake*, 1941. The Adirondack Museum, Blue Mountain Lake, N.Y., 2003.5.

ern, approaching the abstract in its bold simplicity. This painting is the only record of Nichols's time in the Adirondacks. Perhaps he came to the mountains through contacts he made at the Macbeth Gallery, his dealer in New York from 1930 to 1950, whose artists and patrons knew the region well. The gallery exhibited *Lake Saranac* in January 1938.

London born and trained, Julius Delbos (1879–1970) came to America in 1923 and quickly established himself first in Chicago and later in New York as an artist of note. He regularly exhibited at major museums and galleries and won significant awards. In 1940 he made his only trip to the Adirondacks. Based with friends in Tupper Lake, Delbos spent the summer sketching and painting mountain and lake vistas as well as making friends in Saranac Lake and Lake Placid. To make visits to friends and painting sites easier, Delbos's Tupper Lake host taught him to drive. Delbos produced many on-the-spot sketches and watercolors that he worked up into oil paintings in his studio in New York. His diary entry dated 12 January 1941 states his pleasure at having completed a major canvas, *The Road from Tupper Lake to Saranac Lake* (fig. 113). It pictures the landscape around the road he had traveled so often in bold, flat planes of azure and green under a characteristically cloudy Adirondack sky.

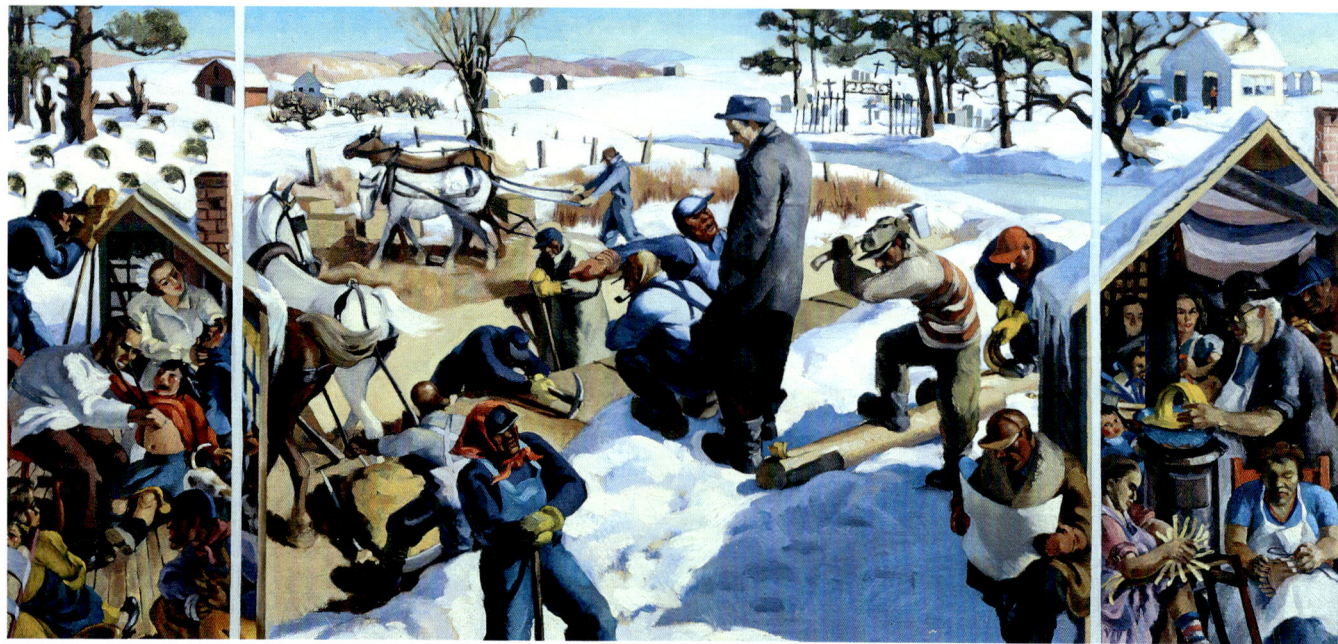

114. Amy Jones, *St. Regis Reservation*, 1937. The Adirondack Museum, Blue Mountain Lake, N.Y., 1986.65.

Adirondack Muralists

The national social, political, and economic conditions during the depression years of the 1930s and early 1940s were also a subject for American art. Franklin Delano Roosevelt's programs and policies for recovery from the depression included the Public Works of Art Project (1933–35) and the Federal Art Project (1935–41), which employed 3,500 artists, including Adirondack artists Amy Jones, Rockwell Kent, Peppino Mangravite, and Harold Weston. Under the aegis of these programs 4,500 murals, 19,000 sculptures, and nearly 1 million easel paintings were produced. Subjects were primarily historical events, local scenes, and vignettes of daily life depicting an idealized world in which people found dignity in productive work, a profound contrast to the harsh realities of the times. Rockwell Kent painted two murals for the new U.S. Post Office building in Washington, D.C., in 1935, commissioned by the federal Public Works Administration. Weston's critically acclaimed murals of national-recovery public-works projects, completed in 1938, were for the General Services Administration Building in Washington, D.C., through a commission from the Treasury Relief Art Project.

Amy Jones (1899–1992), painter, printmaker, and sculptor, won national recognition in the 1930s as a muralist while living in Saranac Lake with her husband, who was being treated for tuberculosis. The triptych *St. Regis Reservation*, 1937 (fig. 114), was her entry for the Treasury Department's post office mural project; she painted murals for three post offices, in Winsted, Connecticut, and in Painted Post and Scotia, both in New York. Her competition entry captures little-documented aspects of Native American life in the North Country: a doctor checks Mohawk children for tuberculosis; a foreman supervises Mohawks on construction and logging jobs; and a Mohawk basketmaker prepares ash splint for making the tribe's trademark basket.

Peppino Mangravite (1896–1978) was a distinguished artist and teacher in the 1920s, 1930s, and 1940s. During the 1930s he painted murals for the Department of Labor, for the Treasury Building in Washington, D.C., and for post offices in Hempstead, New York; Pittsburg, Pennsylvania; and Atlantic City, New Jersey. His connection to the Adirondacks began when he married Frances Teall, daughter of Adirondack newspaperwoman and author Edna West Teall. The Mangravites bought a large farm near Elizabethtown, pictured in his work *Reunion* (fig. 115), painted in the summer of 1936. His expressionistic style and narrative realism bring life and verve to this alfresco family picnic captured on canvas. The Weston and Mangravite families were friends, sharing many happy summer outings in the Adirondacks.[39] Mangravite wrote to Weston in May 1934: "I shall be delighted to see you and am looking forward to many hours of pleasure, smoking our pipes and talking ourselves sick."[40] A May 1935 letter from "Gino to Harold" reveals an ongoing conversation about the murals the two artists were working on. In April 1937 Mangravite critiqued two of Weston's murals: "Briefly and plainly let me say that you have done a competent, conscientious and exquisite piece of work. They both look superb in place. Extraordinarily rich in color and a design that makes one think of the weaving and interweaving, lacing and interlacing of Coptic tapestry."[41]

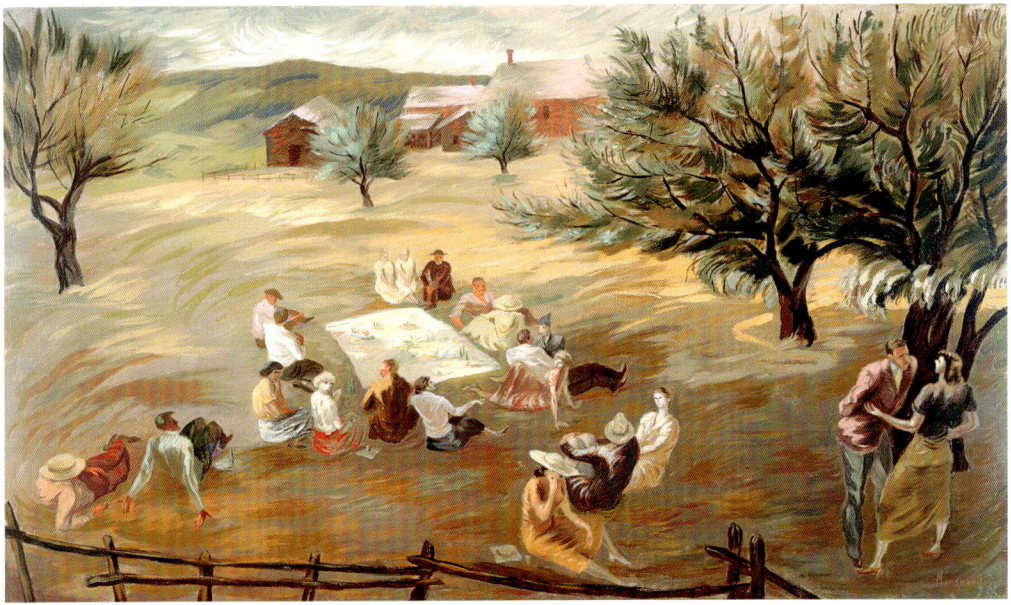

115. Peppino Mangravite, *Reunion*, 1936. The Adirondack Museum, Blue Mountain Lake, N.Y., 1995.21.

Adirondack Art and the New York School

By the 1930s more than 75 percent of America's artists lived in New York City. New York galleries proliferated in the 1940s, and the American version of abstract expressionism, or the New York School, became the most important modernist art movement in the world by the end of the decade. Abstract expressionism, in contrast to the social realism of the New Deal and regionalism, was not about recognizable landscapes or people, but a search for eternal and timeless meanings drawn from the depths of the unconscious mind. David Smith, one of the leaders of this avant-garde movement, and Mark Rothko came to the Adirondacks: Smith to live at Bolton Landing near Lake George and Rothko to summer at Trout Lake near Glens Falls. Robert Motherwell and Kenneth Noland visited David Smith at Bolton Landing.[42]

David Smith (1906–65) launched his abstract sculpture in 1930 and created in 1933 his first welded-steel art in a garage at Bolton Landing on Lake George. His sculptural vocabulary grew out of the railroads, industry, and farms of his childhood in Decatur, Indiana: "We used to play on trains and around factories. I played there just like I played in nature, on hills and in creeks."[43] Connecting industry and nature became implicit in Smith's art. Smith and his first wife, the artist Dorothy Dehner, discovered Bolton Landing through their artist friends Thomas and Weber Furlong. Smith and Dehner purchased the eighty-six-acre Old Fox Farm in the hills overlooking Lake George in 1929. Eleven years later they made the farm their permanent home, renaming it Terminal Iron Works after Smith's original studio in Brooklyn.

Critically acclaimed as the foremost sculptor of his generation, Smith was a painter, draftsman, and sculptor, working constantly to integrate the three media into one art. The sweeping vistas and tree-covered mountain ridges he could see from his farm profoundly shaped the look of his art. He made just-larger-than-human-scale, organically shaped sculptures of inorganic steel or industrial or agricultural machinery and parts he found on his land. He placed his sculptures in rows or groups outside in nature, where the highly reflective stainless steel or painted surfaces mirrored the sun, stars, sky, and the colors of trees, grass, and snow.[44] Situated on the landscape around his studio, the sculptures constantly drew the eye to the horizon and sky, referencing nature, evolution, and change. Smith felt that "It is impossible for any artist not to be of nature or to deal with problems of nature. Nature is everything and everybody's."[45] He made six hundred sculptures and hundreds of drawings and paintings. His drawings are also nonobjective while employing primordial shapes to reference nature's elemental, biomorphic forms in earth tones (fig. 116).

Dorothy Dehner (1901–94), born in Cleveland, Ohio, grew up in Pasadena, California, and studied art in California and New York. She met David Smith in 1926 and married him the following year. At their farm near Bolton Landing, Weston-like without electricity or running water, Dehner raised vegetables, made their clothes, and continued her drawing and painting. In the 1940s and early 1950s she captured the rolling mountain scenery near the farm, often incorporating human activity and anecdotal detail. She would reminisce later, "There was much beauty in our lives in that unspoiled countryside, both in our way of life and the natural setting around it."[46] *Finger of Winter*, 1948 (fig. 117), is a graceful abstraction of trees brushed by ice and snow, painted in gouache and pen and ink on brown paper.

Born in Nagano, Japan, Bumpei Usui (1898–1991) grew up on a silkworm farm before moving to London in 1917. He came to the United States in 1921 and settled in New York City, where he earned a living designing furniture and making frames for many of the leading artists of the time. He decided to become an artist, exhibiting his work as early as 1925.

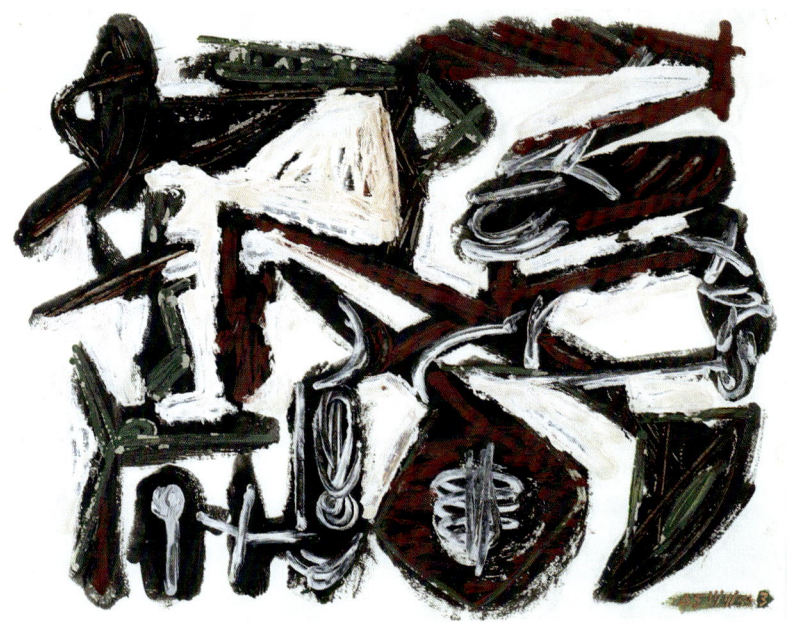

116. David Smith, *Untitled: Abstract*, 1954. The Adirondack Museum, Blue Mountain Lake, N.Y., 1998.18.

117. Dorothy Dehner, *Finger of Winter*, 1948. The Adirondack Museum, Blue Mountain Lake, N.Y.,

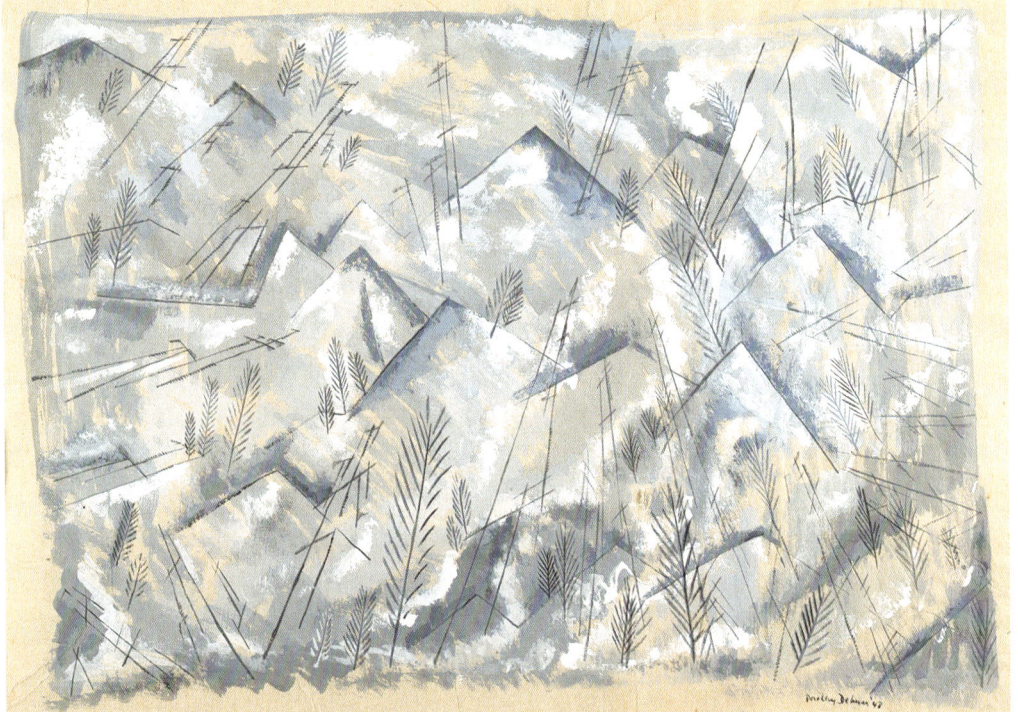

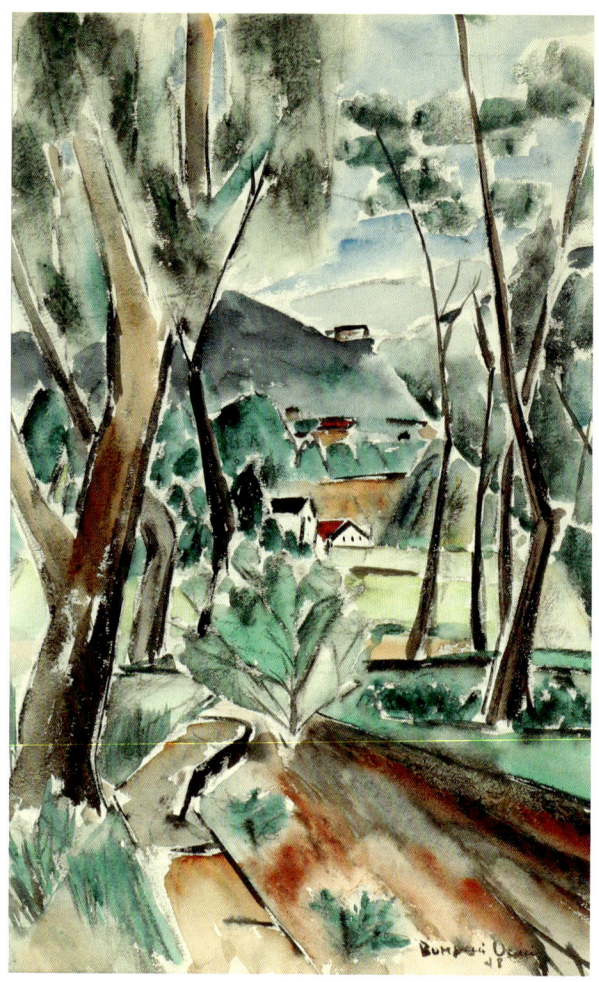

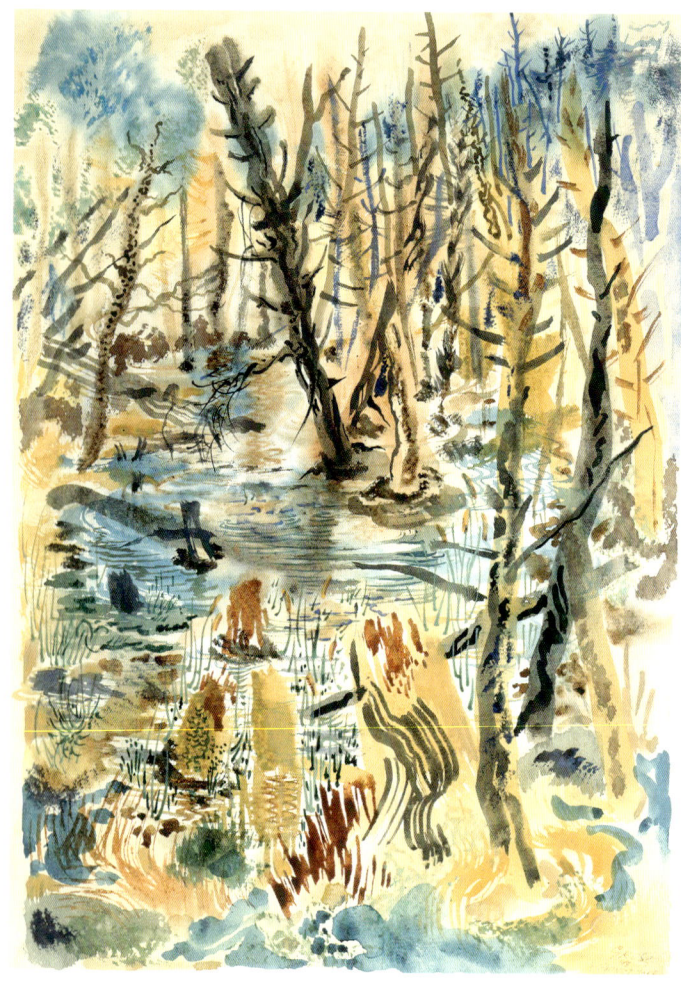

118. Bumpei Usui, *Adirondack Landscape*, 1948. The Adirondack Museum, Blue Mountain Lake, N.Y., 2002.66.2.

119. George Grosz, *Garnet Lake*, 1943. The Adirondack Museum, Blue Mountain Lake, N.Y., 2002.3.

His paintings, acclaimed for their color and expressive line, are reminiscent of John Marin's; *Adirondack Landscape*, 1948 (fig. 118), is one such example. What brought Usui to the Adirondacks in 1948 is not known, but he was friends with many artists, including Marin and Yasuo Kuniyoshi, who vacationed and painted in the region.

George Grosz (1893–1959) came to America in 1933 to escape Nazi Germany. In the eighteenth- and nineteenth-century tradition of William Hogarth, Francisco de Goya, and Honoré Daumier, Grosz's bitter satires chronicled the corruption of German society between the First and Second World Wars. When he became an American citizen, he announced, "I will do no more satire work. I want to forget politics."[47] His rich palette and surging brushwork captured nudes, still lifes, portraits, and landscapes in oil and water-color. His Adirondack works reveal an ardent love of nature; gnarled trees, dead stumps, mountain and lake vistas fascinated him. The "disorderly order" of Grosz's *Garnet Lake*, 1943 (fig. 119), embodies Weston's description of wilderness: "One of the rich rewards of a wilderness tract is the apparently disorderly order which the laws of nature unpredictably produce with infinite variations the complex confusion of a mass of fallen timber or a wind-blown collection of autumn leaves that result in both dissonances and harmonies which seem totally accidental but give forth vibrations akin to those of which beauty is composed."[48]

Ludwig Sander (1906–75) began his career as a landscapist. Born on Staten Island, New York, he studied art in Paris, New York, and Munich during the 1920s and 1930s. His work evolved toward abstraction, and by the 1950s he had identified the geometric color format that makes him one of the few nonobjective renderers of Adirondack scenery. For Sander, painting was about provoking sensory and intellectual experiences, and color was his focus. Through interrelationships of colors within rectilinear geometric forms, he demonstrated that "color begets form and classical harmony is its purpose."[49] *Adirondack V,* 1972 (fig. 120), is part of a fifteen-painting series, all modulations of the color green. Sander's widow believed that the series was inspired by the artist's childhood visits to the

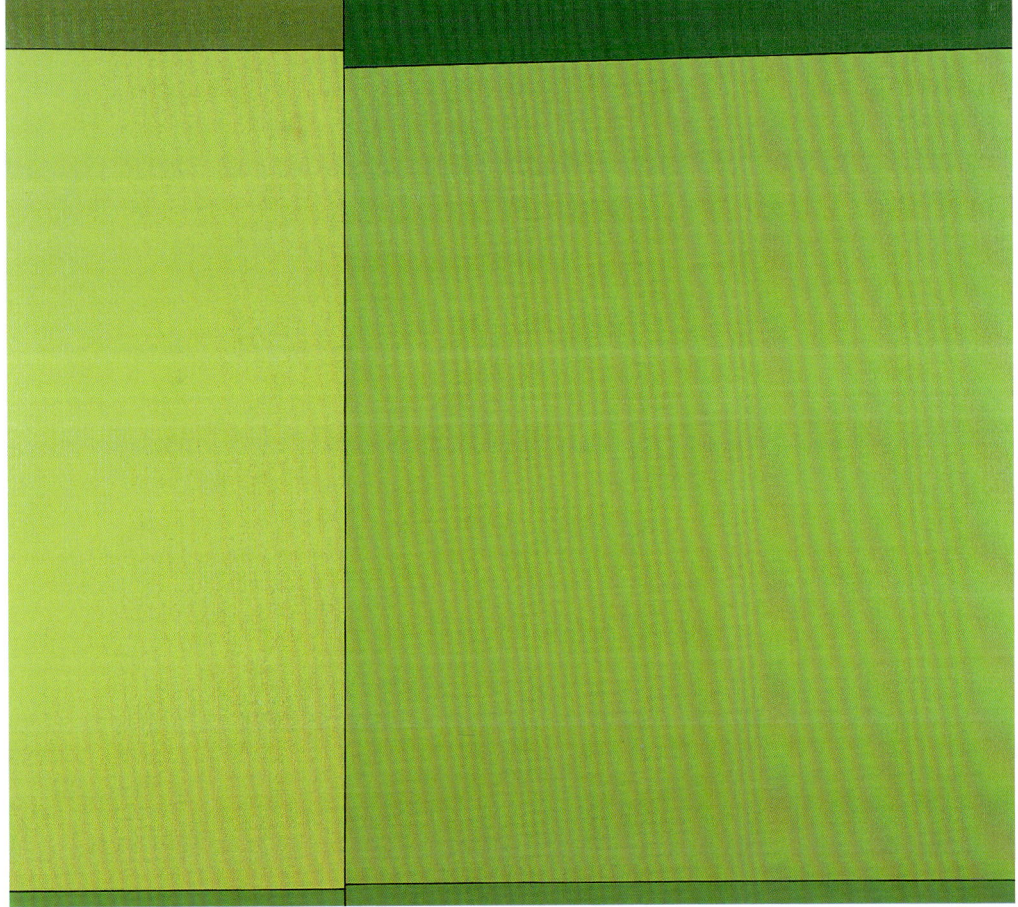

120. Ludwig Sander, *Adirondack V,* 1972. The Adirondack Museum, Blue Mountain Lake, N.Y., 1997.9.

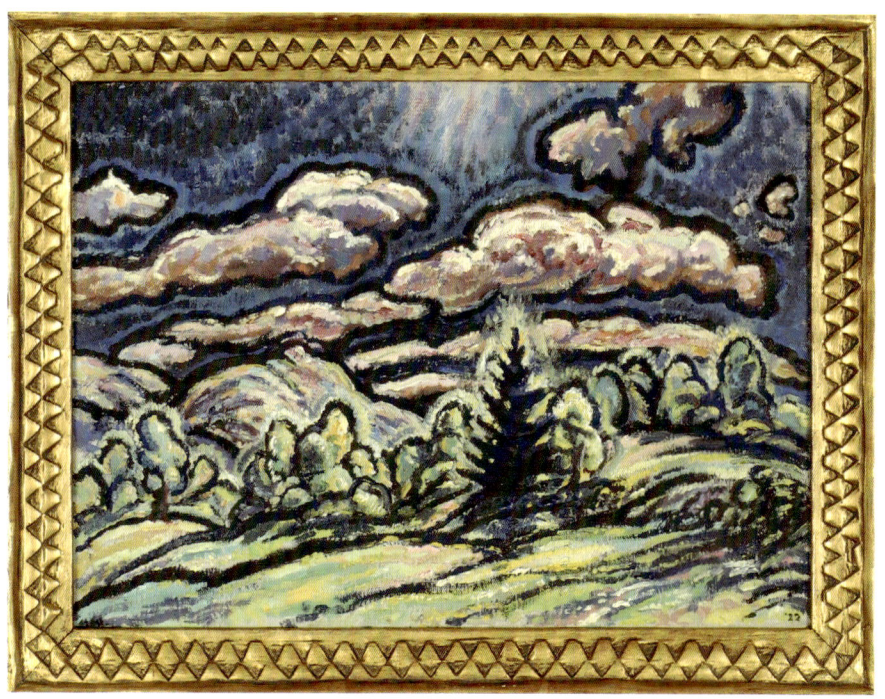

121. Harold Weston, *Noonday Sun*, 1922. The Adirondack Museum, Blue Mountain Lake, N.Y., 1989.75.

Adirondacks. Like artists who preceded him, he was drawn to the Adirondack landscape, which he distilled to color alone.

Twentieth-century Adirondack artists, for the most part, continued to portray the sanctity of nature and to acknowledge its tenuous balances or, in Weston's musical metaphor, the "dissonances and harmonies" of nature. Harold Weston's Adirondack art manifests the latent energy of ancient rock, rushing waters, and mighty wind; the vivid palettes of sunrise and sunset; nature's ordinary and sublime. His Adirondack art is a testament to his abiding passion for the Adirondack wilderness, ignited when he was a child and kept aflame for more than seventy years. He and a host of artists have reminded us of the rich rewards of wilderness in their art of the Adirondacks (fig. 121).

Notes

1. Quoted in Louis L. Noble, *The Course of Empire, Voyage of Life and Other Pictures of Thomas Cole N.A. with Selections from His Letters and Miscellaneous Writings* (New York: Cornish, Lamport, 1853), 241.

2. See Sue Rainey, *Creating Picturesque America: Monument to the National and Cultural Landscape* (Nashville: Vanderbilt Univ. Press, 1994), for a thorough discussion of this subject.

3. Thomas Cole, "Essay on American Scenery," 1835. Cole wrote: "The ravages of the axe are daily increasing—the most notable scenes are made destitute, and often times with a wantonness and barbarism scarcely credible in a civilized nation." Quoted in *Thomas Cole: Landscape into History*, edited by William H. Truettner and Alan Wallach (New Haven, Conn.: Yale Univ. Press, for the National Museum of American Art, Washington, D.C., 1994), 67.

4. Robert Hughes, *American Visions* (New York: Alfred A. Knopf, 1997), 142.

5. For a complete discussion of the creation and history of the Adirondack Park, see Philip Graham, *The Adirondack Park: A Political History* (New York: A. A. Knopf, 1978); and Philip G. Terrie, *Contested Terrain: A New History of Nature and People in the Adirondacks* (Syracuse, N.Y.: Syracuse Univ. Press, for the Adirondack Museum, 1997).

6. Robin Pell, *Keene Valley: The Landscape and Its Artists*, exhibition catalogue (New York: Gerald Peters Gallery, 1994), unpaginated.

7. Roswell M. Shurtleff, "Recollections of Keene Valley," manuscript, n.d., Keene Valley Library Archive, Keene Valley, N.Y.

8. The Adirondack Museum Artist Files and the Margaret O'Brien Artist Files, Adirondack Museum Library, document the artists who worked in the region. See also Richard Plunz, ed., *Two Adirondack Hamlets in History: Keene and Keene Valley* (Fleischmanns, N.Y.: Purple Mountain Press, 1999), 132–46; and Pauline Goldmark, "Keene Valley Artists," manuscript, Adirondack Museum Library.

9. Quoted in Alice Korff, eulogy to Weston, Aug. 1972, Harold Weston Foundation, West Chester, Pa.

10. Duncan Phillips, *The Artist Sees Differently: Essays Based upon the Philosophy of a Collection in the Making*, 2 vols. (New York: E. Weyhe; Washington, D.C.: Phillips Memorial Gallery, 1931), 1: 138.

11. Harold Weston, *Freedom in the Wilds: A Saga of the Adirondacks* (St. Huberts, N.Y.: Adirondack Trail Improvement Society, 1971), 62.

12. William P. Dunham, eulogy to Weston, Aug. 1972, Harold Weston Foundation.

13. Weston, *Freedom in the Wilds*, 93.

14. Ibid., 152.

15. Ibid., 105.

16. Ibid., 107.

17. Plunz, *Two Adirondack Hamlets in History*, 132–46.

18. Charles C. Cunningham, as quoted in Lee Malone, *An Exhibition of Paintings by James Rosenberg*, exhibition catalogue (New York: Kaufman Art Gallery, 1963), Adirondack Museum Artist Files, Rosenberg file.

19. Marin quoted in Dorothy Norman, *John Marin Memorial Exhibition*, exhibition catalogue (Los Angeles: Art Galleries, University of California, 1955), n.p.

20. Kristina Wilson, "The Intimate Gallery and the Equivalents: Spirituality in the 1920s Work of Stieglitz," *Art Bulletin* 85 (Dec. 2003): 746.

21. John Szarkowski, *Alfred Stieglitz at Lake George*, exhibition catalogue (New York: Museum of Modern Art, 1995), 9–30.

22. Erika D. Passantino, ed., *The Eye of Duncan Phillips* (Washington, D.C.: Phillips Collection, 1999), 378.

23. Georgia O'Keeffe to Sherwood Anderson, 1923, in Adirondack Museum Artist Files, O'Keeffe file.

24. Christopher B. Fulton, *Modernist Idylls: Nature and the Avant-Garde, 1905–1930*, exhibition catalogue (Allentown, Pa.: Allentown Art Museum, 1987), n.p.

25. Sheldon Reich, *John Marin: A Stylistic Analysis and Catalogue Raisonné* (Tucson: Univ. of Arizona Press, 1970), pt. 1, p. 376, no. 13.18; pt. 2, p. 373, no. 13.1, p. 592, no. 28.30, p. 588, no. 28.3, p. 592, no. 28.29, p. 636, no. 31.30, p. 751, no. 47.6, p. 758, no. 47.40.

26. John Marin, *John Marin by John Marin*, edited by Cleve Gray (New York: Holt, Rinehart and Winston, n.d.), 161, quoted in John I. H. Baur, *John Marin's Mountains*, exhibition catalogue (New York: Kennedy Galleries, 1983), 161, Adirondack Museum Artist Files, Marin file.

27. Weston, *Freedom in the Wilds*, 124.

28. Marin quoted in Nanette V. Maciejunes, *Trees as Seen Through the Eyes of John Marin and Charles Burchfield*, exhibition catalogue (New York: Kennedy Galleries, 1991), n.p.

29. Rockwell Kent, *It's Me, O Lord* (New York: Dodd, Mead, 1955), 211.

30. Rockwell Kent, *This Is My Own* (New York: Duell, Sloan and Pearce, 1940), 38.

31. Rockwell Kent, *Rockwell Kent: The Early Years*, exhibition catalogue (Waterville, Maine: Bowdoin College Museum of Art, 1969), n.p.

32. Kent, *It's Me, O Lord*, 198.

33. Nina Weston Foster, in conversation with Caroline M. Welsh, 13 Jan. 2004, West Chester, Penn.

34. Adirondack Museum Artist Files, Adams file, and Margaret Bartley, "Model Citizens: Posing, Painting, and Partying at Elizabethtown's Old Mill Art School," *Adirondack Life* 34, no. 6 (Sept.–Oct. 2003): 64–73, 80–82.

35. Mrs. Adler quoted in Weston, *Freedom in the Wilds*, 154.

36. Lie quoted in Christian Brinton, "Jonas Lie—An Interpretation," in *Paintings by Jonas Lie*, exhibition catalogue (New York: Ainslie Galleries, 1923), n.p. Also see "Jonas Lie of Norway and America: A Painter Who Has Found the Secret of Suggesting on Canvas Nature's Manifold Moods," *Craftsman* 13 (Nov. 1907): 135–39, Adirondack Museum Artist Files, Lie file.

37. Margaret Bourke-White to Harold Weston, 22 Aug. and 20 Sept. 1934, Harold Weston Papers, 1916–72, Archives of American Art, Smithsonian Institution, Washington, D.C. (hereafter AAA).

38. Margaret Bourke-White to Harold Weston, 4 Mar. 1934, Harold Weston Papers, AAA.

39. Nina Weston Foster, in conversation with Caroline M. Welsh, 13 Jan. 2004, West Chester, Pa.

40. Peppino Mangravite to Harold Weston, 22 May 1934, Harold Weston Papers, AAA.

41. Peppino Mangravite to Harold Weston, 27 Apr. 1937, Harold Weston Papers, AAA.

42. James Kettlewell, *Artists of Lake George, 1776–1976*, exhibition catalogue (Glens Falls, N.Y.: Hyde Collection, 1976), 38–39.

43. Hughes, *American Visions*, 502.

44. Ibid., 504.

45. Smith quoted in Fairfield Porter, "David Smith: Steel into Sculpture," *Art News* 56 (1959): 42.

46. Dorothy Dehner, in Adirondack Museum Artist Files, Dehner file.

47. Grosz quoted in *The Art Digest* 13 (1 Jan. 1939), Adirondack Museum Artist Files, Grosz file.

48. Weston, *Freedom in the Wilds*, preface, n.p.

49. Robert C. Morgan, *Ludwig Sander: The Elegance of Painting*, exhibition catalogue (New York: ACA Galleries, 1992), Adirondack Museum Artist Files, Sander file.

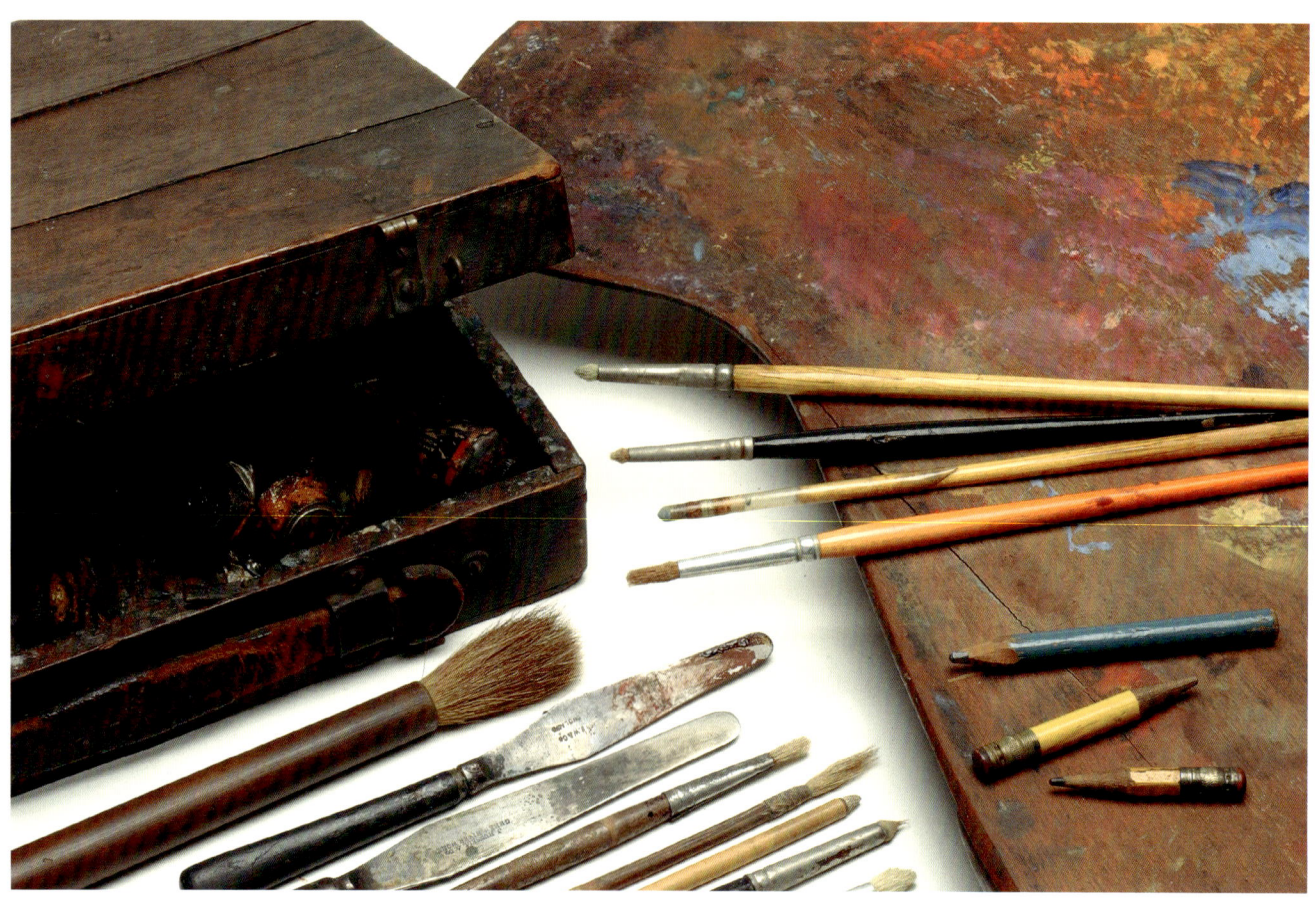

122. Weston's palette, paint box, and brushes. Harold Weston Foundation.

CHECKLIST

Kathleen V. Jameson and Nina Weston Foster

All the objects included in the exhibition are reproduced in this catalogue. Full citations to almost all references listed here are given in the bibliography (or the listed item can be located through the Harold Weston Foundation).

LANDSCAPE SKETCHES

Afternoon's Glory
1920
Oil on cardboard
7⅞ × 9½ in.
15 × 16½ in. (framed)
Signed and dated l.l. "W. 20"
St. Huberts Trust

Afternoon Shower
1920
Oil on cardboard
5⅞ × 8¼ in.
15¼ × 17¼ in. (framed)
Signed and dated l.l. "Weston 20"
Donna and Michael O'Rourke

Spring Light
1920
Oil on cardboard
6½ × 8 in.
12⅝ × 13¾ in. (framed)
Signed and dated l.r. "Weston 20"
St. Huberts Trust

Sunset over Baxter Mountain
1920
Oil on cardboard, mounted on cardboard
8 × 10 in.
14½ × 16 in. (framed)
Signed l.l. "Weston"
St. Huberts Trust

Windy Brow—Autumn (original sketch for oil on canvas *Indian Summer* [1922])
1920

Oil and pencil on cardboard
7¼ × 9½ in.
13½ × 15¾ in. (framed)
Signed and dated l.l. "W. '20"
Private Collection
EXHIBITED: Montross Galleries, New York, 1922; Adirondack Center Museum, Elizabethtown, N.Y., 1976; Atea Ring Gallery, Westport, N.Y., 1991; St. Huberts, N.Y., 1993.

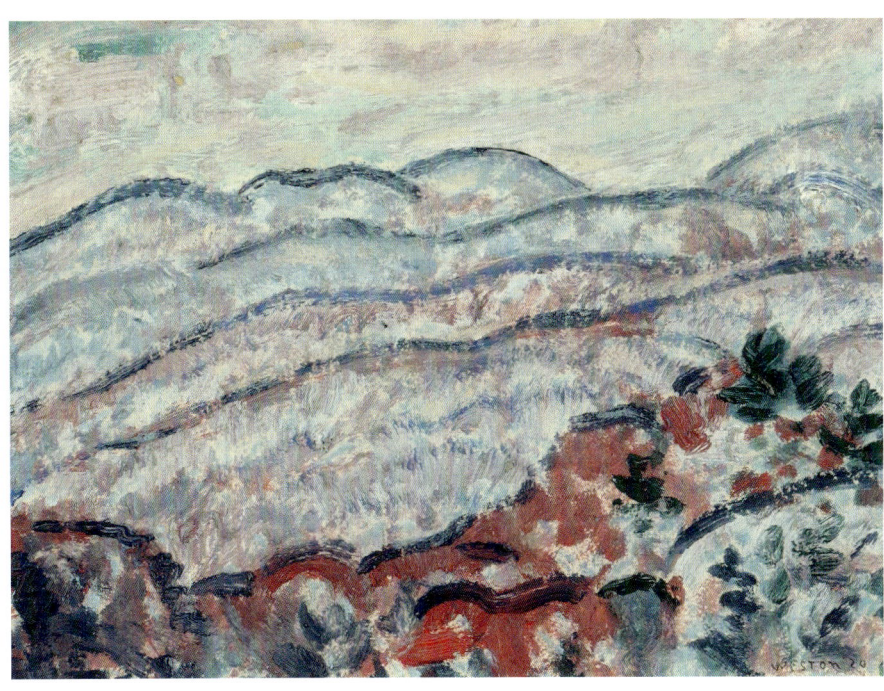

Winter Wilderness
1920
Oil on cardboard
6¼ × 8½ in.
11 × 13½ in. (framed)
Signed and dated l.r. "Weston 20"
Private Collection
EXHIBITED: St. Huberts, N.Y., 1989; Atea Ring Gallery, Westport, N.Y., 1991.

Autumn Trees
1921
Oil and pencil on cardboard
9¾ × 7½ in.
15½ × 13¼ in. (framed)
Signed and dated l.r. "Weston 1921"
St. Huberts Trust
EXHIBITED: St. Huberts, N.Y., 1989, 1993; Atea Ring Gallery, Westport, N.Y., 1991.

123. Harold Weston, *Winter Wilderness*, 1920. Private Collection.

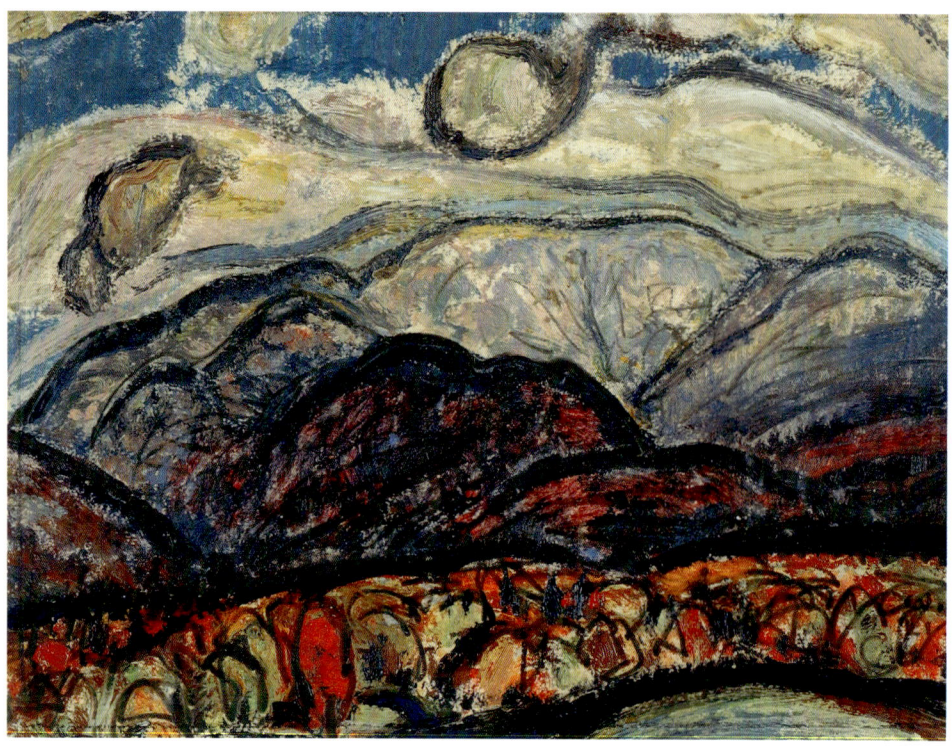

Early Snow on Giant
1921
Oil and pencil on cardboard
5⅞ × 7⅞ in.
11½ × 13½ in. (framed)
Signed l.r. "Weston"
Suzanne and Seymour Preston Jr.
EXHIBITED: St. Huberts, N.Y., 1993.

Last Glow
1921
Oil on cardboard
8 × 9 in.
14¾ × 16 in. (framed)
Signed l.r. "H. Weston"
The Adirondack Museum, Blue Mountain Lake, N.Y., 1967.199.0003
EXHIBITED: The Adirondack Museum, Blue Mountain Lake, N.Y., 1990–91, 1999–2000, 2003–2004.

Lower Ausable Lake
1921
Oil on cardboard
8½ × 12 in.
14½ × 18 in. (framed)
Signed l.r. "W"
Baird and Nancy Edmonds
EXHIBITED: Art Club of Philadelphia, 1923, no. 76; St. Huberts, N.Y., 1989.

Nubble—Coming Night
1921
Oil and pencil on cardboard
7½ × 9⅜ in.
14⅜ × 16¾ in. (framed)
Signed and dated l.l. "Weston 20," l.r. "W"
Private Collection
EXHIBITED: Montross Galleries, New York, 1922, no. 154.

On McIntyre
1922
Oil on cardboard
7½ × 9¼ in.
13¼ × 15 in. (framed)
Signed and dated l.r. "W. 22"
St. Huberts Trust

EXHIBITED: Adirondack Center Museum, Elizabethtown, N.Y., 1976.

Clouds at Sunset
1924
Oil and pencil on cardboard
7½ × 9½ in.
14¾ × 16½ in. (framed)
Signed and dated l.l. "H. Weston 24"
St. Huberts Trust
EXHIBITED: St. Huberts, N.Y., 1993.

Range Sunset
1924
Oil and pencil on cardboard
8 × 10 in.
11 × 13 in. (framed)
Signed and dated l.l. "Weston '24"
Edward Bear Miller
EXHIBITED: St. Huberts, N.Y., 1993.

LANDSCAPE PAINTINGS

Pine Tree
1920
Oil on canvas
18¾ × 14 in.
20¾ × 16½ in. (framed)
Signed l.l. "W"
Collection of Katherine Merle-Smith
EXHIBITED: D. Wigmore Fine Art, New York, 1999.
REPRODUCED: *Harold Weston, 1894–1972* (D. Wigmore Fine Art, 1999), 6.

Windy Brow—Spring (related to oil on canvas *Spring Wind* [1922])
1921
Oil on canvas
18 × 20 in. (unframed)
Signed l.l. "W"
Private Collection
EXHIBITED: Salander-O'Reilly Galleries, New York, 1984.
REPRODUCED: *Harold Weston, 1894–1972: A Selection of Landscapes* (Salander-O'Reilly Galleries, 1984), n.p.

Winter Lower Lake (also titled *Indian Head*; related to oil on canvas *Winter—Lower Ausable Lake* [1922])
1921
Oil on canvas
15 × 20 in.
16½ × 21½ in. (framed)
Signed l.r. "W"
Harold Weston Foundation
EXHIBITED: Adirondack Center Museum, Elizabethtown, N.Y., 1976; Salander-O'Reilly Galleries, New York, 1984.
REFERENCE: *Harold Weston, 1894–1972: A Selection of Landscapes* (Salander-O'Reilly Galleries, 1984), n.p.

Birch Tree (also titled *The Birch*)
1922
Oil on canvas
22 × 16 in.
24 × 18 in. (frame carved by Harold Weston)
Signed l.l. "Weston"; dated l.r. "1922"
Baird and Nancy Edmonds
EXHIBITED: Memorial Art Gallery, Rochester, N.Y., 1925, no. 97; The Adirondack Museum, Blue Mountain Lake, N.Y., 1992; Lake Placid Center for the Arts, Lake Placid, N.Y., 1994.
REPRODUCED: Mackinnon, *Adirondack Life* (Jan.–Feb. 1994), 32.
REFERENCE: *A Wild Sort of Beauty* (Adirondack Museum, 1992), 35, 55.

Clouds—Upper Ausable Lake
1922
Oil on canvas
16 × 20 in.
19¾ × 23¾ in. (frame carved by Harold Weston)
Signed l.l. "H.W."; dated l.r. "22"
Private Collection
EXHIBITED: Montross Galleries, New York, 1922, no. 6; The Adirondack Museum, Blue Mountain Lake, N.Y., 1992; Lake Placid Center for the Arts, Lake Placid, N.Y., 1992, no. 18.
REFERENCE: *A Wild Sort of Beauty* (Adirondack Museum, 1992), 35, 55.

Forest—Winter, No. 2
1922
Oil on canvas
21½ × 15¾ in.
22½ × 16¾ in. (framed)
Signed l.l. "Weston"; dated l.r. "1922"
Michael and Susan Mahoney
EXHIBITED: Montross Galleries, New York, 1922, no. 17.
REFERENCE: Tyrell, *New York World*, 12 Nov. 1922.

From Studio Window (also titled *Giant Mountain No. 2*)
1922
Oil on canvas
18 × 14 in.
22 × 18 in. (frame carved by Harold Weston)
Signed l.l. "Weston"; dated l.r. "1922"
Collection of Stephen Bennett Phillips
EXHIBITED: Montross Galleries, New York, 1922, no. 58, 1931, no. 38; Memorial Art Gallery, Rochester, N.Y., 1925, no. 94; Phillips Collection, Washington, D.C., 1932, no. 69; Adirondack Center Museum, Elizabethtown, N.Y., 1976.

Giant Mountain from Windy Brow
1922
Oil on canvas
16 × 18 in.

17½ × 19½ in. (framed)
Signed l.l. "W"; dated l.r. "'22"
Kathryn and Robert Preyer
EXHIBITED: Mount Holyoke College, South Hadley, Mass., 1975, no. 3; Adirondack Center Museum, Elizabethtown, N.Y., 1976; Philadelphia Art Alliance, 1978.
REPRODUCED: *A Retrospective Exhibition* (Mount Holyoke College, 1975), cover; "Weston Landscapes," Plattsburg (N.Y.) *Press-Republican*, 17 July 1976, 6; *Harold Weston* (Art Alliance Press, 1978), cover.

The Lumberman
1922
Oil on canvas
14 × 18 in.
19⅞ × 23¾ in. (frame carved by Harold Weston)
Signed and dated l.l. "Weston 22"
Private Collection
EXHIBITED: Montross Galleries, New York, 1922, no. 14; Kokoon Arts Klub, Cleveland, Ohio, 1923; Memorial Art Gallery, Rochester, N.Y., 1925, no. 74.
REPRODUCED: Bell, *The Younger Set* (Nov. 1922), 10.
REFERENCES: "Palette and Brush," *Town Topics*, 11 Nov. 1922; "Weston's Persian and American Views," *American Art News*, 11 Nov. 1922, sec. 2, 6; Bell, *The Younger Set* (Nov. 1922), 11.

Noonday Sun (formerly titled *Spring—Sky to Earth*)
1922
Oil on canvas
16 × 22 in.
19¾ × 25¾ in. (frame carved by Harold Weston)
Signed l.l. "HW"
The Adirondack Museum, Blue Mountain Lake, N.Y., 1989.075.0001
EXHIBITED: Memorial Art Gallery, Rochester, N.Y., 1925, no. 93; Crosslands, Kennett Square, Pa., 1986; The Adirondack Museum, Blue Mountain Lake, N.Y., 1997.
REPRODUCED: Kannewisher, "Would Add Richness" (Jan. 1925); Mackinnon, *Adirondack Life* (Jan.–Feb. 1994), 30; Welsh, *American Art Review* (Aug. 1997), 82.

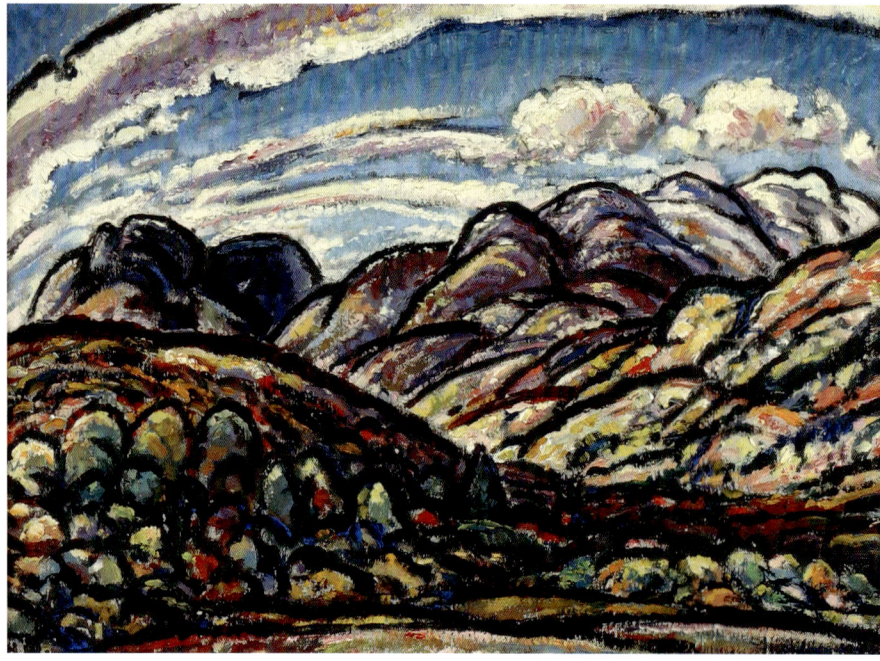

Resigonia and Gothics—Autumn (also titled *Autumn Snow, Resigonia*)
1922
Oil on canvas
16 × 22 in.
21 × 27 in. (framed)
Signed l.l. "HW"
Collection of Mr. and Mrs. William H. B. Hamill
EXHIBITED: Montross Galleries, New York, 1922 (not listed); Lake Placid Center for the Arts, Lake Placid, N.Y., 1994.

Sunrise from Marcy
1922
Oil on canvas
16 × 22 in.
18½ × 24½ in. (framed)
Signed l.l. "HW"
Private Collection
EXHIBITED: Montross Galleries, New York, 1922 (not listed).

Wilderness—Marcy, Dvôrák New World Symphony, Largo
1922
Oil on canvas
18 × 20 in.

22 × 24 in. (framed, approx.)
Signed l.l. "W."
Museum of Fine Arts, Boston. Robert Jordan Fund, 1999.504
EXHIBITED: Montross Galleries, New York, 1922, no. 22; Memorial Art Gallery, Rochester, N.Y., 1925, no. 76; Salander-O'Reilly Galleries, New York, 1984; Bissell House, Lakeville, Conn., 1993; Lake Placid Center for the Arts, Lake Placid, N.Y., 1994; Atea Ring Gallery, Westport, N.Y., 1999.
REPRODUCED: *Harold Weston, 1894–1972: A Selection of Landscapes* (Salander-O'Reilly Galleries, 1984), n.p.; *Harold Weston: Beyond the Known* (Lake Placid Center for the Arts, 1994), n.p.; Moody, "The Arts," 5 Aug. 1994.
REFERENCES: "Palette and Brush," *Town Topics*, 11 Nov. 1922; McBride, *New York Herald*, 12 Nov. 1922, sec. 7, 7; Tyrell, *New York World*, 12 Nov. 1922; R. F., *Christian Science Monitor*, 17 Nov. 1922, 8; Weiss, *Rochester (N.Y.) Herald*, 25 Jan. 1925, 11.

Winds—Upper Ausable Lake
1922
Oil on canvas
16 × 22 in.

20⅞ × 26⅞ in. (frame carved by Harold Weston)
Signed l.l. "Weston"; dated l.r. "1922"
The Phillips Collection, Washington, D.C. Gift of Mrs. Harold Weston, 1981
EXHIBITED: Montross Galleries, New York, 1922, no. 53; Phillips Collection, Washington, D.C., 1999.
REPRODUCED: *Phillips Collection* (Phillips Collection, 1985), 249.
REFERENCE: Passantino, ed., *Eye of Duncan Phillips* (Phillips Collection and Yale Univ. Press, 1999), 483.

Winter Hill
1922
Oil on canvas
20 × 16 in.
25 × 20¾ in. (frame carved by Harold Weston)
Signed and dated l.l. "Weston 22"
Private Collection

LANDSCAPE NUDES

Self-Portrait (also titled *Self-Portrait with Pipe*)
1923
Oil on canvas

15½ × 13¼ in.

20 × 18¼ in. (frame carved by Harold Weston)

Signed and dated l.l. "Weston '23"

Charles and Marietta Weston

EXHIBITED: Kokoon Arts Klub, Cleveland, Ohio, 1923; Pennsylvania Academy of the Fine Arts, Philadelphia, 1924, no. 216; Memorial Art Gallery, Rochester, N.Y., 1925, no. 96; Philadelphia Art Alliance, 1978 (not listed); Adirondack Center Museum, Elizabethtown, N.Y., 1976.

REPRODUCED: *Philadelphia Art Alliance* (quarterly calendar, Sept.–Dec. 1978), cover.

REFERENCE: Karr, *Cleveland Sunday News-Leader*, 22 Apr. 1923, 8.

Mountain Nude
1924
Oil on canvas
21⅞ × 25¾ in.
23¼ × 27 (framed)
Signed and dated u.r. "HW 24"
Collection of Springfield Art Museum, Springfield, Mo., S.A.M. 1977.19
EXHIBITED: Springfield Art Museum, Springfield, Mo., 1977.
REPRODUCED: *Accessions/1976–77* (Springfield Art Museum, 1977), 5.

The Studio Stove
1924
Oil on canvas
22½ × 18 in.
30½ × 26½ in. (framed)
Signed l.l. "Weston"
D. Wigmore Fine Art, New York
EXHIBITED: Memorial Art Gallery, Rochester, N.Y., 1925, no. 83; D. Wigmore Fine Art, New York, 1999.
REPRODUCED: *Harold Weston, 1894–1972* (D. Wigmore Fine Art, 1999), 8.

Torso (also titled *Lap Nude*)
1924
Oil on canvas
16 × 20 in.
21¾ × 25¾ in. (framed)
Signed and dated u.r. "Weston 24"
Collection of Burns H. and Marta C. Weston
EXHIBITED: Montross Galleries, New York, 1927, no. 24 (listed but not exhib-

ited), 1932, no. 32; San Francisco Museum of Art, 1939 (traveled to Portland, Ore., Seattle, Wash., and Butte, Mont., in 1940); Bissell House, Lakeville, Conn., 1993; Atea Ring Gallery, Westport, N.Y., 1997.

REPRODUCED: Weston, *Freedom in the Wilds* (Adirondack Trail Improvement Society, 1971), 145.

Narcissus in Bowl
1925
Oil on canvas
20 × 18 in.
22½ × 20½ in. (frame carved by Harold Weston)
Signed and dated l.r. "HW 25"
Harold Weston Foundation
EXHIBITED: Bissell House, Lakeville, Conn., 1993; Lake Placid Center for the Arts, Lake Placid, N.Y., 1994.

Sleeping Nude
1925
Oil on canvas
24 × 20 in.
31⅛ × 27 in. (framed)
Signed l.l. "Weston"
Wichita Art Museum, Wichita, Kans. Gift of Dr. Martin H. Bush, 1974.11
EXHIBITED: Edwin A. Ulrich Museum of Art, Wichita, Kans., 1980.

Torso Prone
1925
Oil on canvas
20 × 26½ in.
20¾ × 27¾ in. (framed)
Signed and dated u.l. "H. Weston '25"
Private Collection

Headland
1925, 1931
Oil on canvas
18 × 20 in.
19 × 21 in. (framed)
Signed l.r. "Weston"
Private Collection
REPRODUCED: Mackinnon, *Adirondack Life* (Jan.–Feb. 1994), 33.

FRANCE

Green Hat (also titled *Eye in a Green Hat*, *Girl with Green Hat*, and *Girl in Green Hat*)

1927
Oil on canvas
19⅞ × 25⅜ in.
29¾ × 35½ in. (framed)
Signed and dated u.l. "Weston '27"
San Francisco Museum of Modern Art. Gift of the Ladies' Auxiliary of the Palace of Fine Arts, 39.129
EXHIBITED: Montross Galleries, New York, 1928, no. 31; Little Gallery of Contemporary Art, Philadelphia, 1930; Boyer Galleries, New York, 1937, no. 14; Golden Gate International Exposition (won third prize in American painting), San Francisco, 1939; San Francisco Museum of Art, 1939 (traveled to Portland, Oreg., Seattle, Wash., and Butte, Mont., in 1940); Tacoma Art League, Tacoma, Wash., 1948; San Francisco Theological Seminary, 1965.

REPRODUCED: "News and Comment," *Magazine of Art* (Sept. 1939), 536; Weston, *Freedom in the Wilds* (Adirondack Trail Improvement Society, 1971), 157.

REFERENCES: J. K., *New York Times*, 16 Dec. 1928, sec. 10, pt. 2, 14; "News and Views," *Brooklyn Daily Eagle*, 16 Dec. 1928, E7; "Little Gallery Opens," *Philadelphia Inquirer*, 2 Nov. 1930; Devree, *New York Times*, 9 July 1939, sec. 10, 12; Frankenstein, *San Francisco Chronicle*, 30 July 1939, 20; "Bring Work of Weston," *Tacoma (Wash.) News Tribune*, 13 Sept. 1939; "New Art Exhibit," *Tacoma (Wash.) Times*, 9 Nov. 1939, 12; Jones, *The Oregonian*, 17 Dec. 1939; "Weston Gives Up Painting," *Syracuse (N.Y.) Post-Standard*, 11 May 1941; *Magazine of Art* (Nov. 1946), San Francisco sec., vi; Mackinnon, *Adirondack Life* (Jan.–Feb. 1994), 34.

Man Looking
1927
Oil on canvas
22 × 13½ in.
25¼ × 17 in. (framed)
Signed u.l. "W"
The Adirondack Museum, Blue Mountain Lake, N.Y., 2003.005.0002
EXHIBITED: Montross Galleries, New York, 1927, no. 27; Galerie Joseph Billiet & Co., Paris, 1927; Little Gallery of Contemporary Art, Philadelphia, 1930; Mellon Galleries, Philadelphia, 1933, no. 61; Norfolk Museum of Arts and

Sciences (now the Chrysler Museum of Art), Norfolk, Va., 1969, no. 152.

REPRODUCED: *Harold Weston* (Galerie Joseph Billiet & Co., 1927), n.p.; "Weston," *La Semaine à Paris*, 25 July–3 Aug. 1927, 51; *Alfred Khouri Memorial Collection*, vol. 2 (Norfolk Museum of Arts and Sciences, 1969), no. 152.

REFERENCES: "Who's Who Abroad," *Chicago Tribune*, Paris ed., 7 July 1926, 4; McBride, *New York Sun*, 22 Oct. 1927, 5; "Exhibited in the New York Galleries," *New York Times*, 23 Oct. 1927, sec. 8, 12; "1-Man Show," *New York American*, 23 Oct. 1927; Grafly, *Philadelphia Public Ledger*, 17 Dec. 1933, 12.

THE 1930S

The Arena
1930
Oil on canvas
18 × 24 in.
22¾ × 28¾ in. (framed)
Signed and dated l.l. "W 30"
The Phillips Collection, Washington, D.C.

EXHIBITED: Montross Galleries, New York, 1930, no. 6; Phillips Collection, Washington, D.C., 1931, no. 64, 1931, no. 9, 1932, no. 83, 1976; Choate School, Wallingford, Conn., 1933; Corcoran Art Gallery, Washington, D.C., 1956; Mount Holyoke College, South Hadley, Mass., 1975, no. 22.

REPRODUCED: Breuning, *New York Evening Post*, 16 Nov. 1930; Sayre, *International Studio* (Dec. 1930), 106; *Magazine of Art* (June 1939), frontispiece; Phillips, *The Artist Sees Differently* (E. Weyhe and Phillips Memorial Gallery, 1931), plate 229; Buchalter, *Washington Daily News*, 9 Jan. 1932, 11; Phillips, *Phillips Collection Catalogue* (Phillips Collection, 1952), 108, 225; *Phillips Collection* (Phillips Collection, 1985), 246; *The Cat Postcard Book* (Running Press, 1987).

REFERENCES: *Harold Weston Exhibition* (Montross Galleries, 1930); Phillips, *The Artist Sees Differently* (Phillips Collection, 1931), 139.

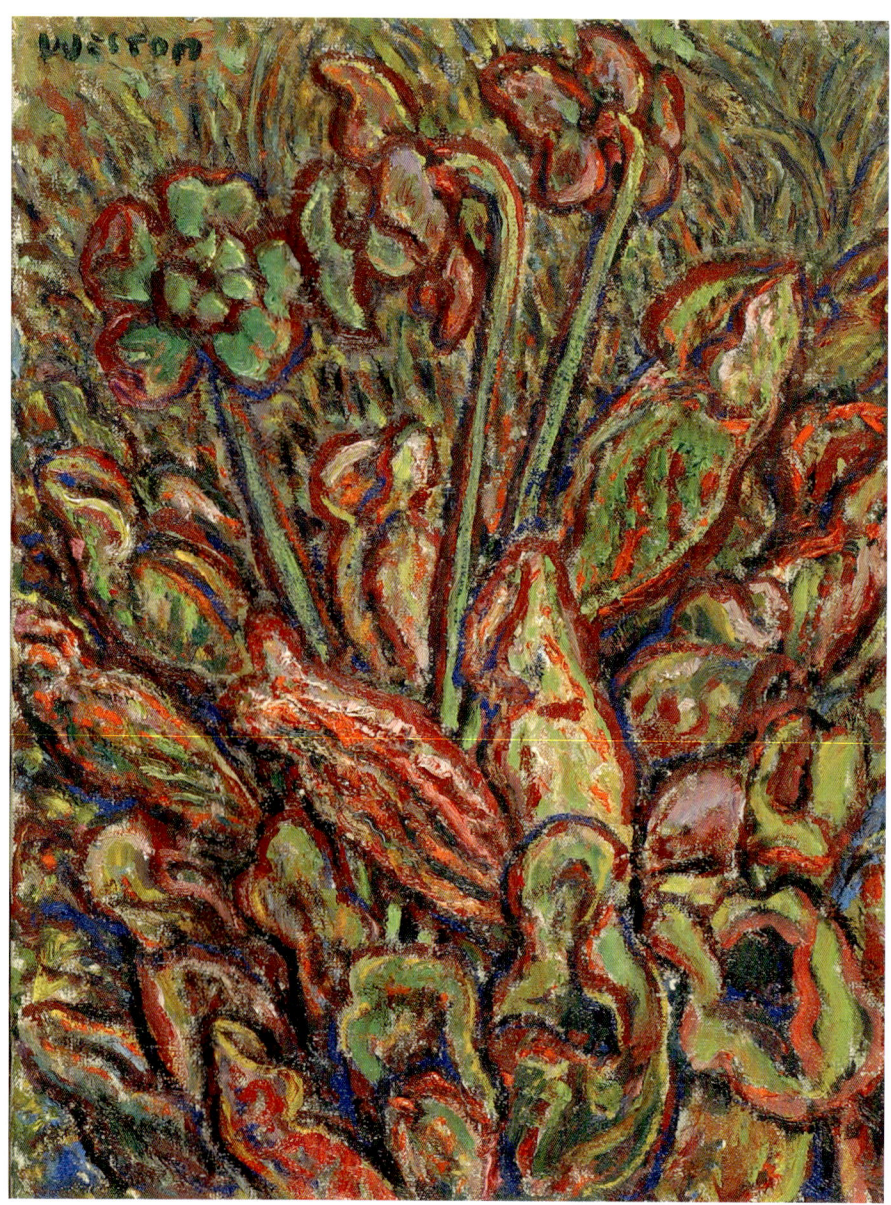

Pitcher Plant
1930–32
Oil on canvas
18 × 14 in.
18¾ × 14¾ in. (framed)
Signed u.l. "Weston"
Private Collection

126. Harold Weston, *Pitcher Plant*, 1930–32. Private Collection.

Palette on Couch
1931
Oil on canvas
22⅛ × 16⅛ in.
26 × 20 in. (frame carved by Harold
    Weston)
Signed u.r. "Weston"
Bill Sudduth
EXHIBITED: Montross Galleries, New
    York, 1932, no. 19; Bissell House,
    Lakeville, Conn., 1993; Dahl Arts Cen-
    ter, Rapid City, S.D., 2001, no. 2.
REFERENCES: Jewell, *Harold Weston* (Mon-
    tross Galleries, 1932), n.p.; "Art Roster,"
    New York Times, 2 Dec. 1932, 24; *New
    York Times*, 4 Dec. 1932, sec. 9, 8.

Profile
1931, 1933
Oil on canvas
20 × 22 in.
22 × 24 in. (framed)
Signed l.l. "Weston"
Private Collection
EXHIBITED: Montross Galleries, New
    York, 1931, no. 27; Phillips Collection,
    Washington, D.C., 1932, no. 65; Mellon
    Galleries, Philadelphia, 1933, no. 24;
    San Francisco Museum of Art, 1939
    (traveled to Portland, Oreg., Seattle,
    Wash., and Butte, Mont., in 1940); Lake
    Placid Center for the Arts, Lake Placid,
    N.Y., 1994; Atea Ring Gallery, West-
    port, N.Y., 1999, 2000.
REFERENCES: Burrows, *New York Herald
    Tribune*, 22 Nov. 1931, sec. 7, 9; *Harold
    Weston* (Mellon Galleries, 1933), n.p.;
    Moody, "The Arts," 5 Aug. 1994; Passan-
    tino, ed., *The Eye of Duncan Phillips*
    (Phillips Collection and Yale Univ.
    Press, 1999), 486 n. 26.

Rhubarb in Bud
1931
Oil on canvas
29 × 19½ in.
35 × 29 in. (framed)
Signed l.l. "Weston"
Private Collection
EXHIBITED: Montross Galleries, New
    York, 1931, no. 18; Atea Ring Gallery,
    Westport, N.Y., 1999.
REFERENCES: McBride, *New York Sun*, 21
    Nov. 1931, 12; [Foster], *Antiques and the
    Arts Weekly*, 3 Sept. 1999, 101.

Seated Back Nude (related to charcoal on
    paper *Base for Oil "Greco"* [1925] and oil
    on canvas *Greco* [1925, 1934, 1939])
1932
Gouache on brown paper
12 × 10 in.
18½ × 16 in. (framed)
Signed and dated l.l. "Weston 32"
Harold Weston Foundation
EXHIBITED: Lake Placid Center for the
    Arts, Lake Placid, N.Y., 1994.
REPRODUCED: *Harold Weston: Beyond the
    Known* (Lake Placid Center for the Arts,
    1994), n.p.
REFERENCE: Foster, *Lake Placid News*, 20
    July 1994, 12.

Squash Enthroned
1932
Oil on canvas
16 × 20 in.
20¾ × 24¾ in. (framed)
Signed l.r. "Weston"
Private Collection
EXHIBITED: Boyer Galleries, New York,
    1939, no. 17; San Francisco Museum of
    Art, 1939 (traveled to Portland, Oreg.,
    Seattle, Wash., and Butte, Mont., in
    1940); Riverside Museum, New York,
    1958; Gross-McCleaf Gallery, Philadel-
    phia, 1979; Lake Placid Center for the
    Arts, Lake Placid, N.Y., 1994.
REPRODUCED: *Harold Weston: Beyond the
    Known* (Lake Placid Center for the Arts,
    1994), n.p.
REFERENCES: Devree, *New York Times*, 8
    Jan. 1939, sec. 10, 10; Pillsbury, "Pre-
    Hitler Paintings Due in German
    Exhibit," *Portland Oregonian*, 31 Dec.
    1939, sec. 4, 4.

Horizons
1934
Oil on canvas
20 × 26 in.
21⅛ × 27⅛ in. (framed)
Signed l.l. "Weston"
Private Collection
EXHIBITED: Boyer Galleries, Philadelphia,
    1935, no. 18; New Gallery, Wellfleet,
    Mass., 1935, no. 13; Eighth Street
    Gallery, New York, 1935, no. 5.
REPRODUCED: *Exhibition: Recent Work,
    1935. Harold Weston* (Eighth Street
    Gallery, 1935), cover; "Solid, Rugged
    Things," *Art Digest*, 15 March 1935, 23.

REFERENCES: Grafly, *Philadelphia Record*, 6
    Jan. 1935, sec. 4, 12; Upton, *New York
    Sun*, 15 Mar. 1935, 25; Mumford, *New
    Yorker*, 23 Mar. 1935.

My Snow Shoes
1934
Oil on canvas
38 × 26⅛ in.
46½ × 34¾ in. (artist-designed frame)
Signed l.l. "Weston"
The Phillips Collection, Washington, D.C.
EXHIBITED: Whitney Museum of Ameri-
    can Art, New York, 1934–35, no. 75
    (Whitney Biennial); Dorothy Paris
    Gallery, New York, 1935; City Art
    Museum, St. Louis, Mo., 1936, no. 53;
    Studio House, Washington, D.C., 1936;
    Boyer Galleries, Philadelphia, 1936, no.
    4; Phillips Collection, Washington,
    D.C., 1939, 1976, 1997; Corcoran
    Gallery of Art, Washington, D.C., 1956;
    Mount Holyoke College, South Hadley,
    Mass., 1975, no. 27.
REPRODUCED: Jewell, *New York Times*, 2
    Dec. 1934, sec. 10, 9; *Oil Paintings and
    Water Colors: Harold Weston* (Boyer Gal-
    leries, 1936), cover; *Art and Artists of
    Today* (June–July 1938), back cover;
    Hall, *Eyes on America* (Studio Publica-
    tions, [1939]), 141; Weston, *Freedom in
    the Wilds* (Adirondack Trail Improve-
    ment Society, 1971), 111; Burton, *Gar-
    den City (N.Y.) Newsday*, 18 Dec. 1971,
    Magazine sec., 16W; Weston, *Adiron-
    dack Life* (winter 1972), 35; Bury, *Oil
    Painting of Today* (The Studio Publica-
    tions, 1975), 83; *Phillips Collection*
    (Phillips Collection, 1985), 248; Mack-
    innon, *Adirondack Life* (Jan.–Feb. 1994),
    cover; Phillips, *Twentieth-Century Still-Life
    Painting* (Phillips Collection, 1997), 112.
REFERENCES: Lowrie, *Philadelphia Evening
    Public Ledger*, 7 Sept. 1934, 12; Mechlin,
    Washington, D.C., Evening Star, 29 Feb.
    1936, B3; Bonte, *Philadelphia Inquirer*, 22
    Nov. 1936, Society sec., 17; "Oils and
    Water Colors Exhibited," *Washington,
    D.C., Sunday Star*, 23 Apr. 1939, pt. 5;
    Watson, *Washington Post*, 23 Apr. 1939,
    sec. 6, 6; "Weston Outdoors," *Art Digest*,
    15 Nov. 1940, 11; Phillips, *Phillips Collec-
    tion* (Phillips Collection, 1952), 109;
    Phillips, *Twentieth-Century Still-Life Paint-
    ing* (Phillips Collection, 1997), 14, 18,
    111, 112.

Snow on Balsams
1934
Oil on canvas
24 × 16⅛ in.
25½ × 17¾ in. (framed)
Signed l.r. "Weston"
Syracuse University Art Collection,
    1972.35
EXHIBITED: Mount Holyoke College,
    South Hadley, Mass., 1975, no. 28.

Gothics from Sawtooth
1935
Watercolor on paper
9 × 13⅜ in.
15⅞ × 20 in. (framed)
Signed and dated l.r. "Weston '35"
Private Collection
EXHIBITED: Lake Placid Center for the
    Arts, Lake Placid, N.Y., 1994.

REALISM

Upstate Farm (also titled *Winter Farm*)
1939
Watercolor and gouache on orange paper
12½ × 15½ in.
19¾ × 22 in. (framed)
Signed and dated l.l. "Weston 39"
Harold Weston Foundation
EXHIBITED: Ferargil Galleries, New York,
    1940, no. 27; Fieldston Galleries,
    Riverdale, N.Y., 1940, no. 37; D. Wig-
    more Fine Art, New York, 1999.
REFERENCE: "Weston Outdoors," *Art
    Digest*, 15 Nov. 1940, 11.

Adirondacks in Winter
1940
Watercolor on paper
10 × 14 in.
17 × 20½ in. (framed)
Signed and dated l.l. "Weston 40"
Private Collection
EXHIBITED: D. Wigmore Fine Art, New
    York, 1999.

North Wind on East Hill
1940
Watercolor on paper
11½ × 19½ in.
18½ × 26 in. (framed)

Signed and dated l.l. "Weston 40"
Collection of Jackie Day and David
    Hansen
EXHIBITED: Lake Placid Center for the
    Arts, Lake Placid, N.Y., 1994.

Pheasant
1940
Gouache on paper
10½ × 18½ in.
19³⁄₁₆ × 27⅛ in. (framed)
Signed and dated l.l. "Weston '40"
Collection of Jonathan and Jennifer Ring
EXHIBITED: Ferargil Galleries, New York,
    1940, no. 5; Atea Ring Gallery, West-
    port, N.Y., 1992, 1997, 2000; Lake
    Placid Center for the Arts, Lake Placid,
    N.Y., 1994.
REFERENCES: Burrows, *New York Herald
    Tribune*, 19 Nov. 1940, sec. 6, 8; Caudell,
    Plattsburgh (N.Y.) Press-Republican, 4 Sept.
    1997, B6.

Chapel Pond
1947
Gouache on gray paper
18¾ × 11 in.
25½ × 17 in. (framed)
Signed and dated l.l. "Weston '47"
Private Collection
EXHIBITED: Mount Holyoke College,
    South Hadley, Mass., 1975, no. 46.

Copper Pond
1947
Watercolor on paper
9¾ × 13½ in.
15½ × 19¼ in. (framed)
Signed and dated l.l. "Weston '47"
Private Collection

Chapel Pond—Autumn
1949
Watercolor and gouache on paper
19¼ × 14¼ in.
27¼ × 21½ in. (framed)
Signed and dated l.l. "Weston 1949"
Private Collection

ABSTRACTION

Fungus
ca. 1959
Oil on canvas
18 × 24 in.
19 × 25 in. (framed)
Signed l.l. "Weston"
Sarah Hamill
EXHIBITED: D. Wigmore Fine Art, New
    York, 1999.
REPRODUCED: *Harold Weston, 1894–1972*
    (D. Wigmore Fine Art, 1999), 9.

Silent Barriers
1961
Watercolor on paper
19½ × 25½ in.
24 × 30 in. (framed)
Signed l.l. "Weston"
Laura Weston
EXHIBITED: St. Huberts, N.Y., 1964.

Morning Wind
1964
Gouache on sage green paper
24 × 18 in.
30¼ × 24¼ in. (framed)
Signed l.l. "Weston"
Harold Weston Foundation

Spring Ritual
1964
Gouache on gray paper
11¾ × 20 in.
20 × 28½ in. (framed)
Signed l.r. "Weston"
Private Collection
EXHIBITED: St. Huberts, N.Y., 1965.

Wind-Swept
1964
Watercolor on tan paper
25¼ × 19½ in.
31⅞ × 25⅞ in. (framed)
Signed l.l. "Weston"
C. Corscaden Galbraith
EXHIBITED: St. Huberts, N.Y., 1964.

Wood Script
1967
Oil on canvas
22 × 48 in.

23 × 49 in. (framed)
Signed l.l. "Weston"
Private Collection
EXHIBITED: Adirondack Center Museum, Elizabethtown, N.Y., 1976.

THE STONE SERIES

Conference (Stone Series No. 3)
1968
Gouache on brown paper
20 × 26 in.
27½ × 33 in. (framed)
Signed l.l. "Weston"
Harold Weston Foundation, courtesy of the Atea Ring Gallery, Westport, N.Y.
EXHIBITED: Philadelphia Art Alliance, 1978; Harold Weston Art Trust, New York, 1990; Atea Ring Gallery, Westport, N.Y., 1992; Bissell House, Lakeville, Conn., 1993.
REPRODUCED: *Harold Weston* (Art Alliance Press, 1978), n.p.; *Early Figures and the Stone Series* (privately printed, 1990), n.p.

Blue Beyond Blues (Stone Series No. 17)
1968
Gouache on blue paper

24¾ × 18¾ in.
40¾ × 30¾ in. (framed)
Signed l.l. "Weston"
The Phillips Collection, Washington, D.C.
EXHIBITED: Phillips Collection, Washington, D.C., 1969, 1991.
REPRODUCED: *Phillips Collection* (Phillips Collection, 1985), 247; Mackinnon, *Adirondack Life* (Jan.–Feb. 1994), 34.
REFERENCES: *Loan Exhibition of Contemporary Paintings* (Phillips Collection, 1969), n.p.; Passantino, ed., *The Eye of Duncan Phillips* (Phillips Collection and Yale Univ. Press, 1999), 483.

Tibetan Dawn (Stone Series No. 38)
1969
Gouache on rose paper
26 × 20⅜ in.
35½ × 29½ in. (framed)
Signed l.r. "Weston"
Harold Weston Foundation, courtesy of Platt Fine Art, Chicago
EXHIBITED: Phillips Collection, Washington, D.C., 1982, no. 13; Virginia Polytechnic Institute, Blacksburg, Va., 1983, no. 13; Lake Placid Center for the Arts, Lake Placid, N.Y., 1983, no. 13; Harold

Weston Art Trust, New York, 1990; Atea Ring Gallery, Westport, N.Y., 1992; Bissell House, Lakeville, Conn., 1993.
REFERENCE: *Harold Weston: The Stone Series, 1968–1972* (Phillips Collection, 1982), n.p.

Spring (Stone Series No. 61)
1970
Gouache on gray paper
20 × 25 in.
27 × 32½ in. (framed)
Signed l.r. "Weston"
Harold Weston Foundation
EXHIBITED: Harold Weston Art Trust, New York, 1990.

Suspense (Stone Series No. 62)
1970
Gouache on brown paper
20 × 26 in.
27 × 33 in. (framed)
Signed l.l. "W."
Harold Weston Foundation

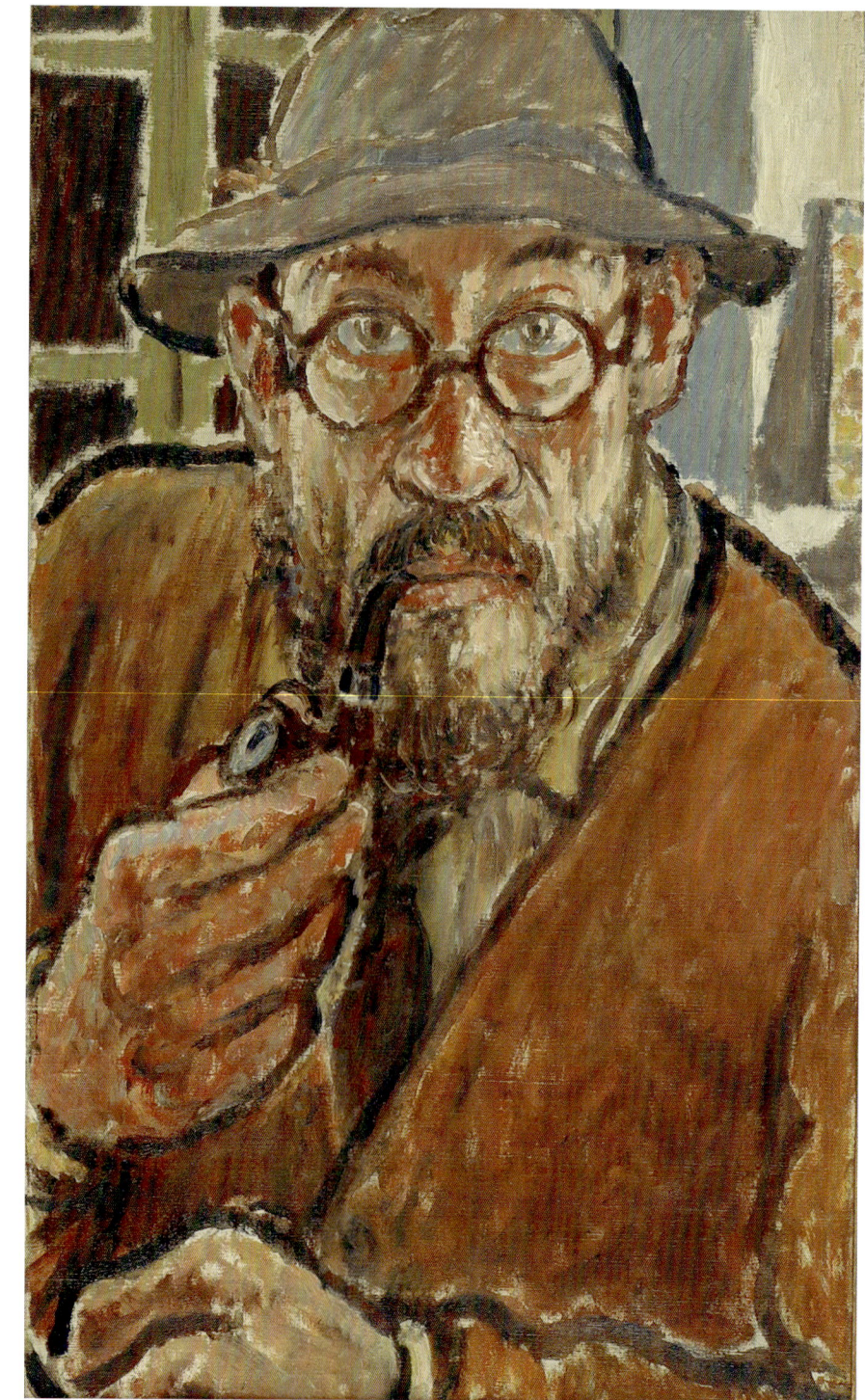

127. Harold Weston, *Man Looking*, 1927. The Adirondack Museum, Blue Mountain Lake, N.Y., 2003.5.2.

CHRONOLOGY

1894 14 February, born in Merion, Pa.

1909–10 Traveled around Europe and attended school in Lausanne, Switzerland, and Hannover, Germany.

1911 Struck by infantile paralysis (polio) in left leg.

1912–16 Attended Harvard University, graduated magna cum laude in Fine Arts, Phi Beta Kappa, editor of *The Lampoon.*

1914 Attended Summer School of Graphic Arts in Ogonquit, Maine.

1916–19 Attached to the British army as a YMCA volunteer in India and Mesopotamia (now Iraq). Organized Baghdad Art Club in 1917. Appointed Official Painter for the British Army in 1918. Returned to the United States through the Far East.

1920 Built one-room studio in St. Huberts, N.Y.

1922 Held first one-person exhibition at Montross Galleries, New York City.

1923 12 May, married Faith Borton.

1926–30 Lived in France (Pyrenees and Paris).

1930 Returned to New York City, then later to St. Huberts.

1936–38 Commissioned by Treasury Relief Art Project to paint murals for the General Services Administration Building in Washington, D.C.

1939 Won prize in American painting in the Golden Gate International Exposition in San Francisco.

1940–47 Organized and led the Committee to Defend America by Aiding the Allies in Essex County, N.Y., in 1940–41; the Reconstruction Service Committee in Washington, D.C., in 1942–43; and Food for Freedom in Washington, D.C., in 1943–47.

1948–68 Served as secretary of the Adirondack Trail Improvement Society, St. Huberts, N.Y.

1949–52 Painted *Building the United Nations.*

1953–57 President of the Federation of Modern Painters and Sculptors (charter member from 1940 to 1972).

1954 Moved winter home to Greenwich Village, New York City.

1954–70 Founding member, vice president, and president of the National Council on Arts and Government.

1954–67 Early organizer and later president of the International Association of Plastic Arts (later the International Association of Arts [IAA]), an affiliate of the United Nations Educational, Scientific, and Cultural Organization (UNESCO). President of the U.S. Committee of the IAA, 1961–67.

1957–58 December–January, painted in Rhodes, Greece.

1961–65 Advisor to the New York State Council for the Arts.

1963 Elected Life Fellow of the World Academy of Art and Science as a "distinguished artist with worldwide humanitarian achievements."

1964 Received Annual Award from the American Society of Contemporary Artists. (Honorary memberships included Society of American Mural Painters, Society of American Graphic Artists, National Educational Theatre Technology, and U.S. Institute of Theatre Technology.)

1968–72 Painted the Stone Series.

1971 Published *Freedom in the Wilds: A Saga of the Adirondacks.*

1972 10 April, died in New York City.

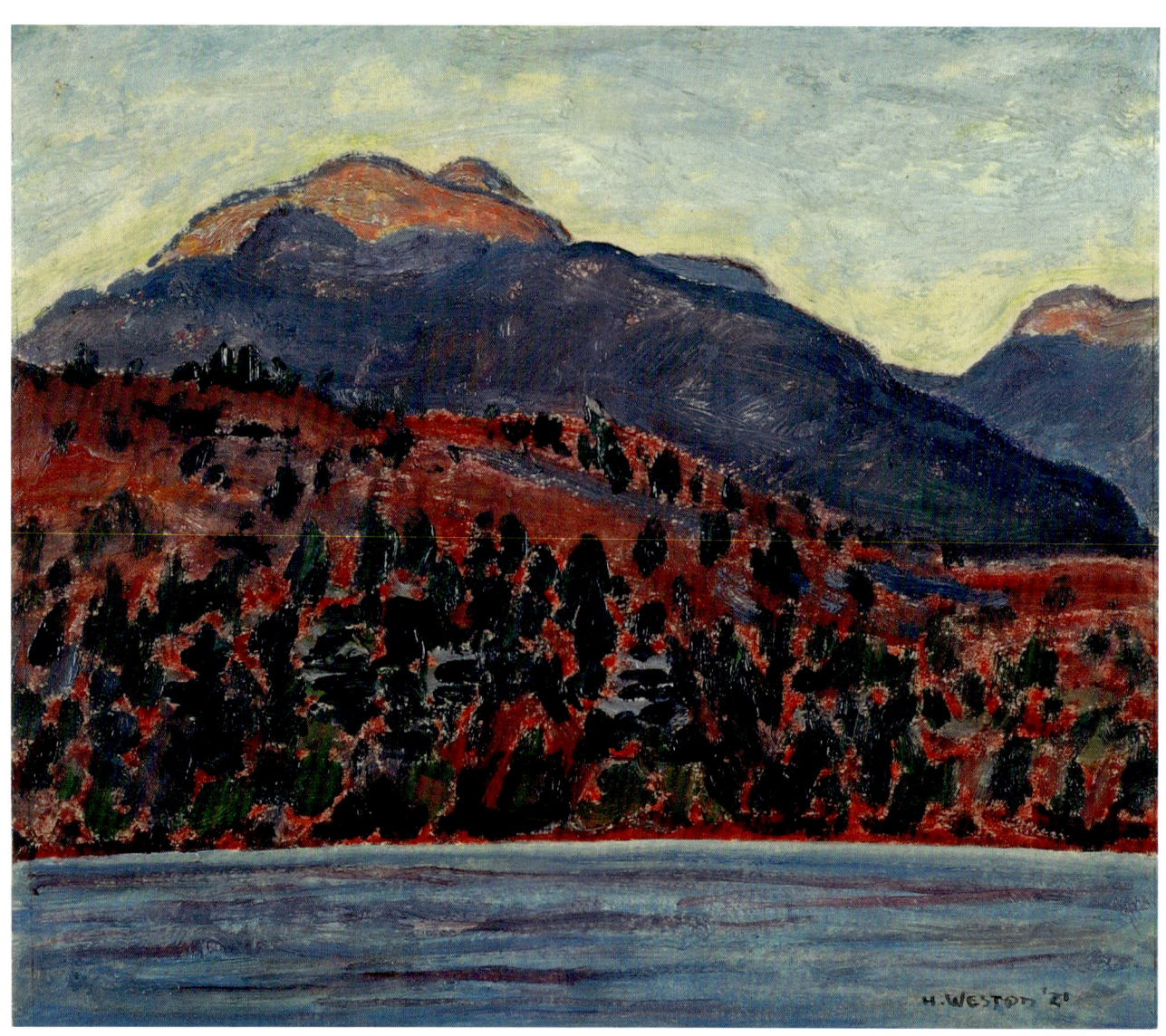

128. Harold Weston, *Last Glow*, 1921. The Adirondack Museum, Blue Mountain Lake, N.Y., 1967.199.3.

EXHIBITIONS

ONE-PERSON EXHIBITIONS

1922   Exhibition of Paintings: Adirondack Mountains and Persia by Harold F. Weston. Montross Galleries, New York. 8–25 Nov. Catalogue.

1923   Kokoon Arts Klub, Cleveland, Ohio. Apr.

1925   Paintings by Harold Weston, Memorial Art Gallery. Rochester, N.Y. Jan.–Feb.

1927   Harold Weston. Galerie Joseph Billiet & Co., Paris. 8–23 July. Catalogue.

Harold Weston: Exhibition of Pictures. Montross Galleries, New York. 17–29 Oct. Catalogue.

1928   Exhibition: Paintings in Oil and Water Color, Etchings and Lithographs by Harold Weston. Montross Galleries, New York. 10–29 Dec. Catalogue.

1929   Philadelphia Art Alliance. 20 Feb.–4 Mar.

1930   An Exhibition of Recent Paintings by Harold Weston. Phillips Memorial Gallery, Washington, D.C. 1–30 Apr.

Harold Weston Exhibition: Paintings—Water Colors—Etchings. Montross Galleries, New York. 10–29 Nov. Catalogue.

Paintings by John Steuart Curry, Louis Ritman, and Harold Weston. Art Institute of Chicago. 23 Dec.–18 Jan. 1931. Catalogue.

1931   Paintings by Harold Weston. City Art Museum, St. Louis. 1–15 Mar.

Recent Paintings by Harold Weston. Phillips Memorial Gallery, Washington, D.C. 1–31 Mar. Catalogue.

Harold Weston. Phillips Memorial Gallery, Washington, D.C. 5 Apr.–3 May. Catalogue.

Harold Weston: Exhibition of Recent Paintings. Montross Galleries, New York. 16–28 Nov. Catalogue.

1932   Paintings by Harold Weston: 1921–1931. Phillips Memorial Gallery, Washington, D.C. Jan. Catalogue.

Harold Weston: Exhibition of Recent Paintings. Montross Galleries, New York. 28 Nov.–10 Dec. Catalogue.

1933   Harold Weston. Mellon Galleries, Philadelphia. 16 Nov.–5 Dec. Catalogue.

Sarah Lawrence College, Bronxville, N.Y. Dates unknown.

1935   Recent Paintings by Harold Weston. Boyer Galleries, Philadelphia. 4–24 Jan. Catalogue.

Exhibition: Recent Work, 1935. Harold Weston. Eighth Street Gallery, New York. 11–30 Mar. Catalogue.

1936   Paintings by Harold Weston. Studio House, Washington, D.C. 24 Feb.–7 Mar. Catalogue.

J. B. Speed Art Museum, Louisville, Ky. 29 Mar.–12 Apr.

Oil Paintings and Water Colors: Harold Weston. Boyer Galleries, Philadelphia. 18 Nov.–8 Dec. Catalogue.

1939   Harold Weston. Phillips Memorial Gallery, Washington, D.C. 16 Apr.–7 May.

Painting—Harold Weston. San Francisco Museum of Art. 20 July–9 Aug.

Tacoma Art Association, Tacoma, Wash. 12 Nov.–10 Dec.

Exhibition of Paintings by Harold Weston. Greenwich Library, Greenwich, Conn. 11–31 Dec.

Eighteen Paintings by Harold Weston. Portland Art Museum, Portland, Oreg. 15 Dec.–Jan. 1940.

1940   Harold Weston: Exhibition of Oils and Water-Colors. Fieldston Galleries, Fieldston School, Riverdale, N.Y. 5–29 Feb. Catalogue.

Ferargil Galleries, New York. 11–23 Nov.

Seattle Museum of Art. Dates unknown.

Vassar College, Poughkeepsie, N.Y. Dates unknown.

1950   Recent Oils and Water Colors by Harold Weston. Babcock Galleries, New York. 13 Feb.–4 Mar. Catalogue.

1951   Paintings by Harold Weston. Library and Acquisition Committee, Ausable Club, St. Huberts, N.Y. 26 Aug.–7 Sept.

1956   Building the United Nations: Six Oil Paintings by Harold Weston. Corcoran Gallery of Art, Washington, D.C. 17–29 Apr. Catalogue. Retrospective, including paintings in addition to the murals.

1961   Harold Weston. Babcock Galleries, New York. 7–25 Mar. Catalogue.

1975   A Retrospective Exhibition of Paintings by Harold Weston 1894–1972. Mount Holyoke College, South Hadley, Mass. 8 Sept.–8 Oct. Catalogue.

1976   Harold Weston: Early Adirondack Landscapes. Adirondack Center Museum, Elizabethtown, N.Y. 18 July–28 Aug. Catalogue.

1978   Harold Weston. Philadelphia Art Alliance. 3 Dec.–7 Jan. 1979. Catalogue.

1979   Harold Weston Paintings. Gross McCleaf Gallery, Philadelphia. 8–29 Sept.

1980   Harold Weston: Paintings. Ulrich Museum, Wichita, Kans. 9 Apr.–4 May.

1982   Harold Weston: The Stone Series, 1968–1972. The Phillips Collection, Washington, D.C. 5 June–18 July. Catalogue.

1983   Harold Weston: The Stone Series, 1968–1972. Virginia Polytechnic Institute, Blacksburg, Va. 22 Mar.–22 Apr. Catalogue.

Harold Weston: The Stone Series, 1968–1972. Lake Placid Center for the Arts, Lake Placid, N.Y. 13 Aug.–7 Sept. Catalogue.

1984   Harold Weston 1894–1972: A Selection of Landscapes, 1920 to 1934. Salander-O'Reilly Galleries, New York. 5 July–24 Aug. Catalogue.

1990   Early Figures and the Stone Series: Watercolors by Weston. Harold Weston Art Trust, New York. 20 Apr.–25 May. Catalogue.

1991   Works on Paper: Harold Weston. The Phillips Collection, Washington, D.C. 19 Feb.–7 June.

Harold Weston: Adirondack Landscapes. Atea Ring Gallery, Westport, N.Y. 29 June–19 July.

1993   Harold Weston 1894–1972: A Retrospective. Bissell House Gallery, Lakeville, Conn. 5 June–4 Sept.

1994   Harold Weston: Beyond the Known. Lake Placid Center for the Arts, Lake Placid, N.Y. 20 July–14 Aug. Catalogue.

1995   Harold Weston: Double Take. Atea Ring Gallery, Westport, N.Y. 22 July–11 Aug.

Harold Weston: Waves of the Land, Waves of the Sea. Good News Café, Woodbury, Conn. 12 Nov.–31 Dec.

1997   Harold Weston: Up Close. Atea Ring Gallery, Westport, N.Y. 5 Sept.–13 Oct.

1999   Harold Weston, 1894–1972. D. Wigmore Fine Art, New York. 2 Feb.–31 Mar. Catalogue.

2001   Harold Weston Retrospective: Paintings, 1927–1955. The Dahl Arts Center, Rapid City, S.D. 6 Apr.–21 May.

2003   Harold Weston: 20th Century Modernist. Washington Pavilion, Sioux Falls, S.D. 10 Jan.–23 Mar.

GROUP EXHIBITIONS

Harold Weston's paintings have been in more than two hundred group exhibitions, from the Baghdad Art Club in 1918 to the Phillips Collection in Washington, D.C., in 2000. Weston was represented in nineteen annual exhibitions at the Pennsylvania Academy of the Fine Arts in Philadelphia from 1923 to 1967 and in twelve biennials at the Corcoran Gallery of Art in Washington, D.C. The Whitney Museum of American Art hung paintings by Weston in four exhibitions, including its first and second biennials in 1932 and 1934. Works by Weston could be seen in five exhibitions at the Art Institute of Chicago, including its Century of Progress Exhibition of Paintings and Sculpture in both 1933 and 1934. The 1933 exhibition American Sources of Modern Art at the Museum of Modern Art in New York City showed two of his works, and *Green Hat* was awarded third prize in American painting at the Golden Gate International Exposition in San Francisco in 1939. In addition to the seven one-person exhibitions at the Phillips Collection, eight group shows there have included works by Weston. The Federation of Modern Painters and Sculptors had Westons in twenty-four of its annual group exhibitions and mounted a memorial exhibition of his work in 1973.

Paintings by Weston went on tour with the College Art Association, the American Federation of Art, the Chicago Art Institute midwestern museum circuits, and others. An exhibition of paintings selected from Corcoran biennials traveled in 1947–48 to Alabama, Indiana, Kentucky, Minnesota, New Hampshire, New York, Pennsylvania, and Texas. His work was included in two other notable traveling exhibitions: Seventy-five Living American Painters, which was circulated by the U.S. Information Agency in 1956–57 to cities in France and Germany; and The Expressionist Landscape, organized by the Birmingham Museum of Art, which traveled from Birmingham to New York, Syracuse, Akron, and Vancouver in 1987–88. Weston's works were part of group shows at, among other venues, The Adirondack Museum, the Brooklyn Museum, the Metropolitan Museum of Art, the Oregon Art Museum, the Philadelphia Museum of Art, Salons of America, the Tate Gallery in London, the Virginia Museum of Fine Arts, and the 1939 World's Fair in New York. The Harold Weston Foundation has a complete listing of group exhibitions.

SELECTED BIBLIOGRAPHY

INDEX

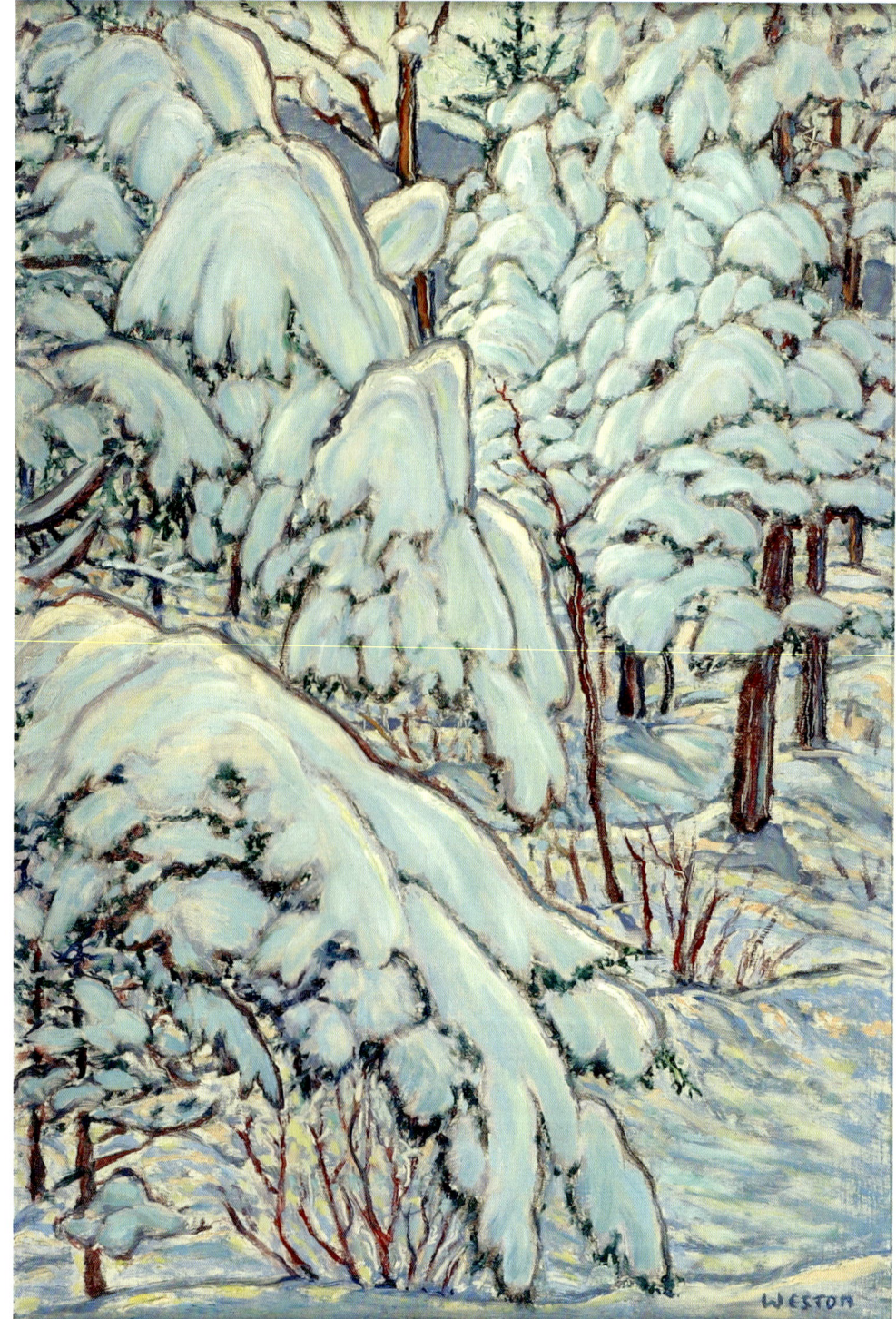

129. Harold Weston, *Snow on Balsams*, 1934. Courtesy of the Syracuse University Art Collection.

Selected Bibliography

Kathleen V. Jameson

This bibliography is limited to references related to works included in the Wild Exuberance exhibition, Harold Weston's Adirondack work, and general citations of major importance. Each section is arranged chronologically rather than alphabetically so that the exhibition checklist, the chronology, the one-person and group exhibitions, and this bibliography can be cross-referenced easily. The best available information has been provided. Copies of almost all articles and essays listed in this bibliography are housed in the archives of the Harold Weston Foundation.

ARCHIVAL SOURCES

Harold Weston Manuscript Collection, George Arents Research Library, Syracuse Univ., Syracuse, N.Y.

Harold Weston Manuscript Collection, Harold Weston Foundation, West Chester, Pa.

Harold Weston Manuscript Collection, Library of Congress, Washington, D.C.

Harold Weston Papers, 1916–72, Archives of American Art, Smithsonian Institution, Washington, D.C.

ARTICLES

Bell, Harold C., Jr. "Art Notes: Landscapes by Harold F. Weston." *The Younger Set* 1, no. 8 (Nov. 1922): 10–11.

de Rochemont, Ruth. "Notes on Painting and Sculpture: Comments on the Current Exhibitions in New York." *Vanity Fair* 19, no. 3 (Nov. 1922): 29.

"Harold F. Weston: An Adirondack Painter." *Art Review*, Nov. 1922, 21.

"Palette and Brush." *Town Topics*, 11 Nov. 1922.

"Weston's Persian and American Views." *American Art News*, 11 Nov. 1922, sec. 2, 6.

McBride, Henry. "Art News and Reviews: Attractive Shows in Many Galleries." *New York Herald*, 12 Nov. 1922, sec. 7, 7.

"Random Impressions in Current Exhibitions." *New York Tribune*, 12 Nov. 1922, sec. 5, 6.

Tyrell, Henry. "A Roundabout Modernist." *New York World*, 12 Nov. 1922.

Nelson, H. C. "Art and Artists." *New York Globe and Commercial Advertiser*, 13 Nov. 1922.

F[lint], R[alph]. "Adirondack Hills and Persian Vales Painted by Harold F. Weston." *Christian Science Monitor*, 17 Nov. 1922, 8.

Breuning, Margaret. "Galleries Show Many Phases of Modern Art." *New York Evening Post*, 18 Nov. 1922, 11.

Milton, Ray. "The Artist Who Conquered Fate." *New York World*, 19 Nov. 1922, Magazine sec., 13, 16.

Karr, Benjamin. "A Pathetic Exhibition." *Cleveland Sunday News-Leader*, 22 Apr. 1923, 8.

Glasier, Jessie C. "Hermit's Pictures Unusual." *Cleveland Plain Dealer*, 29 Apr. 1923, 3.

F[lint], R[alph]. "Old Color Prints to the Fore." *Christian Science Monitor*, 18 June 1923, 9.

Watson, Forbes. "Portraits That Are Efficient." *New York World*, 11 Nov. 1923, M8.

"Final Group at Montross: Gallery Sums Up Season's Exhibitions with a Diversified Show." *New York World*, 11 May 1924.

Breuning, Margaret. "About Artists and Their Work: Fifty Pictures in Group Show at Montross's Reveal Work by Prominent Artists." *New York Evening Post*, 17 May 1924, 5.

Kannewisher, Bertha. "Would Add to Richness of Life of Others, Declares Artist" (Jan. 1925).

Weiss, Ernest A. "Art in Rochester." *Rochester (N.Y.) Herald*, 18 Jan. 1925, 9.

———. "Art in Rochester." *Rochester (N.Y.) Herald*, 25 Jan. 1925, 11.

Darling, Thurston V. "Painter of Adirondack Views Visits Memorial Art Gallery Where His Work Is on Display." *Rochester (N.Y.) Times Union*, 27 Jan. 1925, 19.

"Artist Tells of Ideals That Inspire His Work." *Rochester (N.Y.) Herald*, 28 Jan. 1925, 12.

"Noted Painter Praises Design of Art Gallery." *Rochester (N.Y.) Democrat and Chronicle*, 28 Jan. 1925, 3.

"Who's Who Abroad: Harold Weston." *Chicago Tribune*, Paris ed., 7 July 1926, 4.

"Weston." *La Semaine à Paris*, 25 July–3 Aug. 1927, 51.

"Around the Studios." *New York Herald*, Paris ed., 29 Aug. 1927, 9.

"Harold Weston: Montross Galleries." *Art News*, 22 Oct. 1927.

McBride, Henry. "Modern French Art at Kraushaar Galleries Proves Reigning Attraction of the Week: Harold Weston's Recent Work." *New York Sun*, 22 Oct. 1927, 5.

"Eventful Opening Gives Bright Promise to 1927–1928 Art Season: Paintings in Oils Like Mosaics." *New York World*, 23 Oct. 1927.

"Exhibited in the New York Galleries: Some of Harold Weston's Pictures Reveal Affinity with Van Gogh." *New York Times*, 23 Oct. 1927, sec. 8, 12.

"1-Man Show Is Big Feature of Art Week." *New York American*, 23 Oct. 1927.

"Random Impressions in Art Exhibitions." *New York Herald Tribune*, 23 Oct. 1927, sec. 6, 10.

Mannes, Marya. "Gallery Notes." *Creative Art* 1, no. 2 (Nov. 1927): vii, ix.

Moss, Arthur. "Around the Town." *New York Herald*, Paris ed., 4 Dec. 1928.

Breuning, Margaret. "Other Shows." *New York Evening Post*, 15 Dec. 1928, M11.

McBride, Henry. "Varied Attractions." *New York Sun*, 15 Dec. 1928, 9.

"Fresco Texture Marks Weston's Paintings." *New York World*, 16 Dec. 1928.

J. K. "Further Comment on the Week's Art Exhibits in Various Galleries." *New York Times*, 16 Dec. 1928, sec. 10, pt. 2, 14.

"News and Exhibitions of the Week in Art: At the Montross Gallery." *New York Herald Tribune*, 16 Dec. 1928, sec. 7, 10–11.

"News and Views on Current Art: Harold Weston." *Brooklyn Daily Eagle*, 16 Dec. 1928, E7.

"Portrait by Harold Weston." *New York American*, 16 Dec. 1928.

"Highly Significant Exhibit of Paintings by Americans." *Rochester (N.Y.) Democrat and Chronicle*, 20 Jan. 1929.

Sayre, Ann. "Through the Galleries." *Town & Country*, 1 Nov. 1930, 90, 92.

Grafly, Dorothy. "Art News and Comment about Current Exhibits: Oils by Weston Feature Exhibit by Phila. Group." *Philadelphia Public Ledger*, 2 Nov. 1930, 8.

"Little Gallery Opens Tuesday with Display by Local Artists." *Philadelphia Inquirer*, 2 Nov. 1930.

"Exhibitions in New York: Edward [sic] Weston." *Art News*, 15 Nov. 1930, 13.

Flint, Ralph. "Presenting 4 Artists: Interesting One-Man Shows in Three Galleries." *New York Sun*, 15 Nov. 1930, A26.

Sayre, Ann. "Through the Galleries." *Town & Country*, 15 Nov. 1930, 72.

Breuning, Margaret. "Harold Weston." *New York Evening Post*, 16 Nov. 1930.

Harris, Ruth Green. "Seen in the Galleries: Water-Colors, Oils, Etchings, and Drawings Compose a Richly Diversified Display." *New York Times*, 16 Nov. 1930, sec. 8, 11.

"Weston's Versatile Art." *New York World*, 16 Nov. 1930, M7.

Klein, Jerome. "Where Was Weston When 'The 19' Ruled?" *Chicago Evening Post*, 18 Nov. 1930, Magazine of the Art World sec.

Comstock, Helen. "New Works by H. Weston Now on View." *New York American*, 23 Nov. 1930, M5. Also published as "Air of Familiarity Marks Weston's Spanish Paintings." *Cleveland Plain Dealer*, 16 Nov. 1930, Society sec., 17.

Sayre, Ann. "Exhibitions." *International Studio* 97 (Dec. 1930): 96–106.

"New York Season." *Art Digest*, 1 Dec. 1930, 16.

Rosenfeld, Paul. "Harold Weston's Adventure." *New Republic*, 31 Dec. 1930, 190–91.

Mechlin, Leila. "Notes of Art and Artists: Paintings of Harold Weston on View." *Washington, D.C., Sunday Star*, 8 Mar. 1931, Magazine sec., 19.

Rainey, Ada. "Weston Lone Show at Phillip's Gallery Independent and Daring in His Work." *Washington Post*, 8 Mar. 1931, sec. 2, 6.

D[evree], H[oward] V. "Weston's Oils on Display." *New York Times*, 17 Nov. 1931, 30.

Breuning, Margaret. "Whitney Museum Opening Event of the Week—New Yorkers at the Resorts: Other Art Events." *New York Evening Post*, 21 Nov. 1931, D3.

Flint, Ralph. "Exhibitions in New York: Harold Weston, Montross Gallery." *Art News*, 21 Nov. 1931, 13.

McBride, Henry. "Brilliant Opening of Whitney Museum of American Art Has Far-Reaching Effect. Attractions in Other Galleries." *New York Sun*, 21 Nov. 1931, 12.

Burrows, Carlyle. "News and Comment on Current Art Events." *New York Herald Tribune*, 22 Nov. 1931, sec. 7, 9.

Read, Helen Appleton. "In the Galleries: Harold Weston." *Brooklyn Daily Eagle*, 22 Nov. 1931, E6.

Vaughan, Malcolm. "Today in the Realm of Art: Recent Paintings by Harold Weston." *New York American*, 22 Nov. 1931, M5.

"On View in the New York Galleries: Harold Weston. Montross Gallery." *Parnassus* 3, no. 8 (Dec. 1931): 10.

Phillips, Duncan. "Original American Painting of Today." *Formes* 21 (Jan. 1932): 197–201.

Buchalter, Helen. "A Modernist Sees Life in Unique Symbols. Too Much Prettiness in Art Like Ice Cream Diet Claims Harold Weston, Artist, in Gallery Talk." *Washington Daily News*, 9 Jan. 1932, 11.

Jewell, Edward Alden. "Art: Works by American Group." *New York Times*, 29 Mar. 1932, 22.

"Spring Displays in 5 Galleries: Contemporary Americans at Montross." *New York Sun*, 31 Mar. 1932, 24.

Flint, Ralph. "Whitney Museum Opens Its First Biennial Show." *Art News*, 26 Nov. 1932, 1, 4.

Grafly, Dorothy. "News of Art, Artists, and Current Exhibitions: Whitney Biennial: A Strong Salon." *Philadelphia Public Ledger*, 27 Nov. 1932, 6.

"Harold Weston at Montross's: Artist Exhibits His Late Work in Varied Fields." *New York Sun*, 30 Nov. 1932, 16.

Jewell, Edward Alden. "Art in Review: Exhibition of Recent Paintings by Harold Weston Opens at Montross Gallery." *New York Times*, 2 Dec. 1932, 24.

Breuning, Margaret. "Winter Exhibition of Academy of Design Leads Week's Art Showings: Harold Weston." *New York Evening Post*, 3 Dec. 1932, sec. 3, 3.

Flint, Ralph. "Exhibitions in New York: Harold Weston, Montross Gallery." *Art News*, 3 Dec. 1932, 5.

Vaughan, Malcolm. "Current Events in the Realm of Art, Antiques: In the Parade of New York Art Shows This Week." *New York American*, 3 Dec. 1932, 32.

"Art Roster: New Exhibitions." *New York Times*, 4 Dec. 1932, sec. 9, 8.

Burrows, Carlyle. "Briefer Comment on Current Art Attractions in New York: A New Exhibition by Harold Weston." *New York Herald Tribune*, 4 Dec. 1932, sec. 7, 10.

"New York Criticism: With Vehemence and Violence." *Art Digest*, 15 Dec. 1932, 14.

Mumford, Lewis. "The Art Galleries: Assorted Americana." *New Yorker*, 17 Dec. 1932, 62.

"Harold Weston Shows 39 Oils." *Philadelphia Evening Bulletin*, 18 Nov. 1933, 20.

Bailey, Weldon. "Weston's Oils Show Rugged, Bold Strength." *Philadelphia Record*, 19 Nov. 1933, sec. 4, 4.

Bonte, C. H. "In Gallery and Studio." *Philadelphia Inquirer*, 19 Nov. 1933, Society sec., 10.

Grafly, Dorothy. "Crudity Vies with Culture in Weston's Rough-Hewn Art." *Philadelphia Public Ledger*, 19 Nov. 1933, 12.

———. "News of Art, Artists, and Current Exhibitions: Many Debuts in Mellon Show." *Philadelphia Public Ledger*, 17 Dec. 1933, 12.

Lowrie, Sarah D. "As One Woman Sees It: Painters of Pictures, When They Do the Things They Really Want to Do." *Philadelphia Evening Public Ledger*, 7 Sept. 1934, 12.

Jewell, Edward Alden. "Paintings Shown by 153 Americans." *New York Times*, 28 Nov. 1934, 19.

———. "In the Realm of Art: The Whitney's Second Biennial." *New York Times*, 2 Dec. 1934, sec. 10, 9.

"Galleries Show 3 Artists' Work." *Philadelphia Evening Bulletin*, 5 Jan. 1935, 2.

Bonte, C. H. "What Is Now to Be Seen in the Art Galleries of Philadelphia." *Philadelphia Inquirer*, 6 Jan. 1935, Society sec., 13.

Grafly, Dorothy. "Weston Takes to More Color on His Canvas." *Philadelphia Record*, 6 Jan. 1935, sec. 4, 12.

Jewell, Edward Alden. "Oils by Paul Klee Now on Exhibition: Openings of the Week." *New York Times*, 11 Mar. 1935, 20.

"Solid, Rugged Things Make Up Weston's World." *Art Digest*, 15 Mar. 1935, 23.

Upton, Melville. "Weston's Late Work Shown." *New York Sun*, 15 Mar. 1935, 25.

J[ewell], E[dward] A[lden]. "Mahonri Young, Etcher: Complete Set of Veteran's Work in Show at Kraushaar's—Other Exhibitions." *New York Times*, 17 Mar. 1935, sec. 10, 7.

Genauer, Emily. "Weston Paintings Rugged and Pure." *New York World-Telegram*, 23 Mar. 1935, 27.

Mumford, Lewis. "The Art Galleries: Spring and Renoirs." *New Yorker*, 23 Mar. 1935, 30–32.

———. "Goings On about Town: Weston." *New Yorker*, 23 Mar. 1935, 6.

Graeme, Alice. "Phillips Memorial Gallery Has on Display Interesting Arrangement of Paintings." *Washington Post*, 12 Jan. 1936.

Mechlin, Leila. "Inspiration Marks Etchings by World Leader in Art. Harold Weston's Virile Paintings." *Washington, D.C., Evening Star*, 29 Feb. 1936, B3.

"Weston Defies Tradition." *Washington Times*, 29 Feb. 1936, Magazine sec., 7.

"Harold Weston Offers Paintings of U.S. Industrial Scene." *Washington Post*, 1 Mar. 1936.

"Weston Exhibit in Capital." *Art Digest*, 1 Mar. 1936, 12.

Mumford, Lewis. "The Art Galleries: The Treasury's Murals." *New Yorker*, 17 Oct. 1936, 70–71.

Bonte, C. H. "Current Exhibitions in Philadelphia." *Philadelphia Inquirer*, 22 Nov. 1936, Society sec., 17.

Grafly, Dorothy. "The Gallery Gazer: Harold Weston's Murals Seen at Boyer." *Philadelphia Record*, 22 Nov. 1936, sec. 4, 8.

G[raeme], A[lice]. "Latest Weston Art on Display in Philadelphia." *Washington Post*, 29 Nov. 1936, sec. 7, 7.

Bonte, C. H. "Art: Forty-third Annual of Oils at the Art Club and a Personally Chosen Trio of Prize Winners." *Philadelphia Inquirer*, 6 Dec. 1936, Society sec., 11.

Devree, Howard. "Among the New Group Exhibitions." *New York Times*, 27 June 1937, sec. 10, 7.

———. "A Reviewer's Notebook: In Galleries." *New York Times*, 19 Dec. 1937, sec. 10, 11.

Weston, Harold. *My Snow Shoes* (reproduction). *Art and Artists of Today* (New York) 1, no. 6 (June–July 1938): back cover, illus.

Weston, Harold. "A Painter Speaks." *Magazine of Art* 32 (Jan. 1939): 16–21. Reprinted in *Painters and Sculptors of Modern America*, introduction by Monroe Wheeler, 85–88. New York: Thomas Y. Crowell, 1942.

Devree, Howard. "A Reviewer's Notebook." *New York Times*, 8 Jan. 1939, sec. 10, 10.

"Oils and Water Colors Exhibited." *Washington, D.C., Sunday Star*, 23 Apr. 1939, pt. 5.

Poe, Elisabeth E. "Society of Etchers Exhibition Reveals Many Splendid Works: Gabrielle Clement's Mastery Shown in Etchings; Weston Scores in Phillips Show." *Washington, D.C., Times-Herald*, 23 Apr. 1939, C16.

Watson, Jane. "Weston in One-Man Show at Phillips." *Washington Post*, 23 Apr. 1939, sec. 6, 6.

Weston, Harold. *The Arena* (reproduction). *Magazine of Art* 32, no. 6 (June 1939): frontispiece.

Devree, Howard. "In the Realm of Art: Events in New York and Afield: Prizes and Popularity." *New York Times*, 9 July 1939, sec. 10, 12.

Frankenstein, Alfred. "The East's Weston Comes West." *San Francisco Chronicle*, 30 July 1939, 20.

"News and Comment." *Magazine of Art* 32, no. 9 (Sept. 1939): 536.

"Bring Work of Weston." *Tacoma (Wash.) News Tribune*, 13 Sept. 1939.

"New Art Exhibit at C.P.S. Nov. 12." *Tacoma (Wash.) Times*, 9 Nov. 1939, 12.

"Tacoma Art Group Preview on Sunday." *Tacoma (Wash.) News Tribune*, 11 Nov. 1939 [as David Weston].

"Appeal Is Varied." *Tacoma (Wash.) News Tribune*, 12 Nov. 1939.

Jones, Catherine. "Artists Hosts to Art Group." *Portland Oregonian*, 17 Dec. 1939.

[Pillsbury, Elinor]. "Museum Calendar Includes Two Exhibits of Paintings, Two Casts of Bronze Statue." *Portland (Oreg.) Journal*, 17 Dec. 1939, sec. 4, 4.

Pillsbury, Elinor. "Art Museum Hours Changed for Sundays and Holidays; Weston Exhibit Now Here." *Portland (Oreg.) Journal*, 24 Dec. 1939, sec. 4, 4.

———. "Pre-Hitler Paintings Due in German Exhibit; Lecture at Museum Thursday Night." *Portland Oregonian*, 31 Dec. 1939, sec. 4, 4.

Maguire, Cecilia. "Artist Takes Center of Stage at Own Show in Fieldston." *Yonkers (N.Y.) Herald Statesman*, 6 Feb. 1940, 4.

"Weston Outdoors." *Art Digest*, 15 Nov. 1940, 11.

"New Exhibitions of the Week." *Art News*, 16 Nov. 1940, 17.

Jewell, Edward Alden. "In the Realm of Art: Attractions Many and Diverse." *New York Times*, 17 Nov. 1940, sec. 9, 9.

Burrows, Carlyle. "Notes and Comment on Events in Art: Harold Weston." *New York Herald Tribune*, 19 Nov. 1940, sec. 6, 8.

"Weston Gives Up Painting to Work on Aid for Allies." *Syracuse Post-Standard*, 11 May 1941.

"News of Art: Harold Weston Paintings at Fogg." *Boston Herald*, 25 Jan. 1942, 22.

Pilat, Oliver. "Art, Food, and Freedom." *New York Post*, 6 Jan. 1945, 7.

Weston, Harold. *Green Hat* (reproduction). *Magazine of Art* (Nov. 1946): San Francisco sec., vi.

F[lint], R[alph]. [No article title]. *Pictures on Exhibit*, Mar. 1961, 24.

V. R. "In the Galleries: Harold Weston." *Arts* 35, no. 6 (Mar. 1961): 51.

"Art Openings in Galleries." *New York Times*, 5 Mar. 1961, sec. 2, 18.

C. B. "Art Exhibition Notes." *New York Herald Tribune*, 11 Mar. 1961.

"Goings On about Town: Art." *New Yorker*, 11 Mar. 1961, 13.

Preston, Stuart. "Moderns in Art's House of Many Mansions." *New York Times*, 12 Mar. 1961, sec. 2, 25.

"Goings On about Town: Art." *New Yorker*, 18 Mar. 1961, 12.

V. P. "Reviews and Previews: Harold Weston." *Art News* 60, no. 2 (Apr. 1961): 62.

Johnson, Grant. "Paintings of Essex Co. Artists Exhibited at N.Y. State Capitol." *Elizabethtown (N.Y.) Valley News*, 15 Feb. 1962.

Burton, Hal. "Books . . . Adirondack Original." *Garden City (N.Y.) Newsday*, 18 Dec. 1971, Magazine sec., 16W.

Goodwin, James A. "Wilderness in Adirondacks" (book review). *Hartford (Conn.) Times*, 26 Dec. 1971, C7.

"Notes: *Freedom in the Wilds*" (book review). *Adirondack Life* 3, no. 1 (winter 1972): 42.

Weston, Harold. "Freedom in the Wilds: A Saga of the Adirondacks." *Adirondack Life* 3, no. 1 (winter 1972): 32–35.

"Death of Harold Weston." *Congressional Record*, 21 June 1972, S9848–50.

Jamieson, Paul F. "*Freedom in the Wilds*" (book review). *Forest History* 16, no. 2 (July 1972): 27.

"Mt. Holyoke Friends of Art Plan Retrospective Exhibit." *Holyoke (South Hadley, Mass.) Transcript-Telegram*, 3 Sept. 1975, 16.

Hart, Tom. "Impressionist Brushwork with Expressionist Individuality." *Springfield (Mass.) Daily News*, 10 Sept. 1975, 25.

Canonico, Vanieta. "MHC Pays Homage to Harold Weston." *Choragos* (South Hadley, Mass.), 18 Sept. 1975, 4.

"Calendar." *Lake Placid (N.Y.) News*, 15 July 1976, 18.

"Weston Landscapes Show Adirondack Wilderness." *Plattsburgh (N.Y.) Press-Republican*, 17 July 1976, 6.

M. E. B. "A Review: Weston's Adirondack Landscapes." *Lake Placid (N.Y.) News* 29 July 1976, 14.

Weston, Harold. *Self-Portrait* (reproduction). *Philadelphia Art Alliance* (quarterly calendar) 57, no. 1 (Sept.–Dec. 1978): cover, 6.

Donohoe, Victoria. "A Forgotten Painter, a Local Artist in Paper." *Philadelphia Inquirer*, 1 Dec. 1978, 24.

MacCormack, Mrs. H. J. W. "Adirondack Art in Philadelphia." *Plattsburgh (N.Y.) Press-Republican*, 6 Dec. 1978, 8.

Forman, Nessa. "Harold Weston: The Hermit Painter." *Philadelphia Bulletin*, 10 Dec. 1978, 9.

Jarmusch, Ann. "The Nation: Philadelphia." *Art News* 79 (Jan. 1980): 150.

Ostrow, Joanne. "Galleries & Museums: Weston, McLaughlin: Two at the Phillips." *Washington Post*, 4 June 1982, Weekend sec., 38.

Shaw-Eagle, Joanna. "Capital Life: Art. Capturing Life's Essences in 2 Shows at the Phillips." *Washington Times*, 8 June 1982, B1–B2.

Richard, Paul. "A Phillips Tribute to Friends: McLaughlin and Watson [*sic*] Exhibits in Memoriam." *Washington Post*, 14 June 1982, C8.

O'Brien, Peggy. "Harold Weston, 1894–1972." *Glens Falls (N.Y.) Adirondac*, 47, no. 7 (Aug. 1983): 28, 32.

MacCormack, Margaret. "Exhibit to Feature St. Huberts Artist." *Plattsburgh (N.Y.) Press-Republican*, 11 Aug. 1983, 17.

Lumsden, Linda. "Work of Weston of Keene Valley Is on Display at Art Center in Placid." *Saranac Lake (N.Y.) Adirondack Enterprise*, 16 Aug. 1983, 1.

McLeod, Helen. "Hawkins Dance, Weston Works Blend Modern Art." *Plattsburgh (N.Y.) Press-Republican*, 18 Aug. 1983, 8.

Thill, Mary. "Keene Valley Art Retrospective at Placid Arts Center." *Plattsburgh (N.Y.) Press-Republican*, 31 July 1992, 8.

Mackinnon, Anne. "A Passionate Nature: The Consummate Art of Harold Weston." *Adirondack Life* 25, no. 1 (Jan.–Feb. 1994): 28–35, 65–66.

Foster, Rebecca. "Review: Harold Weston: Beyond the Known. A Look at the Life of an Artist's Work." *Lake Placid (N.Y.) News*, 20 July 1994, 12.

Welsh, Caroline M. "Masterworks of the Adirondacks." *American Art Review* 9, no. 4 (Aug. 1997): 78–85.

Caudell, Robin. "Atea Ring Gallery Exhibit Honors Adirondack Artist." *Plattsburgh (N.Y.) Press-Republican*, 4 Sept. 1997, B6.

[Worth, Alexi]. "Goings On about Town: Art. Galleries: Uptown. Harold Weston." *New Yorker*, 8 Mar. 1999, 13.

[Foster, Rebecca]. "Harold Weston's Paintings from the 1920s and 1930s at Atea Ring Gallery Through October 4." *Antiques and the Arts Weekly*, 3 Sept. 1999, 101.

Holland, Deb. "Dahl Hosts Paintings by Harold Weston." *Rapid City (S.D.) Journal*, 29 Mar. 2001, B1.

BOOKS

Phillips, Duncan. *The Artist Sees Differently: Essays Based upon the Philosophy of a Collection in the Making.* 2 vols. New York: E. Weyhe; Washington, D.C.: Phillips Memorial Gallery, 1931.

Hall, W. S. *Eyes on America.* New York: Studio Publications, [1939].

Weston, Harold. "Interlude in the Adirondacks." In *Paul Rosenfeld: Voyager in the Arts*, edited by Jerome Mellquist and Lucie Wiese, 182–85. New York: Creative Age Press, 1948.

———. *Abridged Guide to Adirondack Trails: St. Huberts and Keene Valley Regions.* St. Huberts, N.Y.: Adirondack Trail Improvement Society, 1948. New ed., 1960.

———. *Freedom in the Wilds: A Saga of the Adirondacks.* St. Huberts, N.Y.: Adirondack Trail Improvement Society, 1971.

Bury, Adrian. *Oil Painting of Today.* London: The Studio; New York: The Studio Publications, 1975.

Marling, Karal Ann. *Wall-to-Wall America: A Cultural History of Post-Office Murals in the Great Depression.* Minneapolis: Univ. of Minnesota Press, 1982.

Weston, Harold. "A Visual Happening." In *The Adirondack Reader*, edited with an introduction by Paul Jamieson, 251–54. Glens Falls, N.Y.: Adirondack Mountain Club, 1982.

EXHIBITION AND COLLECTION CATALOGUES AND BROCHURES

Exhibition of Paintings: Adirondack Mountains and Persia by Harold F. Weston. New York: Montross Galleries, 1922.

Harold Weston. Paris: Galerie Joseph Billiet & Co., 1927.

Harold Weston: Exhibition of Pictures. New York: Montross Galleries, 1927.

Exhibition: Paintings in Oil and Water Color, Etchings and Lithographs by Harold Weston. New York: Montross Galleries, 1928.

Harold Weston Exhibition: Paintings—Water Colors—Etchings. New York: Montross Galleries, 1930.

Paintings by John Steuart Curry, Louis Ritman, and Harold Weston. Chicago: Art Institute of Chicago, 1930.

Harold Weston. Washington, D.C.: Phillips Memorial Gallery, 1931.

Harold Weston: Exhibition of Recent Paintings. New York: Montross Galleries, 1931.

Recent Paintings by Harold Weston. Washington, D.C.: Phillips Memorial Gallery, 1931.

Harold Weston: Exhibition of Recent Paintings. New York: Montross Galleries, 1932.

Paintings by Harold Weston, 1921–1931. Washington, D.C.: Phillips Memorial Gallery, 1932.

A Century of Progress: Exhibition of Paintings and Sculpture, June 1 to November 1, 1933. Chicago: Art Institute of Chicago, 1933.

Harold Weston. Philadelphia: Mellon Galleries, 1933.

Exhibition: Recent Work, 1935. Harold Weston. Text by Paul Rosenfeld. New York: Eighth Street Gallery, 1935.

Recent Paintings by Harold Weston. Text by Paul Rosenfeld. Philadelphia: Boyer Galleries, 1935.

Oil Paintings and Water Colors: Harold Weston. Philadelphia: Boyer Galleries, 1936.

Paintings by Harold Weston. Washington, D.C.: Studio House, 1936.

Harold Weston: Exhibition of Oils and Water-Colors. Riverdale, N.Y.: Fieldston Galleries, Fieldston School, 1940.

Recent Oils and Water Colors by Harold Weston. New York: Babcock Galleries, 1950.

Phillips, Duncan. *The Phillips Collection Catalogue: A Museum of Modern Art and Its Sources.* New York: Phillips Collection, 1952.

Federation of Modern Painters and Sculptors, 1955–56. Introduction by Harold Weston. Foreword by Duncan Phillips. New York: Federation of Modern Painters and Sculptors, 1955.

Building the United Nations: Six Oil Paintings by Harold Weston. Washington, D.C.: Corcoran Gallery of Art, 1956.

Harold Weston. New York: Babcock Galleries, 1961.

The Alfred Khouri Memorial Collection.. Vol. 2. Norfolk, Va.: Norfolk Museum of Arts and Sciences [now the Chrysler Museum of Art], 1969.

Loan Exhibition of Contemporary Paintings. Washington, D.C.: Phillips Collection, 1969.

A Retrospective Exhibition of Paintings by Harold Weston (1894–1972). Text by Jean C. Harris. South Hadley, Mass.: Mount Holyoke College, 1975.

Harold Weston: Early Adirondack Landscapes. Text by Frank Owen. Elizabethtown, N.Y.: Adirondack Center Museum, 1976.

Accessions/1976–77. Springfield, Mo.: Springfield Art Museum, 1977.

Harold Weston. Text by Ben Wolf. Philadelphia: Art Alliance Press; London: Associated Univ. Press, 1978. [Includes interview with Faith Weston.]

Harold Weston: The Stone Series, 1968–1972. Text by Sasha Newman. Washington, D.C.: Phillips Collection, 1982.

Phillips, Marjorie. *Duncan Phillips and His Collection.* Boston: Atlantic Monthly Press, 1970. Rev. ed., New York: W. W. Norton, in association with the Phillips Collection, 1982.

Harold Weston, 1894–1972: A Selection of Landscapes, 1920 to 1934. Text by Lori Bookstein. New York: Salander-O'Reilly Galleries, 1984.

The Phillips Collection: A Summary Catalogue. Washington, D.C.: Phillips Collection, 1985.

The Expressionist Landscape: North American Modernist Painting, 1920–1947. Text by Ruth Stevens Appelhof, Barbara Haskell, and Jeffrey R. Hayes. Birmingham, Ala.: Birmingham Museum of Art, 1988.

Early Figures and the Stone Series: Watercolors by Weston. Text by Brooks Adams. New York: privately printed, 1990.

Fair Wilderness: American Paintings in the Collection of The Adirondack Museum. Text by Patricia C. F. Mandel. Blue Mountain Lake, N.Y.: Adirondack Museum, 1990.

A Wild Sort of Beauty: Public Places and Private Visions. Text by Robert L. McGrath. Blue Mountain Lake, N.Y.: Adirondack Museum, 1992.

Harold Weston: Beyond the Known. Text by Rebecca Foster. Lake Placid, N.Y.: Lake Placid Center for the Arts, 1994.

Phillips, Stephen B. *Twentieth-Century Still-Life Painting from the Phillips Collection.* Washington, D.C.: Phillips Collection, 1997.

Harold Weston, 1894–1972. New York: D. Wigmore Fine Art, 1999.

Passantino, Erika D., ed. *The Eye of Duncan Phillips: A Collection in the Making.* Washington, D.C.: Phillips Collection, in association with Yale Univ. Press, 1999.

Index

Page number in italics denotes illustration.